Fundamentals of Digital Computers

by Donald D. Spencer

Howard W. Sams & Co., Inc.
4300 WEST 62ND ST. INDIANAPOLIS, INDIANA 46268 USA

SECOND EDITION
SECOND PRINTING—1982

International Standard Book Number: 0-672-21534-9
Library of Congress Catalog Card Number: 78-54457

Printed in the United States of America.

Preface

Our lives are increasingly involved with computer uses in which we have an active part or which affect our daily activities in obvious or subtle ways. Computer-processed information aids in medical diagnosis, solves problems in chemistry, points the way in scientific research, forms the basis for business management decisions, maintains the records of businesses, aids engineers in designing supersonic aircraft, helps in educating students, and serves in many other ways. Today, thousands of computers can even be found in the home. Low-cost microcomputers are being used by more and more people to do everything from keeping the family budget to playing games such as backgammon, chess, tic-tac-toe, etc.

The purpose of this book is to explain the seeming mysteries of a computer system and how it may be used for useful purposes by humans. It is intended for persons who need to have a general understanding about computers and programming.

Chapter 1 tells you what computers can do. Chapter 2 gives you a brief history of computers. Chapters 3–5 introduce the reader to computer hardware. Chapters 6–11 describe how computers are used to solve problems—programming. The two most popular programming languages, BASIC and FORTRAN, are discussed in Chapters 9 and 10. Chapters 12–13 cover advanced computer concepts. Chapter 14 describes the operation of a typical computer center. Chapter 15 tries to give the reader an insight into what to expect in the future.

Every effort has been made to keep this text as simple and understandable as possible. It should be pointed out, however, that many new and baffling (to the uninitiated) words and phrases have been added to the vocabulary of computer technology since the early days. Therefore, a rather extensive glossary of computer terms is included at the back of the book.

I wish to thank the computer equipment manufacturers, airlines, and government agencies that supplied me with the photographs used in the book, and Theresa B. Balon and William L. Verrill, Jr., for their imaginative drawings and cartoons. I also wish to thank my wife, Rae, for pounding the keys of the IBM Selectric.

DONALD D. SPENCER

Contents

CHAPTER 4

CHAPTER 5

CHAPTER 6

CHAPTER 7

CHAPTER 8

CHAPTER 9

CHAPTER 10

CHAPTER 11

CHAPTER 12

CHAPTER 13

CHAPTER 14

CHAPTER 15

APPENDIX A

APPENDIX B

Chapter 1

Using Computers

Courtesy Sanders Associates, Inc.

The computer, one of the most useful tools that humans have ever developed, has already begun to impinge on the daily lives of practically everyone. Computers are helping to revolutionize education, business, government, communications, science, and industry. Your utility bill, telephone bill, and bank statement are probably all calculated and produced by a computer. Did you also realize that the television program you watch may be following a computer-generated plan and that the pies and cakes you eat may have the quantity of ingredients controlled by a computer?

Fig. 1-1 illustrates how computers are being used in supermarket checkout counters to speed grocery shopping. As the clerk passes items over a reading slot, an optical scanning mechanism reads data from a UPC (*U*niversal *P*roduct *C*ode) symbol printed on the container of each item. This data is transmitted to a computer, which looks up the product code, matches the code with the latest price for the item, computes taxes, and sends the information to the cash-register terminal. The cash register then displays the name and price of the item (bottom photo) and prints a customer receipt (top photo).

The following examples illustrate a few more ways that computers are being used in order to help us solve the complex problems of today. Although the computer can solve problems at fantastic speeds, it is important to remember that a computer is only a machine, and that machines are controlled by humans. Therefore, the value of any machine, including the computer, depends on the skill and knowledge of the humans who direct it.

HOW COMPUTERS HELP DOCTORS

Medicine is facing the problem of information overload similar to that being faced by many professions today. Doctors, nurses, and hospital administrators are not capable of effectively handling the large amounts of information that must be processed in both medical research and patient care.

In recent years, the medical profession has begun to use computers more and more for assistance in the care of hospital patients. What exactly does this mean? Will a computer instead of a doctor diagnose your illness? Is it possible that computers will replace the family physician? At the present time, the an-

Courtesy IBM Corp.

Fig. 1-1. Computerized checkout systems speed supermarket shopping.

swer to these questions must be "no," for however remarkable it may be, the computer is merely a machine. Nevertheless, computers can *help* a doctor diagnose a disease. In medicine, a computer is simply another tool—like a microscope or a stethoscope—that can help a doctor do a better job.

There are many reasons for wanting to use computers in medicine. Computers can help to make more medical care available in the face of an apparently inevitable decrease in the number of trained doctors, nurses, and other health personnel. Through modern information storage, indexing, and retrieval systems, computers can be used to keep doctors abreast of important new advances in the field, thus helping to improve the quality of medical care. In a similar way, computers are also likely to help extend the frontiers of medicine and perhaps help medical research conquer some of today's diseases.

Fig. 1-2 shows the computer terminal of a medical information center. Physicians, nurses, and others requiring information from the system simply identify themselves to one of the

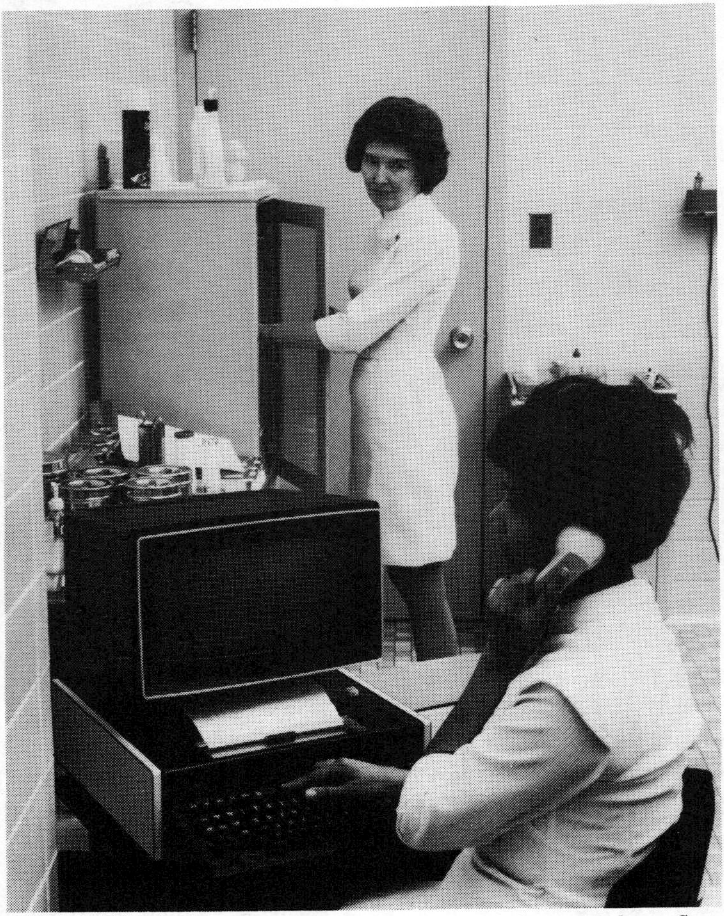

Courtesy Teletype Corp.

Fig. 1-2. Computer terminal of a medical information center.

units located strategically around the hospital. The requesting individual can then perform a wide variety of functions at the terminal—from entering new medical data about a patient, to obtaining the health status of a patient in the intensive care ward.

Today, the largest use of computers in the hospital is in the administrative areas—patient billing, accounts receivable, inventory control, payroll, bed accounting, etc. More and more, however, medical personnel will use these machines for patient care functions. Computers will be used to:

- Study heart disease, cancer, and many other diseases.
- Train doctors and health personnel.
- Free doctors and nurses to spend more time with patients.
- Help speed processing of patients' laboratory tests.
- Analyze brain waves to help investigators learn more about fatigue, stress, and mental illness.
- Monitor pulse, temperature, blood pressure, and other vital clinical facts about critically ill patients.
- Provide immediate information for the diagnosis and treatment of accidental-poisoning victims.
- Provide early warning profiles of mentally ill patients.

Hospitals throughout the country are developing centralized data processing systems which bring administrative, technical, and medical departments into direct and instant contact with a patient's hospital record. With such a system, computer input stations are located at key spots throughout the hospital. From admission to discharge, key information can be entered continually upon a patient's record. At the same time, doctors can instantly receive information on a patient's medical history and check the results of laboratory tests. Nurses can be advised of what drugs a doctor has ordered for a patient from the hospital pharmacy and when they should be administered. The system also provides excellent control over billing for doctors, nurses, drugs, and other hospital services. The result is better and more economical service to patients.

CRIME CONTROL

Crime rates are rising in virtually every part of the country. Law enforcement agencies are finding many practical uses for computers to help them fight crime. Chicago pioneered computer crime fighting in 1962 by putting the license numbers of stolen cars in computer storage. Now the license numbers can be checked out and identified in seconds. Chicago police use the system to warn them if a suspect is dangerous, is driving a stolen car, or is wanted for any crime ranging from murder to parking in front of a fire hydrant.

Fig. 1-3 shows a computer terminal at the Los Angeles Police Department. The computer holds records on stolen cars, missing persons, wanted fugitives, etc. The system enables the police to determine almost instantly whether a particular car is stolen, a person has been reported missing, or a person is wanted by the police. This information is then quickly relayed by radio to officers in the field.

Courtesy Sanders Associates, Inc.

Fig. 1-3. Computer terminal at the Los Angeles Police Department.

In New York City, police use a computer to find a set of matching fingerprints from files of tens of thousands. A computer is helping collect a backlog of traffic and parking fines from San Francisco motorists. In California, a computer keeps track of all weapon sales and stolen property; while in Florida, a computer system is increasing interagency cooperation throughout the state. St. Louis vehicle license plate numbers are stored in a computer file for immediate access. Similar systems are being implemented in many other cities and states.

Computers are also used very effectively in crime mapping. For example, trends in the incidence of crime can be analyzed from computer-plotted maps that illustrate movements from one locality to another.

Some prisons are even teaching inmates how to work with computers. Fig. 1-4 shows inmate trainees working in a computer programming course at Leavenworth penitentiary. Leavenworth officials have found that the enthusiasm some of the inmates develop for computer programming changes their entire outlook. It improves their behavior while in prison, their chances for parole, and their chances for success after parole.

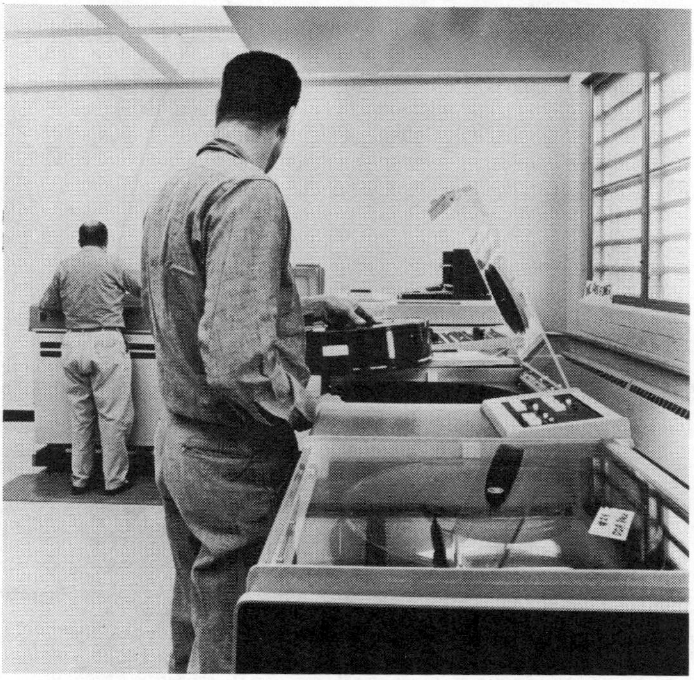

Courtesy NCR Corp.

Fig. 1-4. Inmates at Leavenworth penitentiary learn about computers in a programming course.

HOW COMPUTERS HELP TEACHERS AND STUDENTS

Computers have invaded the schools—not only universities and colleges, but also secondary and elementary schools. These machines are used not only as a source of instruction, but also as an aid to teachers in their teaching assignments. Machines will never replace teachers; but, when coupled with keyboard/display devices and well-developed learning programs, computers may enable the student to learn more quickly and with greater understanding than ever before. Fig. 1-5 shows a classroom microcomputer system with video display and cassette tape unit. This system can be used effectively to aid in the teaching of arithmetic, algebra, science, chemistry, business, or almost any other discipline.

Courtesy Radio Shack, a Division of Tandy Corp.

Fig. 1-5. A classroom microcomputer system with video display and cassette tape unit.

Today, practically every college and university uses computers for administration, student use, or educational research. More and more college students are using computers in the nonscientific and nonbusiness disciplines. In years to come, all college students, regardless of their major, will take at least one course in using and appreciating computers.

Many secondary schools offer some form of computer education (see Fig. 1-6). Within the next decade, most of the high schools in the United States may very well be teaching students

Courtesy Digital Equipment Corp.

Fig. 1-6. Student inserting a floppy disk into the disk storage unit of a minicomputer system designed for use in schools.

how to use computers to solve many algebra, geometry, science, chemistry, and business problems.

COMPUTERS IN THE HOME

The dream of the computer-controlled home is now on the verge of reality. And the driving force that will make it possible is the microcomputer. Today, microcomputer systems are being purchased from manufacturers and computer stores at a rate of several thousand per month.

What is being done with home computers? Most of the first purchasers of these machines were electronic hobbyists who were happy to spend the many hours needed to design, build, test, and fix their new "toys." Today, we find home computer users ranging from ages 5 to 91. They use their machines to play games, to regulate air conditioners, to balance the family budget, to keep track of grocery shopping, to display kitchen menus, and to play video games such as Ping-Pong and Space War (see Fig. 1-7). Home computers can be purchased in kit form or already assembled. A computer kit takes from 50 to 200 hours to assemble; accessory kits generally require less time. Most computer kits require skill and knowledge in electronics work.

Clearly, it is only a matter of time before microcomputers will be as much a fixture in the home as the microwave oven,

Fig. 1-7. Home computer systems can be used by all members of a family to play games, do homework, keep inventory of household items, plan menus, etc.

and as common in the small office as the copying machine. Widespread acceptance of home computing awaits only the marketing of a "Volkskomputer" as a general consumer product, at which time the image of the home computer will be elevated from its present hobby status to the status of appliance or tool. Like the power hand drill, for example, the home computer will be used by the unskilled for a variety of general-purpose tasks as well as by the skilled for more creative projects. Home computers are sold by manufacturers, by computer stores located throughout America and other parts of the world, by mail order companies, and by well-known electronics companies such as Radio Shack and Heathkit. Within the next few years, we can expect other major electronics companies and general retail outlets to sell home computers.

AIRLINE RESERVATIONS SYSTEM

Airline traffic is one of the fastest growing segments of modern transportation. To meet the increasing demand for efficient passenger reservations systems, aircraft flight scheduling, supply and spare-parts inventory control, crew scheduling, airline

administration, freight control, and countless other tasks, the airlines have turned to the computer. Only with the computer can airlines keep up with rapidly changing day-to-day operations.

An airline's most important commodity is its passenger seat. An unsold seat is a complete loss, for it can never be recouped. With a computerized reservations system, the airline can pro-

Courtesy Braniff International

Fig. 1-8. Airline travel agent entering and receiving information on flight availability through a computer display terminal.

vide for optimal use of seats up to the moment of the departure of a plane. Using a computer-controlled reservations system enables the airline agents to "talk" directly with a central computer system. Each agent is equipped with a desk-size console that includes buttons, a keyboard, and a display screen. Within seconds, the agent can reserve flight space or complete any particular action requested by the customer (see Fig. 1-8).

In addition to handling passenger seat reservations, computer systems process information on flight scheduling, cargo

Courtesy Braniff International

Fig. 1-9. Cargo and baggage containers being loaded aboard a Boeing 747 jetliner.

loading (Fig. 1-9), meal planning, crew availability, aircraft maintenance scheduling, and many other tasks of an experimental nature.

BUSINESS USES OF COMPUTERS

It is not surprising that soon after the great potential of the computer became clear, American business became the largest single area of application. Computers are used to control stacks of raw materials and finished products, bill customers, calculate employee pay and taxes, analyze who is buying the company products, and perform hundreds of other administrative functions. Over half of the computers now in use were installed by business to control and reduce administrative paper work and cost.

Banks are large users of computers. Loan accounting, customer account updating, deposits and withdrawals, check processing, and daily report preparation are but a few of the computer applications in banking. With a computerized terminal, a bank teller can process account inquiries, checking transactions, savings transactions, loan payments, and utility bills without leaving the window (see Fig. 1-10).

Automatic check processing is perhaps the most frequent use of these machines, primarily because most money transactions within a bank are completed by the use of checks. The American Banking Association has adopted a special magnetic ink character system to be imprinted on checks. Using this system, check identification can be read by either bank personnel or special reading equipment connected to computers. This equipment can process checks at speeds of more than 2500 per minute. Banks have also developed systems that are used for updating of customer accounts. Such a system prints the trans-

Courtesy NCR Corp.

Fig. 1-10. Computerized terminal speeds banking transactions.

action in the passbook and automatically adds or subtracts the transaction amount from the computer record of the customer's account.

Other banking systems use computers to provide 24-hour banking service to their customers. A self-service, computer-controlled banking machine permits customers to transact their banking business at any hour of the day or night. The unit shown in Fig. 1-11 can be installed in an exterior bank wall, in the bank lobby, or in remote locations such as shopping centers or airports.

In some areas, checking account customers at a local bank are able to make purchases at local stores by using a special plastic banking card. The card is inserted into a reading device

Courtesy NCR Corp.

Fig. 1-11. A self-service banking machine.

at the store, registers an automatic credit to the merchant's account at the bank, and affixes an automatic debit to the customer's account.

Display systems that depict computerized information instantly on television-like screens are used by many banks, insurance companies, and other businesses. One such system is used by Wall Street brokerage firms. With this system, brokerage personnel can call up and display financial data; make additions, changes, or deletions; and send the information back to the computer, all in a matter of seconds. The system computes a master file of all transactions that have taken place, permitting supervisors to summarize vital information instantly.

The computer is rapidly changing the internal financial operating and control system of the modern department store. Sales are automatically used to update accounts, while the computer provides employee pay and commission data, updates inventories, and provides store management with important statistical data. Point-of-sale terminals are being used in many stores to expand and speed service to customers. In a typical sale, for example, a salesperson passes a hand-held wand over a thin magnetic strip on the price tag (see Fig. 1-12). The terminal then reads, records, and prints information describing the item, displays the price on a lighted panel, computes the amount due including applicable taxes, calculates the change to be returned, and prints a cash receipt.

The computer can also be used to determine instantly the credit status and history of a customer. This information may be needed prior to approving large purchases or for checking on delinquent accounts. The storage file of the computer also contains a list of stolen, lost, and discontinued credit cards. The computer can check the account number within seconds and advise the clerk whether the card is acceptable.

Another form of credit where automatic checking is often used is the gasoline credit card. Computer-controlled credit centers are located throughout the country for use by gasoline station managers. To use the system, the manager places a toll-free telephone call to the nearest center giving the oil company name, station number, credit card number, and purchase amount. The manager is informed whether the card is "good" or "bad" in about 20 seconds after receipt of the call.

Courtesy NCR Corp.

Fig. 1-12. Point-of-sale computer terminals speed sales service to department store customers.

Since 1954, when the General Electric Company installed the first computer (UNIVAC I) for data processing activities, business leaders have depended on the computer to help them improve services and products. Today, it would be difficult to imagine a large business conducting everyday operations without the aid of computers. Even small businesses are beginning to use microcomputer and minicomputer systems for processing typical business activities.

HOW COMPUTERS HELP THE GOVERNMENT

The federal government is the largest user of computers. The United States Bureau of the Census was the first group to use the computer for data processing. Today, when the national population is over 200 million, a census could not be taken without the aid of computers. All 50 states use computers to process tax, payroll, and personnel data. Many states have expanded the use of the computer to cover such diverse applications as planning new highways, analyzing laws, controlling new school locations, designing public works projects, and determining teacher requirements.

The Internal Revenue Service has turned to the computer for a faster and more complete method of checking and controlling income tax collections. Tax returns are forwarded to the appropriate regional IRS center where the information from each return is coded on punched cards. The cards are then read into a computer system which checks the mathematical accuracy of the returns and makes preliminary calculations on tax deductions and exemptions. Returns with mistakes are fed into a computer which prints out notices for corrections to the individuals or businesses involved. Correct returns are recorded on magnetic tape (one reel of tape holds about 20,000 individual returns) and forwarded to the IRS National Center in Martinsburg, West Virginia. A record of every taxpayer in the country is available in this center. At a rate of about one per minute, the computer system checks each return against all reports of payments to that individual or business from all

Courtesy Sperry Univac, a Division of Sperry Rand Corp.

Fig. 1-13. Military computer aboard U.S. Navy ship.

sources. If the return is not within certain predetermined guidelines, the computer "flags" it for further checking by IRS tax personnel. The computer has helped the IRS increase collections and has reduced tax evasion and delinquencies.

The Weather Bureau uses computers for forecasting weather, generating computer-printed maps, plotting the course of hurricanes, and communicating with weather satellites such as Tyros and Nimbus. The National Aeronautics and Space Administration (NASA) also uses computers to perform operations in space. Without computers, development, test preflight checkout, launch, control, guidance, navigation, reentry, recovery, and evaluation of space vehicles would not be possible.

The Department of Defense uses computers to tie together Navy, Army, Marine, and Air Force systems, as well as to link other agencies such as the National Security Agency, Civil Defense, and the State Department. Military computers, such as the one shown in Fig. 1-13, are used aboard U. S. Navy ships to provide air and sea surveillance, data communications, and weapons control.

The Atomic Energy Commission uses hundreds of computers to solve complex scientific problems relating to atomic and nuclear energy. With computers, AEC scientists are able to discover and measure phenomena and to solve problems that were beyond exploration a few years ago.

COMPUTERS IN THE ARTS

Most computers are used to perform some straightforward task such as payroll computation, inventory processing, insurance calculations, etc. But there is a lighter side to the role of the computer that is a far cry from the popular view of most people. The computer is used to assist in generating music, producing art, composing poetry, specifying dance movements, making movies, designing sculpture, designing textile fabrics, and making television commercials and programs.

Computer-generated music produces either scores, which are then performed, or music for which the acoustical properties are specified and which is then synthesized by a digital-to-analog converter. Computer-generated scores have ranged from music that is highly random in character to music that is intended to approximate some aspects of the style of a given composer or musical genre. The *Illiac Suite,* one of the best known early computer compositions, was a string quartet comprising rhythms and melodies constructed according to some rules of classical harmony and counterpoint. Another computer-generated composition, *Sonoriferous Loops,* used four parameters: pitch, register, rhythmic unit, and rhythmic mode.

The field of computer-generated motion pictures is often called *computer animation.* Animated movies are commonly made by copying a single frame at a time—an expensive and time-consuming process. Using photo-optic equipment under the control of a computer can be a more economical method to generate films. Bell Telephone Laboratories have even developed a special programming "movie language," called BEFLIX (Bell Flicks), to simplify making computer-produced animated films.

Computer art dates back to the mid 1950s. Since then, artists, engineers, doctors, poets, businessmen, architects, philosophers, and composers have been using the computer to produce

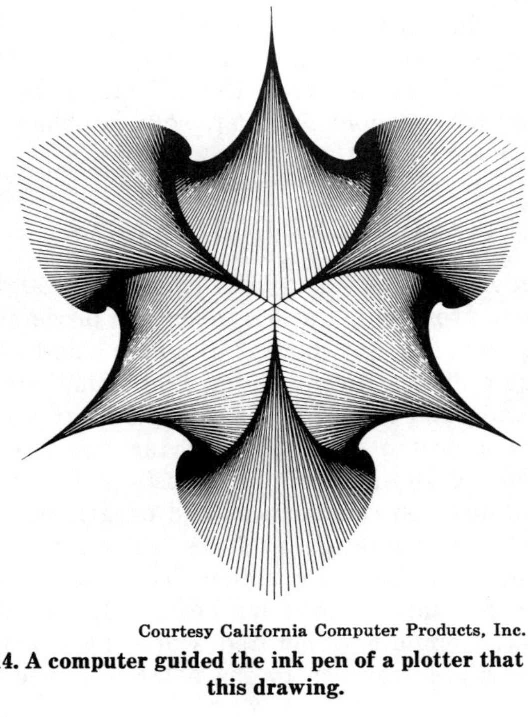

Courtesy California Computer Products, Inc.

Fig. 1-14. A computer guided the ink pen of a plotter that produced this drawing.

pictures. Engineers use the computer to draw airplanes, wiring diagrams, and other works of a scientific nature. The computer also reproduces X-ray images, body organs, and other medical pictures for research doctors. Businessmen use the computer to draw graphs, PERT charts, and statistical diagrams; while architects find the computer helpful in drawing floor layouts, buildings, and perspectives. Most of the previously mentioned drawings have a practical value. However, artists are using the computer to create a form of "computer art." Computer drawings can be made using a digital plotter, a display screen, or a printing device. Fig. 1-14 is a picture drawn by a computer-controlled plotter.

Computers aid sculptors in the design and building of complex sculptures, and are even used to help produce television commercials and programs. For example, computers are used to assemble the "Hee Haw" television show. Each program is composed of up to 200 segments on one particular theme. The computer pieces these segments together to form the show.

Computer-generated dance is in an embryonic state. One experiment used the computer to specify the number of dancers

Courtesy Apple Computer Inc.

Fig. 1-15. Microcomputer being used to generate computer art on a color television screen.

on the stage at any given time and to indicate the positions they would occupy throughout the period of time they were onstage. Another experiment used a computer display to delineate the spatial and arm movements of a group of dancers onstage.

A number of people have used the computer to write poetry. Quite often, the computer-generated poems are sheer nonsense; however, poems of some quality are occasionally generated.

Today, many personal computer users are using their microcomputer systems to compose music and to produce "computer art" in both black and white and color (see Fig. 1-15).

CONTROL COMPUTERS

Computers are used in many control applications: industrial process control, numerical tool control, military command and control, air-traffic control, missile and spacecraft guidance, and traffic-light control.

In controlling a process—like that in a paper plant, steel mill, or oil refinery—the computer reads measuring and sampling instruments, checks the readings for conformity to preset limits, relays corrections to adjusting devices, and prints out a continuous record of instrument readings.

When numerical control of machine tools was introduced in the mid 1950s, a new era in manufacturing began. Numerical control offered economy—a way to produce short runs of complex parts profitably—and it made the entire manufacturing operation much easier and more flexible. Numerical control guides a machine through a complete cycle by means of coded instructions. Thus, once the work is placed in position on the machine, a coded program controls the selection of the tools, feed rate, spindle speed, coolant setting, and the direction and distance of movements until the piece of work is completed.

The United States military uses hundreds of computers in defense command and control systems. These systems keep track of hostile military forces and equipment and are constantly on the alert to detect and monitor enemy movements.

Similarly, many large airports use computerized radar systems to monitor local air traffic. The Atlanta airport was one of the first major airports to install such an air-traffic control system. Such systems have now been installed at every major airport in the United States. Computer systems provide air-

Courtesy Federal Aviation Administration

Fig. 1-16. Computerized radar systems help in identification and tracking of aircraft in the vicinity of an airport.

craft identity, speed, altitude, and other flight data. This information appears in the form of letters, numbers, and symbols next to the radar blip of the plane on the air-traffic controller's visual radar display (see Fig. 1-16). This enables the controllers to direct aircraft into the quickest and safest takeoff and landing patterns.

The computer plays a similar role in spacecraft guidance. When a missile leaves the launch pad, it is continuously controlled and watched by radar and computers. If the missile runs into trouble, a computer command can cause the missile to be destroyed before any damage occurs on the ground. The computer can send signals to the missile to cause it to change course, separate stages, or perform some new function. The past space accomplishments of our nation, such as the Apollo moon landings, would not have been possible without computers.

Computers are also used to control traffic on the ground. By sensing the movement of vehicles and regulating traffic lights, the optimal flow of traffic can be maintained.

PLAYING GAMES WITH COMPUTERS

Until the invention of the computer, game playing was primarily restricted to humans or special-purpose machines. Today, people all over the world are spending a considerable amount of time programming computers to play games. One reason for this is that game programs provide us with excellent opportunities for learning how to solve problems with computers. Beginning computer users can understand the problem in a minimum amount of time; therefore, they can devote more time to learning about the computer, algorithm development, programming languages, and techniques of problem solving with a computer.

Another reason why people are using computers to play games is that games are often good analogies to actual situations involving humans and their environment. Gaming is being applied to business management, scientific experiments, and military tactics. Business executives are playing games with digital computers that simulate the operation of their business. Games of this type allow executives to keep an active study of their employees, to learn more about their company, and to simulate all activities of their company.

Game playing with computers is fun. Many personal computer users are using their microcomputer systems to play games like Space War (see Fig. 1-17), chess, blackjack, backgammon, Ping-Pong, poker, and tic-tac-toe.

How does a computer play a game? It may be pitted against a human player as would be done in a game of checkers or chess. It may also be used as a scorekeeper between two players or teams. The computer can also be directed to generate the solution to a specfic game or puzzle, such as a magic square. The most popular form of play for the computer is for it to participate in the game as an active player. In this type of play, the human player's moves are indicated to the computer on an input device such as a typewriter or display terminal. The com-

Courtesy Compucolor Corp.

Fig. 1-17. Microcomputers are used to play "Space War," a game based on the tv show "Star Trek."

puter then computes its move and reports it to the human player. The report is given on a typewriter or display terminal. The computer also keeps score by recording both its own moves and the human player's moves.

The following printout shows the ease of playing a game of tic-tac-toe with a computer. The computer keeps track of the human player's moves and prints the board configuration every time the computer makes its move. The human player informs the computer of his/her move by indicating the row and column that the desired position lies in. For example, a position in the top right corner of the tic-tac-toe board would be specified as 1, 3 (row 1, column 3).

The human player starts the game by typing 3,1. The computer responds by printing:

```
         *    *
         *    *
         *    *
  ******************
         *    *
         * COM *
         *    *
  ******************
         *    *
   YOU   *    *
         *    *
```

The human player's moves are indicated by YOU and the computer's moves are marked by COM. The game continues by the human player typing 2,1. The computer prints:

```
         *    *
   COM   *    *
         *    *
  ******************
         *    *
   YOU   * COM *
         *    *
  ******************
         *    *
   YOU   *    *
         *    *
```

The player types 1,2 and the computer prints:

```
         *    *
   COM   * YOU *
         *    *
  ******************
         *    *
   YOU   * COM *
         *    *
  ******************
         *    *
   YOU   *    * COM
         *    *
THE COMPUTER WINS THIS TIME—
DO YOU WANT TO PLAY ANOTHER GAME?
```

The player types NO.

Computers have been programmed to play chess for almost three decades. Today, there are computer chess playing tournaments. In 1977, a computer chess program named CHESS 4.6 from the United States swept the international tournament held in Toronto, Canada to become the new world champion.

Charles Fey, a young mechanic who emigrated from Bavaria to San Francisco in 1887, invented the slot machine and put it into operation in the Bay area in 1895. The first one was called *The Liberty Bell,* accepted and paid out nickels, and sat on the bar in a saloon. Today there are thousands of these mechanical coin grabbers operating in casinos throughout the world.

There is also another type of slot machine called the *computer simulated* slot machine. Instead of pulling the handle as one would do on a real slot machine, the action is started by pointing a light pen at a start position on a display console. The computer generates a three-symbol combination composed of the following symbols: cherries, oranges, melons, bars, bells, lemons, and plums. This symbol combination, along with an indicated payoff, is displayed on the cathode ray tube of the display console.

Slot machines are also simulated by crt displays or typewriters connected to computers, as shown in the following printout:

```
THIS IS A SIMULATED SLOT MACHINE
WINNING COMBINATIONS ARE
3 BARS  3 ORANGES  3 CHERRIES
WINNING PAYOFF IS $3.00
HOW MANY 50 CENT PIECES DO YOU
WANT TO PLAY?3
YOU START WITH $1.5
DO YOU WISH TO PLAY
(TYPE 1 FOR YES -- 0 FOR NO)
?1

---ORANGE---
---CHERRY---
---CHERRY---
    TOO BAD --- YOU LOST
YOU NOW HAVE $1
DO YOU WISH TO PLAY
(TYPE 1 FOR YES -- 0 FOR NO)
?1
```

```
---CHERRY---
---CHERRY---
---ORANGE---
   TOO BAD --- YOU LOST
YOU NOW HAVE $.5
DO YOU WISH TO PLAY
(TYPE 1 FOR YES -- 0 FOR NO)
?1

---ORANGE---
---ORANGE---
---BAR---
   TOO BAD --- YOU LOST
YOU HAVE LOST ALL YOUR MONEY
```

There are literally hundreds of games that have been programmed for computer play.

COMPUTERS AND SOCIETY

Much has been said about the computer taking over our lives, putting people out of jobs, and invading our privacy. These topics cannot be discussed intelligently without knowing more about the computer, but they should be given some thought as your knowledge and understanding increase. Remember that the computer cannot do anything unless it is told what to do by human beings. We should control the computer—it should not control us.

Today, there are thousands of businesses and organizations that use computers. While these organizations are making increased use of computers, perhaps the greatest benefits will come from placing the computer at the *direct* service of the individual. If people become more adept in all their activities by using a computer as a knowledgeable and skillful assistant, society as a whole will be improved.

Unfortunately, many people still fear computers and view them as cold, impersonal machines. They also object to being identified by numbers. Such fears and personal objections will probably persist until computers are brought within easy reach of the public and are used as helpful assistants.

A certain amount of apprehension always accompanies new technology. The automobile was disliked because engines were noisy and dirty, and the telephone was initially regarded as an invasion of privacy. Although we often view the abilities of the computer with awe and admiration, several serious and complex issues have been raised by its very accomplishments. In this section we are going to look closely at four of the key issues:

1. Privileged information and privacy.
2. Misuse of computers.
3. Attitudes.
4. Automation and employment.

Privileged Information and Privacy

If computers are to help people in their daily activities, computer memories must accumulate detailed information about the affairs of people—purchases, banking activities, credit information, etc—which amounts to a description of people's lives.

The computer can collect, process, store, and retrieve data more rapidly than any human. This ability, coupled with the ever increasing number of computerized data banks, is making it possible for private businesses and government agencies to compile sizable information files on individual citizens. The potential for good inherent in these data banks is great, but the potential for harm is also present.

A few years ago, a professor of law testifying before the Senate Subcommittee on Constitutional Rights expressed the problem this way: "Whether he knows it or not, each time a citizen files a tax return, applies for life insurance or a credit card, seeks government benefits, or interviews for a job, a dossier is opened under his name and an information profile on him is sketched. It has now reached the point that whenever we travel on a commercial airline, reserve a room at one of the national hotel chains, or rent a car we are likely to leave distinctive electronic tracks in the memory of a computer—tracks that can tell a great deal about our activities, habits, and associations when collected and analyzed. Few people seem to appreciate the fact that modern technology is capable of monitoring, centralizing, and evaluating these electronic entries—no matter how numerous they may be—thereby making credible the fear that many Americans have of a womb-to-tomb dossier on each of us."

There are many reasons why privacy is important to the individual. A person should be able to "unwind," "let it all out," show intimate feelings without fear of events being misinterpreted. A person's hopes, fears, shames, and aspirations should be protected against public scrutiny. A person should be able to seek and utilize counsel (legal, clerical, etc.) without fear of incrimination. A person should be able to choose the recipient of such information as occupation, education, income, family size, number of children, ages of children, religious preference, political preference, taxes paid, attitudes toward social issues, and property ownership.

Government agencies such as the IRS, the FBI, the Social Security Administration, and the Veterans Administration have data banks on people. Each agency generally has its own procedures for collecting data and ensuring its accuracy, value, and appropriateness. But what about when information is shared, as in a data bank? Should an agency have access to information collected by another agency?

The role of privacy, and the role of information about individuals in the operation of society must be clarified. Proper protection of the rights of the individual must be devised, because privacy does indeed play a very important role in our form of society.

Misuse of Computers

The powerful products of our present-day technology such as drugs, chemical and biological warfare, and nuclear weapons offer many opportunities for abuse. It is easy to visualize the misuse of the computer.

One morning, not long ago, an unidentified man walked into a Washington, D.C. bank, deftly pocketed deposit slips at the writing counters and replaced them with his own electronically coded forms. In the next three days, customers who came in without a personal deposit slip used those "blank" forms. Through a computer, their deposits went into the invisible bank robber's account. On the fourth day he withdrew over $100,000, vanished, and still hasn't been caught. That elegant caper is but one of a mounting number of computer-assisted crimes involving uncounted millions of dollars in cash, goods, and services.

In California, an accountant plundered over one million dollars from his company during a six-year period by recording in the computer higher payments for raw material than his company actually paid. Craftily, the accountant had the computer assign the extra cash to his own dummy firm.

A manager of claims in a government-sponsored medical aid scheme introduced false doctor claims and directed the payment checks to an office he had rented under a fictitious name.

Incredibly, someone was able to manipulate Penn Central Railroad computers to divert 277 freight cars, worth one million dollars, to a small Illinois railroad and hide them there.

What is disturbing businesses is that fraud is so hard to detect. Usually, culprits are uncovered merely by accident rather than by audits. A New York savings bank embezzlement, for instance, popped up after a police raid on a bookie joint. The police found records showing the chief teller had been betting as much as $30,000 a day. That led to his undoing.

How do businessses prevent such automated ripoffs? Not surprisingly, the menace has caused many companies to invent all kinds of gadgetry, and computer "audits" have been introduced in efforts to make the machines crime proof.

Attitudes

Results of a national attitude survey of the general public indicated a majority of Americans believe computers are making life better. However, there is a major public concern in several important areas: automation and unemployment, increased dependence on computers, dehumanization, the gathering of information on people by large organizations, and the possible misuse of computerized information files. The survey was based on telephone interviews with 1001 people 18 years of age and older. In analyzing the survey results, analysts found that much of the data could be grouped into eight basic areas. A brief summary of the results follows:

1. *Job Involvement*—Those surveyed indicated that the public has a relatively high degree of job involvement with computers.
2. *Computer Problem*—Thirty-four percent of those surveyed reported that they had a problem "because of a computer."

3. *Computers and the Consumer*—The public view toward the use of computers in providing consumer benefits (products, services, schools, etc.) was positive.
4. *Computers in Business*—Most of those surveyed felt that we can do many things today that would be impossible without computers.
5. *Computers in Government*—In general, the public believed that government should make increased usage of computers in a number of areas.
6. *Computers and Privacy*—There was major concern about the use of large computerized information files.
7. *Computers and Life*—Of those surveyed, almost all agreed that the use of computers is affecting the lives of all of us. Most felt that computers will improve our lives and create more leisure time. However, many felt people are becoming too dependent on computers.
8. *Career Opportunities*—Those surveyed indicated that they were in favor of a young person entering the computer field as a career.

Automation and Employment

Automation is the process of replacing human work done by a machine or system designed to perform a specific combination of actions automatically or repeatedly. It is pointless to argue that automation either destroys or creates employment. Its purpose is to reduce the costs of production or to perform tasks that could not otherwise be done. In either case, it is a substitute as well as a supplement for human labor.

It is true that the computer has displaced some people. Often when an employee's job is to be replaced by a computerized system, the employee is retrained to work in some other area rather than laid off. The installation of a computer system, moreover, always creates new jobs. People are required to maintain, operate, and program the computer system. Displaced persons may very well find new positions as computer operators, keypunch operators, programmers, etc.

THE FUTURE

The future is always uncertain, and predictions are often inaccurate. How many of the predictions made for the 1970s have come to fruition? Certainly landing a man on the moon is one that did. There have even been some unpleasant surprises, such as automobile pollution and soapy rivers. What of the computer? Its future probably includes further miniaturization, lower cost, more reliable machines, greater speed, large capacity memories, and an increased range of communications devices and terminals to connect to computers. Microprocessors and microcomputers will be used widely in all types of appliances, business machines, recreational games, automobiles, and other electrical devices.

Have we tapped the full potential of the computer? The computer has contributed a great deal so far to research in such areas as medicine, space projects, and archeology, uncovering facts and figures that would have taken human beings many years to arrive at. In the society of today can we do without it? As we learn more about its capabilities and limitations, we can probably offer a better judgment about its place in our lives.

Chapter 2

History of Computing

Courtesy Burroughs Corp.

PRIMITIVE CALCULATORS

In ancient times, there was a serious need for a practical calculating device. Both the Romans and the Greeks used clumsy number systems that made addition and subtraction a chore and multiplication and division an exercise for only the experts. One of the earliest calculating devices was the *counting board.* This board consisted of several rods mounted on a wooden frame, with ten sliding beads on each rod (Fig. 2-1). The digits 0 to 9 were represented on each rod by moving an appropriate number of beads toward the bottom of the frame. The counting board in Fig. 2-1 represents the number 6,410,380.

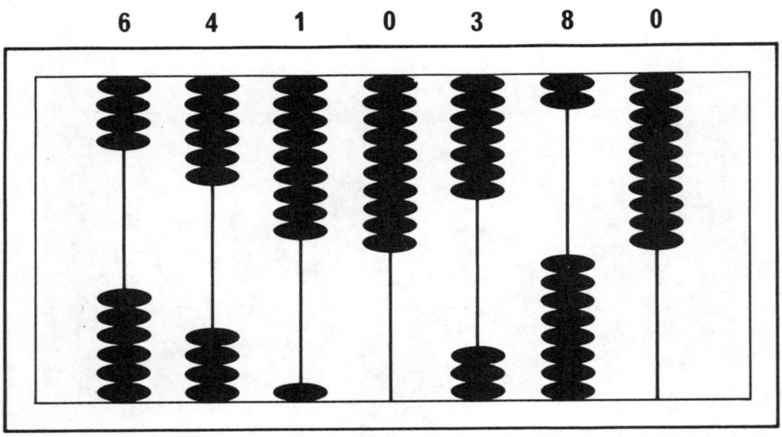

Fig. 2-1. An ancient counting board expressing the number 6,410,380.

The Romans used a counting board that consisted of a metal plate containing seven long vertical slots, with seven short vertical slots above them. Fig. 2-2 illustrates a Roman board expressing the year that Pascal invented the first adding machine, 1642. The seventh long slot to the right represented units, the sixth tens, the fifth hundreds, etc., all the way over to the first long slot on the left which represented millions. The smaller slots each represented five with multiples of 10; the first being 5, the second 50, the third 500, the fourth 5000, the fifth 50,000, etc.

The ancient Chinese modified the counting board into the *abacus*. The abacus has only seven beads on the vertical rods.

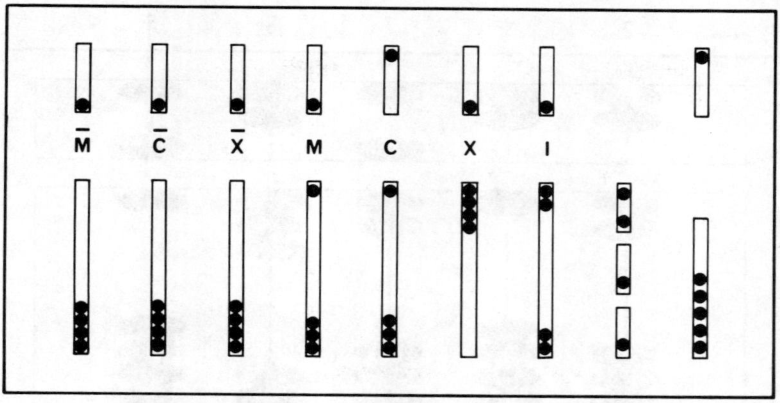

Fig. 2-2. A Roman board expressing the number 1642.

The frame is divided into two sections by a wooden beam. Two beads (known as "five" beads) are above the beam and five "one" beads are below it. One "five" bead is worth five "one" beads. The value of a bead depends on which column is assumed to be the "units" column. The beads in the left-hand column are greater than those in the right-hand column. One unit in the left column is always ten times as large as one unit in the adjacent column to the right. Thus, if we assume that the first column on the right-hand side of the frame is the "units" column, one "one" bead in the first column will be worth one unit; one in the second column will be worth ten units; one in the third column will equal 100 units, etc. Likewise, one "five" bead in the first column will be worth five units; one in the second column will equal 50 units, and so on. By sliding the beads up and down the rods in the proper manner, it is possible to perform all the common arithmetic operations. The Chinese abacus in Fig. 2-3 represents the number 21,736.

The Japanese built a similar device and called it a *soroban.* The soroban used only five beads on a vertical rod as illustrated in Fig. 2-4. One "five" bead is above the separating crosspiece and four "one" beads are below the crosspiece. The number 6,075,001 is represented in Fig. 2-4.

Primitive as it is, the simple abacus should not be underrated as a calculating device. Even today, people still use the abacus.

In solving any problem in arithmetic, however simple it may be, two parts of our mental powers must be used, namely, the

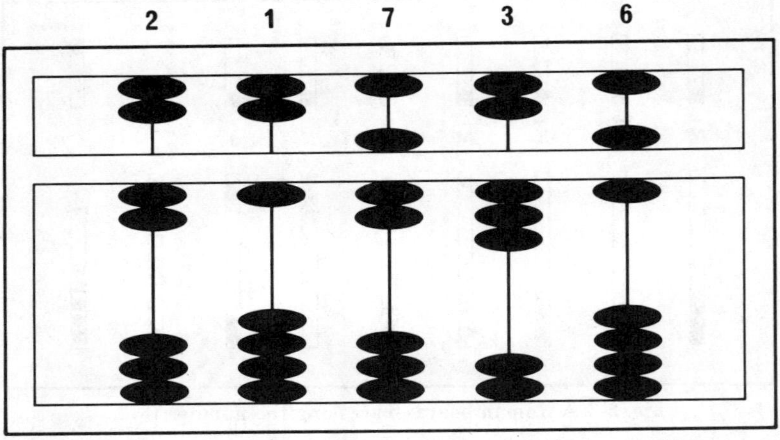

Fig. 2-3. A Chinese abacus expressing the number 21,736.

faculties of computation and of memory. We employ them when we add one and two; for in adding we must first retain the number one in our mind, then we fix our attention upon the other number, two, and finally we compute how much one and two are. With very small numbers, these are very simple operations. But as the problems become more complex, we soon reach the limit of our mental capacity. In dealing with difficult problems, the abacus provides a means of relieving the strain of computation. By using these devices, we can devote our entire attention to accuracy in computing, and leave the memory work to the abacus.

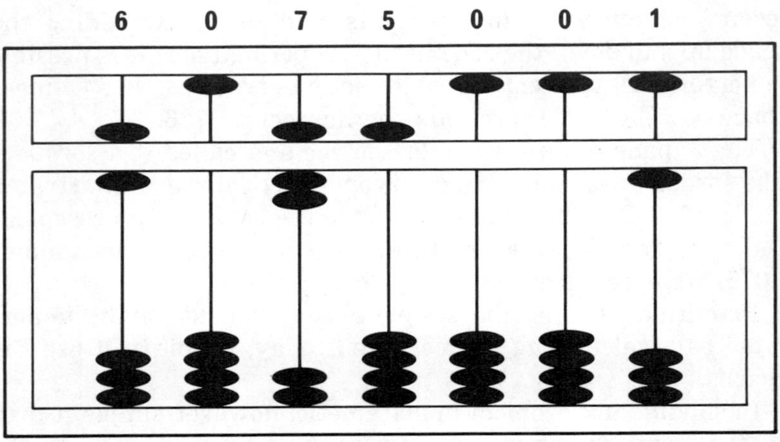

Fig. 2-4. A Japanese soroban expressing the number 6,075,001.

The next significant advancement in computational devices was in 1614, when John Napier invented and published a table of *logarithms*. In 1617, Napier devised a computing system called *Napier's bones*. These were simply a set of numbering rods (Fig. 2-5) which simplified multiplication, division, and the extracting of roots. Each rod was divided into nine sections

Fig. 2-5. Napier's bones.

with a large number at the top. Rod number 1 had a 1 at the top followed by the numbers 2 through 9. Rod number 2 had a 2 at the top and all the other sections contained numbers that were multiples of 2. Rod number 3 had a 3 at the top and all the other sections were multiples of 3. The remaining rods contained numbers in the sections that were multiples of the top number. To multiply 324 by 37, the *bones* would be laid out as in Fig. 2-6. The partial results 972 and 2268 are read from the *bones*, and the answer 11,988 is obtained by the addition of 2268 and 9720.

Napier's *logarithms* were used by William Oughtred in 1630, who inscribed them on ivory and devised the first *slide rule*. This basic *rule* was later modified by Isaac Newton and Lieutenant Amedee Mannheim into the modern version of the slide rule.

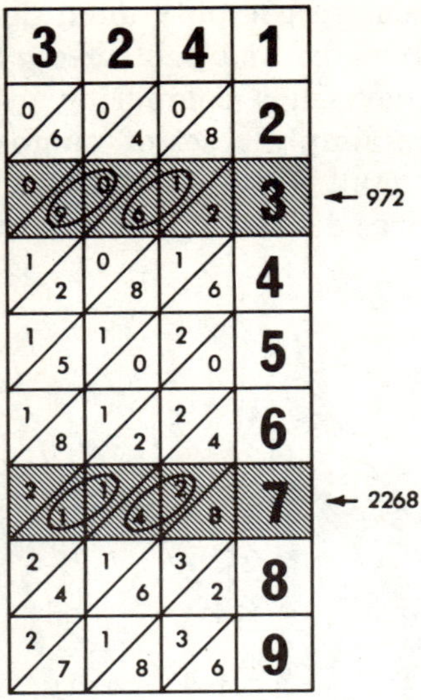

Fig. 2-6. Calculating 324 × 37 on Napier's bones.

MECHANICAL CALCULATORS

In 1642, a nineteen-year-old Frenchman, Blaise Pascal, irritated with the task of adding long columns of figures for his tax-collector father, invented the first mechanical calculating machine (Fig. 2-7). The most important feature of this machine was its built-in and automatic means for *carrying*. It used eight wheels, each containing ten teeth to correspond to the ten digits. When a count of ten was completed on one wheel, the wheel returned to its zero position and caused the wheel on the left to move one position. This introduced a carry of 1 to the next higher position.

Later in the same century (1671), the German mathematician Liebnitz developed a machine that could do multiplication by rapidly repeated addition. Another machine that could multiply was also invented by Sir Samuel Morland in 1673. As time went on, the basic machines of Pascal, Liebnitz, and Morland were improved and eventually new developments led to modern-day calculators.

One of the most used input media to modern-day computing systems is the *punched card*. The punched-card concept is quite old, as a similar media was used in 1725 by Basile Bouchon, a French engineer, in his historic *loom*. Bouchon mechanized a

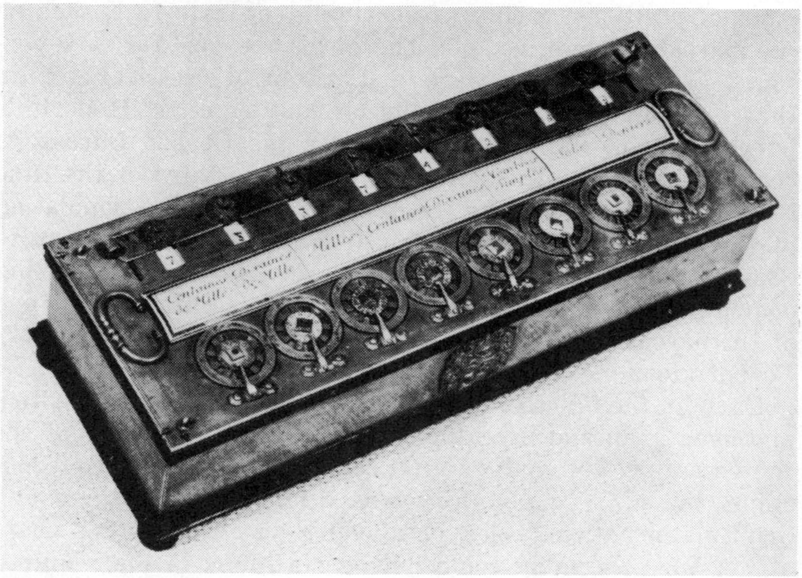

Courtesy IBM Corp.

Fig. 2-7. Pascal's mechanical calculating machine.

loom which could weave a fashionable intricate design into a silk fabric. The loom contained a roll of paper which had instructions coded by lines of punched holes. The holes were punched in the paper in accordance with the design to be woven. Bouchon's machine was simple, but it was a beginning toward modern computing machines.

In 1801, Joseph Marie Jacquard perfected the classic draw-loom action that has remained basically unchanged to this day. The Jacquard punched-card system was more complex than Bouchon's system as it controlled as many as 12,000 needles at once. The punched cards controlled the needles which, in turn, selected the proper threads. Bouchon and Jacquard were essentially communicating with the loom via their punched paper roll and cards. This same type of communication system is used in computers today; *hole* or *no hole, yes* or *no, on* or *off, go* or *no-go, 1* or *0*.

Herman Hollerith, an employee of the United States Census Bureau, applied the punched-hole principle to cards and sorted them mechanically for the 1890 census. Census information was hand-punched on cards, according to a pre-coded arrangement of positions, each representing a separate fact, such as the individual's age, sex, etc. There was one card for each person. The punched cards were used to control electrical circuits that registered the card results on counter dials. Hollerith's punched cards and tabulator enabled the Census Bureau to complete the 1890 census in two years, one third of the time that was required to take the 1880 census, yet the population of the United States had risen from 50,262,000 in 1880, to 63,056,000 in 1890. Hollerith later set up a manufacturing company to build his tabulating device. This company was one of the parents of the *I*nternational *B*usiness *M*achines (IBM) Corporation, one of the giants in the computer business.

Early in the nineteenth century, Charles Babbage, a British mathematician and inventor, developed the forerunner of the contemporary automatic digital computer. Babbage's first machine, the *difference engine,* was designed to calculate and print mathematical tables. It failed because the cogs and gears of his huge assembly could not be machined to the required precision. Before Babbage's difference engine was completed he thought of a new and better machine, the *analytical engine.* This machine used the principles from one of the first automatic machines, the Jacquard loom, which was used in the textile industry. Babbage's analytical engine was to be controlled by the use of holes punched in cards. Again, the concept was brilliant, but the engineering problems were overwhelming and the second machine was never completed because the British government could not continue to finance the development.

Let us take a closer look at Babbage's analytical engine. It was designed in 1833, used punched-card input, and had storage for 50,000 decimal digits. It had an arithmetic unit which performed the actual calculations. It had a unit that controlled the order in which the computations were made. It produced output documents that were either printed forms or punched cards. After looking over these characteristics, it is obvious that Babbage's machine contained all the basic parts of a modern computer: *input, storage, arithmetic unit, control,* and *output.* Although the basic elements of modern computers were known in the early nineteenth century, no major advance took place until shortly before World War II. Charles Babbage was definitely a man ahead of his time.

About the same time Babbage was working with his analytical engine, George Boole, an English mathematician, was developing the foundation for *Boolean Algebra.*

ELECTROMECHANICAL COMPUTING MACHINES

Prior to World War I, manually operated office machines were used to make rapid calculations and to provide information needed by management for carrying out the various activities of a business enterprise. Shortly after World War I, electromechanical machines came into general use. They accomplished four basic operational steps: recording, summarizing, calculating, and, to a limited extent, sorting. These machines were not automatic and they required some form of action by an operator such as depressing a key, bar, or lever, to perform each processing operation.

Courtesy Aiken Computation Laboratory, Harvard University

Fig. 2-8. The *A*utomatic *S*equence *C*ontrolled *C*alculator (ASCC).

In 1944, Dr. Howard Aiken, with assistance from IBM engineers and Harvard graduate students, completed the *A*utomatic *S*equence *C*ontrolled *C*alculator (ASCC) commonly called the Harvard Mark I Computer. The Mark I was built primarily of standard IBM components. The principle of operation was mechanical, although relays operated by electromagnets were used. It had 72 accumulators, each capable of holding a 23-digit decimal number. The operations of the computer were carried out under the control of a punched paper tape.

This control tape contained 24 holes across the width of the tape. The calculator also had facilities for handling punched-card input and output.

The Mark I was a slow calculator because a relay simply cannot operate as fast as an electronic tube or solid-state device. Nevertheless, the Mark I has a permanent place in the history of calculating machines because it was the first automatic calculating machine ever to be built. Fig. 2-8 illustrates the Automatic Sequence Controlled Calculator.

One of the greatest advances in automatic computing came in 1945 when Dr. John von Neumann introduced the *stored-program* concept wherein computer instructions were stored in the internal memory of the computer. Prior to this time, instructions were stored in some external medium such as paper tape, punched cards, or a wired plugboard like the one shown in Fig. 2-9. The stored-program concept was first used in the design of the EDVAC. Most present-day digital computers are of the stored-program type.

Courtesy Sperry Univac, a Division of Sperry Rand Corp.

Fig. 2-9. A wired plugboard.

ELECTRONIC COMPUTING MACHINES

In 1934, Dr. John V. Atanasoff, a professor of physics at Iowa State College (now Iowa State University), modified an IBM punched-card machine to perform calculations mechanically. Five years later, he built a prototype of an electronic digital computer, called the ABC (*A*tanasoff-*B*erry *C*omputer). His assistant on this computing machine was Clifford Berry. The ABC, which had a "memory" consisting of 45 vacuum tubes, was assembled in 1942.

Courtesy U.S. Army Ballistics Research Laboratories

Fig. 2-10. Front view of the *E*lectronic *N*umerical *I*ntegrator *A*nd *C*alculator (ENIAC). Accumulators are on the top row, controls on the left, and function tables on the right.

In 1946, the *E*lectronic *N*umerical *I*ntegrator *A*nd *C*alculator (ENIAC) went into operation at the Moore School of Electrical Engineering of the University of Pennsylvania. This specialized computer was built to compute firing and ballistic tables to help guide army artillerymen in aiming their guns. The ENIAC is shown in Fig. 2-10.

ENIAC, invented by two researchers at the University of Pennsylvania—Dr. John W. Mauchly and J. Presper Eckert—occupied a space of 139.95 m^2 (1500 square feet), weighed about 30 tons, contained about 19,000 vacuum tubes, and required 130 kW of power. The computing elements consisted of many components linked by about a million hand-soldered connections. The input/output system consisted of modified IBM card readers and punches. ENIAC had a limited storage capacity for only 20 ten-digit numbers. (It took 12 vacuum tubes to store one decimal digit). ENIAC could perform 5000 additions or 300 multiplications per second. ENIAC, by today's standards, is relatively slow; however, in 1946, the only other machine that could even compete was the ASCC relay calculator that could perform 10 additions per second. Needless to say, ENIAC made all relay calculators obsolete.

ENIAC could perform several operations simultaneously, a capability that has only recently become possible with the advent of modern digital computer systems. It could perform several additions, a multiplication, and a square root in parallel, as well as solve several independent problems at the same time. It was a fascinating machine that could have been built many years earlier had there been a need for such a machine. Even though there are many amusing stories about ENIAC (stories claiming that all the lights in West Philadelphia would dim when the ENIAC was turned on or that three or more tubes would always burn out when it was started), it was a machine that was so successful that it marked the end of the pioneer stage of automatic computer development. ENIAC was retired from service in 1955.

The *E*lectronic *D*iscrete *V*ariable *A*utomatic *C*omputer (EDVAC) was completed at the Moore School of Electrical Engineering, University of Pennsylvania, in 1949. The EDVAC was designed by Eckert, Mauchley, A. W. Burks, H. H. Goldstine, and Dr. John von Neumann, using the stored-program concept of Dr. von Neumann. This computer was used to compute ballistic- and weapon-systems evaluation problems. It cost around $467,000 and could add in 864 microseconds, multiply in 2.9 milliseconds, and divide in 2.9 milliseconds. This was the first computer that represented numbers in the *binary* scale. The EDVAC had a word size of 44 bits, which corresponds to about 13 decimal digits. The internal memory of the EDVAC could hold 1024 numbers. However, the system had an auxiliary storage that could hold some 20,000 numbers. Fig. 2-11 illustrates the EDVAC.

Several computers were developed during 1949 and 1950. Among the important ones were Eckert-Mauchly Corporation's *BIN*ary *A*utomatic *C*omputer (BINAC), 1949; IBM's Selective Sequence Electronic Calculator (1949); the Bureau of *S*tandard's *E*astern *A*utomatic *C*omputer (SEAC), 1950; Massachusetts Institute of Technology's Whirlwind I (1950) *E*lectronic *D*elay *S*torage *A*utomatic *C*omputer (EDSAC).

The SEAC was retired in 1964. This was one of the first internally programmed digital computers. It was originally developed to help the Air Force attack massive logistics prob-

Courtesy U.S. Army Ballistics Research Laboratories

Fig. 2-11. Front view of the *E*lectronic *D*iscrete *V*ariable *A*utomatic *C*omputer (EDVAC) showing paper-tape reader at right.

lems, and was also used in the design of the first hydrogen bomb.

The MIT Whirlwind I computer used magnetic core as a storage device. This use of core storage was so successful that most of the computers designed after 1952 used magnetic cores for memory.

In 1952, the *I*nstitute for *A*dvanced *S*tudy (IAS) computer was completed. This computer was developed at Princeton University by Dr. von Neumann, Burks, and Goldstein. This computer was much faster than any other computer of its time. In fact, it included many features of modern computers: asynchronous timing, single address, binary number system, and parallel arithmetic mode. Many computers were developed using the IAS design: JOHNNIAC, ILLIAC, MANIAC, ORACLE, and ORDVAC.

The BINAC, which was developed by the Eckert-Mauchly team, was a special-purpose computer of which only one was built. BINAC contained several important features: serial logic, internal programming, magnetic tape input/output, and solid-state elements. With these features, computers began to become practical machines from the commercial standpoint.

The first commercial data-processing computer went into operation in March, 1951. It was installed at the United States Bureau of the Census. This computer was the Sperry Rand Corporation's UNIVAC I (UNIVAC is an acronym for *UNIV*ersal *A*utomatic *C*omputer) and it contained circuitry that was very similar to that used in the BINAC: crystal-diode switches and vacuum-tube circuits.

The UNIVAC I was used by the Census Bureau in their Philadelphia plant location for processing some of the data from the 1950 census. In 1952, the computer was transferred to the Census Building in Suitland, Maryland. By 1955, over 15 UNIVAC Is had been delivered. The commercial users included General Electric, Chesapeake and Ohio Railway Company, University of Pennsylvania, Franklin Institute, Great Northern Railway Company, Franklin Life Insurance Company, U. S. Steel, and Metropolitan Life. In 1963, twelve and one-half years after its installation, the first UNIVAC I was retired to the Smithsonian Institution in Washington, D. C.

One of the most interesting features of the UNIVAC I was that it could read, compute, and write information simulta-

Courtesy Sperry Univac, a Division of Sperry Rand Corp.

Fig. 2-12. The UNIVAC I computer system.

neously, an ability that no other computer would have for several years.

UNIVAC I was a binary-coded decimal machine with a word size of twelve digits. It could perform an addition in 525 microseconds, a multiplication in 2.15 milliseconds, and a division in 3.95 milliseconds. It had an acoustic delay-line memory of 1000 words, with an access time between 40.4 and 404 microseconds. The UNIVAC I is shown in Fig. 2-12.

It was about 1951 when IBM began making significant progress in the computer business. Needless to say, they have been very serious about it ever since. Their first computer was the IBM 701 (first named the Defense Calculator) which was available in 1953. In the next year the popular IBM 650 was delivered. Then came the IBM 702, IBM 704, and IBM 705 in 1955. In 1958, IBM delivered the first 709 and a year later delivered the powerful IBM 7090.

During the 1960s, dozens of companies began to manufacture high-speed computers. All of these machines were much faster and more reliable than the early computers. Most of the machines made during the late 1950s and early 1960s belonged to the second generation of computers. These machines were much smaller, required less power, and produced much less heat. The use of transistors as basic components of internal computer circuits was the main reason for this improvement.

"I DON'T KNOW HIS EXACT AGE, BUT HE SPEAKS OF HAVING PROGRAMMED AN IBM 650 COMPUTER."

MODERN COMPUTERS

The third generation of computers appeared in 1964 when IBM announced the System/360. Most computers made during the late 1960s and 1970s employed microminiature circuits for their internal circuitry. Third-generation machines are smaller, more reliable, and faster than earlier machines. Along with third-generation computers, newer and faster equipment has been introduced for storage and handling of input and output.

A *minicomputer* is a relatively inexpensive computer introduced by Digital Equipment Corporation during the mid 1960s. Minicomputers have been designed for use in a wide variety of application areas. The typical minicomputer has a purchase price of a few thousand dollars. A minicomputer (see Fig. 2-13) is small—often the size of a small suitcase. It is built for simple installation and does not require a closely controlled environment. It can be maintained by the user, and if it is provided with a user-oriented software system, it can be programmed and operated by people who are not computer ex-

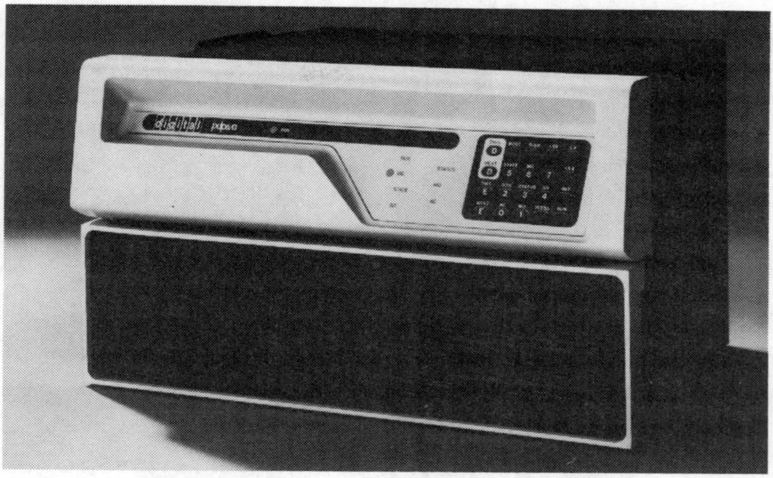

Courtesy Digital Equipment Corp.

Fig. 2-13. A PDP 8/a minicomputer.

Courtesy Digital Equipment Corp.

Fig. 2-14. An LSI-11 microcomputer.

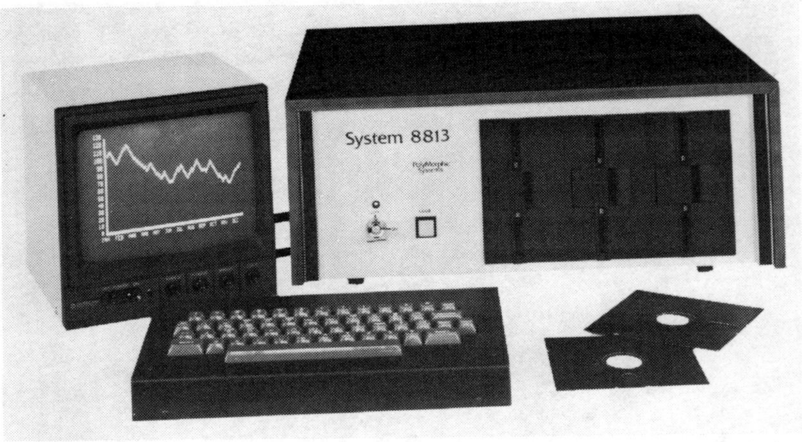

Courtesy PolyMorphic Systems

Fig. 2-15. A microcomputer system—microcomputer, keyboard, display, and floppy-disk storage unit.

perts. In the late 1960s and early 1970s a number of manufacturers got into the minicomputer business, so that now the prospective purchaser has a wide range of models to choose from.

In the mid 1970s, Intel Corporation introduced several *microprocessors,* large-scale integration (LSI) chips containing the calculating and control elements for a computer. Microprocessors are used in video game machines, hand-held calcula-

Courtesy IBM Corp.

Fig. 2-16. An IBM 5100 portable microcomputer.

tors, sewing machines, point-of-sale terminals (cash registers), microwave ovens, automobile ignition systems, phototypesetting machines, gas station pumps, slot machines, paint mixing machines, and as control units for a countless number of other devices.

The first *microcomputer* (Altair 8800) was introduced by MITS in early 1975 (a description of this machine appeared in the January 1975 issue of *Popular Electronics*). The Altair 8800 microcomputer was based on the Intel 8080 microprocessor. The introduction of the Altair 8800 was the beginning of the present wave of personal computers.

" IT'S THE ULTIMATE IN MICROCOMPUTERS... I KNOW I'VE GOT IT HERE SOMEPLACE... "

Today, microcomputers are being manufactured on a 6.4 mm (¼ inch) square silicon chip. Most microcomputers, however, consist of a microprocessor chip, memory chips (ROM, PROM, EPROM, or RAM), and input/output circuitry (see Fig. 2-14). Microcomputer technology is still new and new developments are occurring almost weekly. It is impossible to estimate the future growth of the microcomputer industry or the impact of these small, low-cost machines on our society. Fig. 2-15 shows a microcomputer system consisting of a microcomputer, a display device, a keyboard, and a floppy-disk storage unit. An IBM 5100 portable microcomputer is shown in Fig. 2-16. This small computer contains a keyboard, a small video display, and a magnetic-tape cassette storage unit.

Chapter 3

The Computer System

Courtesy Hawaiian Airlines

Before we consider the operation of a computer system, a look at its makeup and essential components will help us understand how it works and will eliminate some of its mystery. There are four basic parts in a computer system:

1. A central processing unit.
2. A means of putting information into the system.
3. A means of getting information out of the system.
4. Facilities for storing information.

THE CENTRAL PROCESSING UNIT

The central processing unit (CPU) is the heart or nucleus of the computer system. It is made up of two parts: the *arithmetic-logic section,* which performs mathematical and logical operations, and the *control section,* which coordinates the operations of the entire computer system. In its supervision of the system, the control section guides the operation of all input and output devices for entry of information into storage or removal of information from storage, and for routing information between the arithmetic-logic section and the storage section.

The central processsing unit is guided and controlled by computer programs in everything it does. These programs not only control the CPU as it processes data, but they also control the flow of data into and out of the central processing unit.

The central processing unit is the most taken-for-granted component in the computer system. It is always there. It must be ready at all times to receive data, slavishly follow the programs assigned to it, and deliver its results to an output or storage device. Every computer system, whether it is a microcomputer (Fig. 3-1) or a medium-scale computer system (Fig. 3-2), has a central processing unit whose basic function is always the same.

Arithmetic-Logic Section

The arithmetic-logic section is the calculating component of the computer. It carries out arithmetical operations: addition, subtraction, multiplication, and division; logical operations; and makes comparisons. The arithmetic-logic section can calculate the truth or falsity of simple and compound logical sentences using such logical operations as "AND," "OR," and "NOT."

The arithmetic-logic section can also determine such things as whether one number is greater than, less than, or equal to another, or whether two alphabetic characters are the same. It is

Courtesy Radio Shack, a Division of Tandy Corp.

Fig. 3-1. A microcomputer system that can be used in schools, in businesses, and in the home.

through logical and comparison operations that a computer can be programmed to make decisions.

Control Section

The control section performs the most vital function in the computer. When an instruction is obtained (or fetched) from storage, it goes to the control section, which proceeds to generate control signals that cause the other parts of the computer to carry out the instruction. In particular, the control section determines what arithmetical or logical operation the arithmetic-logic section carries out. It also oversees the transfer of information between the arithmetic-logic section and storage. In short, the control section directs the overall functioning of all sections of the computer and controls the information flow between them during the process of solving a problem.

Courtesy NCR Corp.

Fig. 3-2. A medium-scale computer system.

INPUT AND OUTPUT DEVICES

Input devices feed information into the computer system; output devices retrieve information from computer storage for human use. A computer is not very useful unless there are convenient ways of putting the information to be processed into it, and getting the results out. There are numerous types of input and output devices, and these will be discussed in Chapter 5.

COMPUTER STORAGE

The storage (or memory) of a computer is that part of the system that stores information for later use. Most computer systems have both main (sometimes called internal) storage and auxiliary (sometimes called secondary) storage. There are several types of storage devices, and these will be examined in Chapter 4.

COMPUTER CONSOLE

A computer console, such as the one shown in Fig. 3-3, is used to initiate the execution of a program and to monitor the computer system after the computer is under program control. The console is used by a human operator to start and stop the computer as well as to load instructions and data into computer

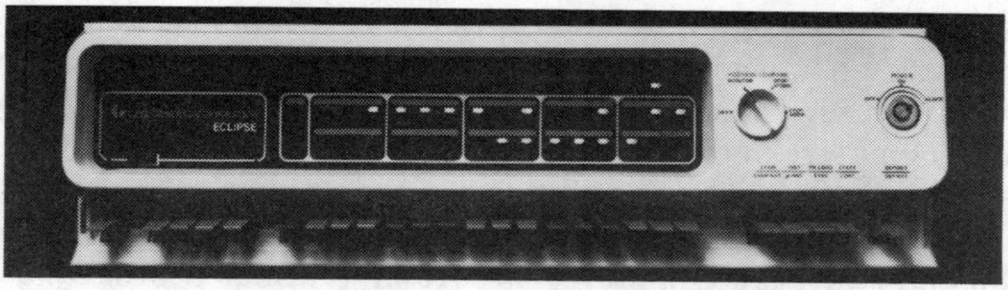

Courtesy Data General Corp.

Fig. 3-3. Control console for a small minicomputer.

storage. The console is equipped with switches, lights, and buttons for entering information into the system and for inspecting information already stored in the computer.

Control consoles can be a panel of switches and lights, such as shown in Fig. 3-3, or a separate typewriter or visual display unit, such as shown in Fig. 3-4. An operator can use the typewriter to enter information into the computer. Computer error messages can also be displayed in this type of console.

Courtesy Digital Equipment Corp.

Fig. 3-4. Operating console for a large minicomputer system.

THE STORED PROGRAM

Control is the process of directing the operation of the computer system, either manually or automatically. *Manual control* is performed by a human operator pressing buttons and switches on a computer control panel. Once a computer program (or set of instructions) is placed in the storage unit of the computer, and the computer is manually started by the operator, the computer will operate automatically under *program control.* The instructions that guide the operation of the computer are called a *stored program.* Without a program, a computer is merely an inert mass of metal, wire, and plastic. With a program, the computer comes to life and slavishly follows its instructions. For this reason, the program is as essential as the computer itself, for without it, no work could be performed.

A different program is written for each new problem to be solved. The program is keyed into computer storage, or recorded on some input media and placed in computer storage. Computer programs are often referred to as *software.* The computer and other data-processing machines are called *hardware.* We will look more closely at programs and how they are developed in later chapters.

THE SHRINKING COMPUTER

Early computers, such as the ENIAC, UNIVAC I, and IBM 704, were built with thousands of vacuum tubes. Walking into a computer room in the 1950s was a "chilly" experience, because the room was very cool, almost cold, in fact. Vacuum tubes gave off a considerable amount of heat, and keeping the machine cool was a very real problem.

By the early 1960s, the vacuum tube was replaced by the transistor. Transistors are smaller and more efficient in their use of energy than vacuum tubes are. They are also cheaper and easier to mass produce. They are made by making "sandwiches" of very thin layers of silicon (obtained by melting and purifying sand) and smaller amounts of other materials. These "sandwiches" are then etched to yield the right electrical prop-

Courtesy NCR Corp.

Fig. 3-5. Circuit board containing microprocessor chip, internal memory chips, and input/output control chips for the central processing unit of the computer system shown in Fig. 3-2.

erties for the circuits, and then sliced up to make one transistor from each small piece of the "sandwich."

The use of transistors greatly increased the reliability of computers. The use of transistor components resulted in much less hardware maintenance, thereby greatly reducing the cost of operating a computer system. The speed of computers using transistors was measured in microseconds, a factor of 1000 times faster than the speed of vacuum-tube machines.

A second dramatic advance came with the introduction of the integrated circuit. Instead of using individual transistors and wiring them together into a circuit, it became possible to etch all the components and all the connections required for the circuit on a single "sandwich" of silicon by using photo-

Courtesy Intel Corp.

Fig. 3-6. The Intel 8748 single-chip microcomputer.

graphic techniques. An integrated circuit of the 1960s could be printed with about 100 components. By using integrated circuits, computer manufacturers were able to produce machines that were smaller, less expensive, and more reliable.

In the mid 1960s, Digital Equipment Corporation introduced the minicomputer, a suitcase size, table-top digital computer. This small computer found widespread use in laboratories and educational institutions. In the late 1960s and early 1970s, a number of other manufacturers got into the minicomputer business, so that now one can find a wide range of available minicomputer models.

In the early 1970s, the Intel Corporation introduced several *microprocessors,* large-scale integration (LSI) chips containing the calculating and control sections for a computer. These microprocessors are used as central controlling units of *minicomputers* and *microcomputers.* Shown in Fig. 3-5 is a circuit board that includes a microprocessor chip as well as a number of internal memory chips and input/output control units. This circuit board accesses the proper terminals within the computer system shown in Fig. 3-2, and controls the transmission, reception, and verification of communicated data.

Today, LSI chips are available that contain over 100,000 components in a space less than 6.4 mm (¼ of an inch) on a side. In fact, a complete microcomputer can be manufactured on a single silicon chip only 6.4 mm square (Fig. 3-6).

With the new LSI circuitry, the trend of falling computer size and prices has continued very dramatically (Fig. 3-7). Today, one can purchase a computer for less than $600 that is a thousand times more powerful than one of the early vacuum-tube machines, which cost several hundred thousand dollars.

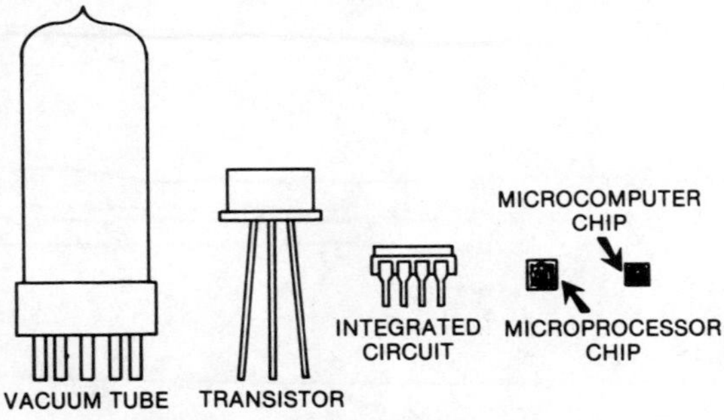

Fig. 3-7. Relative sizes of computer components.

Chapter 4

Computer Storage

Courtesy IBM Corp.

A computer system must have facilities for storing information. It must be able to store both processed information and information that is waiting to be processed. The facilities used for storing information are also used to store computer programs and keep them available for use by the central processing unit whenever needed. The devices for storage of information are often called *computer memory*.

Computer storage is divided into two classes: *internal storage* and *auxiliary storage*. Internal storage is the specific storage unit that serves the central processing unit. Auxiliary storage is either sequential or direct access. *Sequential access*, such as that used with magnetic tape, involves examining sequentially all recorded information. This form of storage necessitates tape searching by starting at the beginning of the tape and continuing to search through all records until the desired information area is found. In contrast, *direct-access* (or *random-access*) devices provide immediate access to individual records and do not require reading from the beginning of a file to find a particular record.

Two terms used in the above paragraph demand further definition. A *record* refers to a group of logically related items read as a single unit into internal storage or written from storage in the same manner. The term *file* refers to a group of logically related records. For example, the name of an employee might be one item. All data about the employee (age, sex, marital status, work experience, number of children, etc.) might be contained in one record. The data for all employees in a company might be contained on a file.

Sequential-access storage is *nonaddressable;* that is, an operator cannot directly refer to the contents of a particular storage location. Direct-access storage is *addressable;* a given item can be selected from anywhere in storage by simply specifying the address where it is located.

The *capacity* of a storage device is expressed as the number of words, bytes, characters or bits it can store at one time. The cost of storage is directly determined by the capacity of the device and its type.

The time the computer takes to locate and transfer information to or from storage is called *access time*. Access to some storage units is so rapid it is measured in nanoseconds (billionths of a second).

For years, magnetic-core storage has been the primary type of storage for computers. Today, however, computer manufacturers are using semiconductor memories in many computers. Almost all minicomputers and microcomputers, and many larger machines as well, use semiconductor memory for their internal storage.

Auxiliary storage devices include magnetic tapes, magnetic disks, and magnetic drums. Magnetic tape is the only sequential storage device discussed in this book; all the other auxiliary storage devices are of the direct-access type. These various forms of storage will be discussed in the remainder of this chapter.

INTERNAL STORAGE

As mentioned earlier, modern computers employ two memory technologies for internal storage: semiconductor (integrated circuit) memory and magnetic-core memory. The trend is toward semiconductor memory, although core memory manufacturers are working to reduce the cost of their product, and so remain competitive. A typical magnetic-core storage unit is made up of thousands of tiny doughnut-shaped rings of a ferromagnetic material assembled on a crosshatch of fine wires (Fig. 4-1).

A *semiconductor memory* uses silicon chips with interconnecting on-off switches (called *flip-flops*). The direction of the electric current passing through each cell determines whether the position of the switch is *on* or *off;* that is, whether the bit is *1* or *0*. Each silicon chip is about 0.32 cm^2 (one-eighth of an inch square). Semiconductor memories provide increased storage capacity and low access time. It is also possible to design logic into these memories.

Semiconductor memories can be found in many large computers (IBM System/370) as well as in small computers like the IBM System/32, NCR Century 151, and Univac 90/60. Semiconductor memories are used as the internal storage in almost all minicomputers and microcomputers.

The most common (and least expensive) kind of microcomputer memory is called RAM (*R*andom-*A*ccess *M*emory). It is used primarily to store user programs and data; however, the contents are lost when the microcomputer's power is shut off.

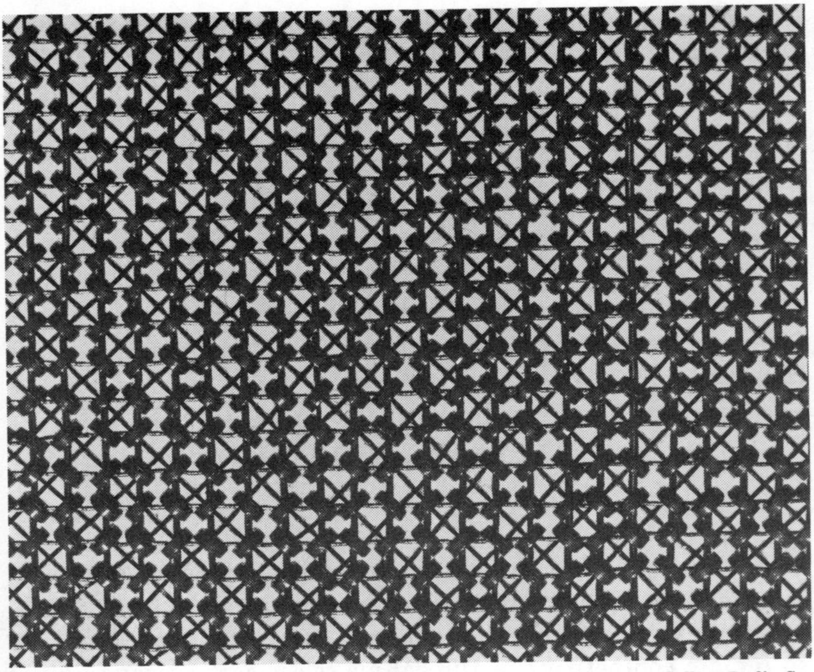

Courtesy Collins Radio Co.

Fig. 4-1. Magnetic cores strung on a crosshatch of fine wires.

So a small amount of another kind of memory is needed in the microcomputer: ROM, PROM, or EPROM.

*R*ead-*O*nly *M*emory (ROM) is used to store monitors, interpreters, input/output drivers, or special application programs. It is not possible to write into ROM memory as it is into RAM memory. ROM memory, however, is not user programmable; the contents of the ROM were put there by the manufacturer.

Another memory, called PROM (*P*rogrammable *R*ead-*O*nly *M*emory), does not forget what it knows when the microcomputer's power is turned off, and is used in many microcomputers to contain monitors, input/out drivers, and special application programs. The PROM chips can be purchased blank and then be programmed by using a special machine called a *PROM programmer* or *PROM burner*. Once programmed, the PROM memory behaves the same as the ROM.

*E*rasable *PROM* (EPROM) is one of the latest types of semiconductor memory. It can be programmed by the user, and it can also be erased and reprogrammed with different information. Once it has been programmed, EPROM memory acts just the same as ROM. The EPROM is the program memory most frequently used by users who must make frequent changes to their programs. They can do it themselves if they have a PROM programmer.

Semiconductor and magnetic-core memories are direct-access memories. That is, the computer can access (transfer information to or from) any memory location chosen at random, instead of having to access the locations in some particular sequence. For this to be possible, every storage location must be provided with an address. When the central processing unit needs the information in a certain storage location, it transmits the address of that location to the storage section. The storage hardware decodes the address and sends back the contents of the specified location. Storing information is accomplished in a similar way. We can thus visualize the internal storage of a computer as a set of post-office boxes. Each box will hold a certain amount of information, and each has a unique address by which it can be identified.

In some computer systems, the working capacity of internal storage can be increased by programming a portion of auxiliary storage to augment internal storage. Called *virtual storage,* this procedure has the effect of increasing the working capacity of internal storage. Virtual storage is discussed later in this chapter.

Other types of internal storage less well known are magnetic-bubble storage, laser-holographic storage, and thin-film storage. These memory types are discussed later in this chapter.

AUXILIARY STORAGE

A computer system may have a number of different storage devices other than internal storage. These devices, called *auxiliary storage* devices, are used to store programs and data. They can be used to receive input information that is to be processed in the central processing unit, or to store the output of the central processing unit and hold it for reference, for printout, or for further processing. There are three commonly used auxiliary memory devices: magnetic tapes, magnetic disks, and magnetic drums. These devices are discussed in the following three sections:

Magnetic Tape

Magnetic tape is one of the more popular media for representing information. It is used not only as a fast way of getting information into and out of the computer, but also as auxiliary storage.

A tape unit reads from and writes on tape. Before the tape unit can perform read or write operations, it must be prepared for operation. This preparation involves loading two reels on the tape unit and threading the tape through the tape transport mechanism. Fig. 4-2 shows an operator loading a magnetic-tape reel on a tape unit.

During tape read or write operations, the tape moves from one reel across a read-write head to the other reel. Writing on tape is *destructive;* that is, as new information is written, old information is destroyed. Reading is *nondestructive;* the same information can be read again and again. Information is written on tape by magnetizing areas in parallel tracks along the length of the tape. In the tape unit, there is one read-write coil in the head for each recording track, where electrical current flowing through the coils magnetizes the iron-oxide coating of the moving tape and erases previously written information. The execution of a "program write" command results in one or more records of data being written. A 15.24-mm *interrecord gap* (IRG) is left after each "write" has been completed. The gap serves to separate one record from another and allows distance for both stopping the tape after an operation and accelerating the tape to the proper speed when starting a new operation.

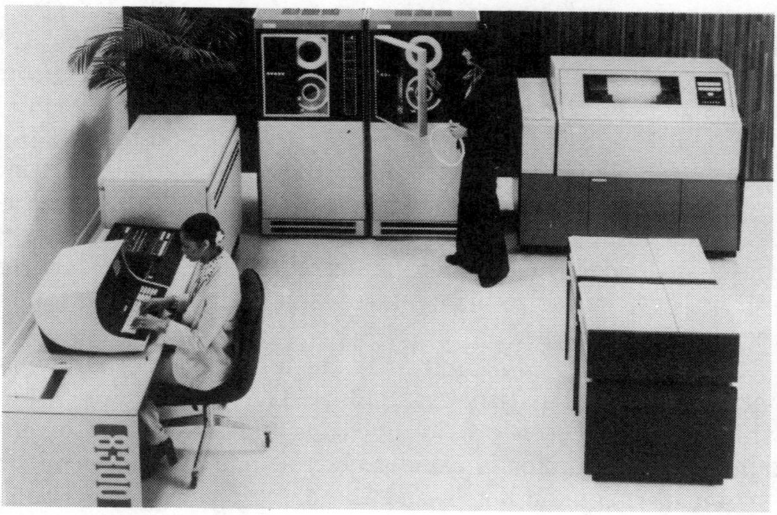

Courtesy NCR Corp.

Fig. 4-2. Operator loading a magnetic-tape reel on a tape unit.

File protection rings are often used with magnetic tape to prevent the accidental writing of information on a tape. This ring, which is made of plastic, fits into a circular groove on the tape reel. Writing is prohibited whenever the ring is absent.

Magnetic-tape units read tapes at speeds up to 285.8 cm (112.5 inches) per second. Information can be recorded on a tape up to 1600 characters per inch. This is referred to as the *tape density*. Data recorded at 1600 characters per inch and reading at 285.8 cm per second allows 180,000 characters to be transmitted each second. This high-speed operation is the primary reason that magnetic tape is used as a primary input/

output method for many medium- and large-scale computer systems.

Many businesses store all their information on magnetic tape, building up large tape *libraries.* Data is often recorded on magnetic tape by using a *card-to-tape conversion* procedure or a *key-to-tape recorder.* In card-to-tape conversion, the source data are initially recorded on punched cards. Then, using the card reader, the computer, and a magnetic-tape unit, the data are recorded on magnetic tape. The key-to-tape recorder is a device that can be used to record data directly onto magnetic tape.

Computer systems often require large quantity storage of data that are used only occasionally. In large systems, this requirement is often met by using a magnetic tape. Minicomputers and microcomputers often have these same requirements, although usually on a smaller scale. The magnetic-tape units available for large systems, although a possible solution, are not often used because their cost is generally higher than that of a minicomputer or microcomputer. Recently, several container-loaded magnetic-tape units, designed as low-cost storage devices for minicomputers and microcomputers, have been made available.

A *cassette/cartridge* unit is a digital tape recorder which operates with tape (usually 3.175 or 6.350 mm (⅛ or ¼ inch wide) that has been previously loaded in some form of container. The container is usually open at one end to permit insertion of magnetic heads and the drive mechanism. The remainder is completely enclosed. The containers come in two forms: *cassette,* which is a tape container in which two reels are mounted; and *cartridge,* which is a container in which the tape is stored in the form of an endless loop. Cassette/cartridge units are basically simple, modest-performance devices. They are relatively easy to operate and their cost is fairly low. Hence, these devices provide a low-cost solution to the problem of large-capacity storage for small digital computer systems.

Magnetic Disk

Magnetic disks are a very popular type of auxiliary storage. The physical characteristics of all magnetic disks are similar. Each one is a thin metal disk coated on both sides with magnetic recording material (Fig. 4-3). Disks are mounted on a

Fig. 4-3. Diagram of a magnetic disk.

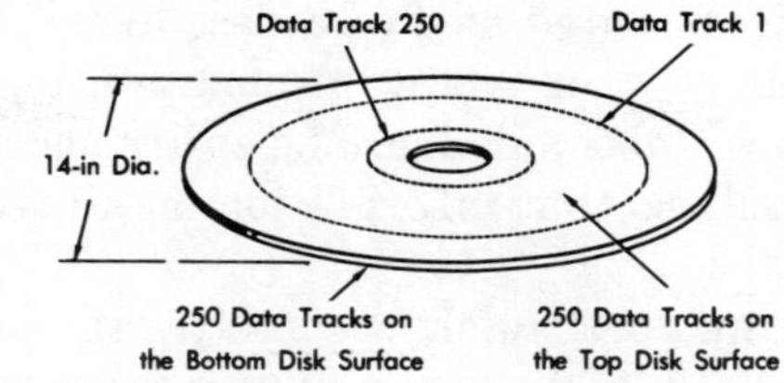

vertical shaft and are slightly separated from each other to provide space for the movement of read-write assemblies. The shaft revolves, spinning the disks. Data are stored as magnetized spots in concentric tracks on each surface of the disk. Disk units have several hundred tracks on each surface for storing data. The tracks are made accessible for reading and writing by positioning the read-write heads between the spinning disks. The read-write head mechanism is hydraulically driven to move all heads simultaneously to any track position. After horizontal movement is completed to a specified track, the read-write heads can be directed to perform the reading and writing on the track.

Fig. 4-4 illustrates a disk assembly. This assembly is composed of six disks mounted on a vertical shaft. The disk assembly provides ten surfaces on which information can be recorded. The top and bottom surfaces are used as protective plates and are not used for recording purposes. Information is read from or written on the disks by read-write heads mounted on a comb-like access mechanism which has ten read-write

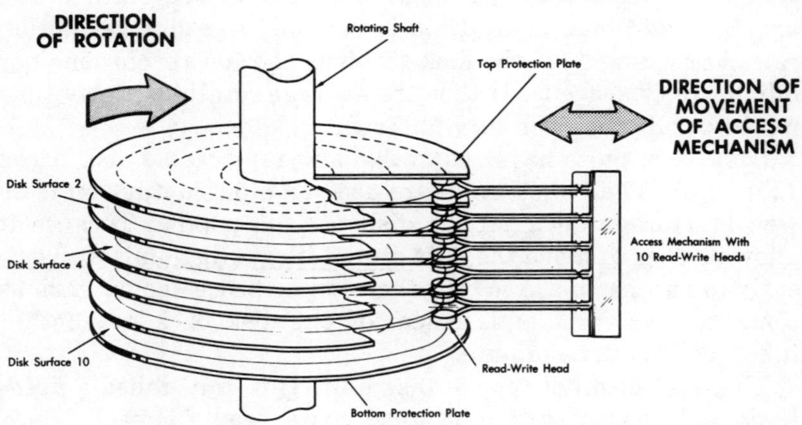

Fig. 4-4. Diagram of a magnetic-disk assembly.

heads mounted on five access arms. Each read-write head can either read or write information on the corresponding upper or lower disk surface. The entire access mechanism moves horizontally so that information on all tracks can be either read or written.

A magnetic-disk assembly can have several disks. A disk unit with 25 disks can have a storage capacity of over 100 million characters of information. This information can be transmitted to and from a computer at rates of over 150,000 characters per second.

The magnetic-disk data surface can be used repetitively. Each time new information is stored on a track, the old information is erased as the new is recorded. The recorded data may be read as often as desired; data remain recorded in the tracks of a disk until they are written over.

The simplified disk assembly shown in Fig. 4-4 illustrates the read-write head mechanism moving in a horizontal direction. In this manner, the disk mechanism is able to position itself at any specified track. The time required to locate a specific track is called the *disk access time.* This time is related to the lateral distance that the read-write head mechanism moves.

In addition to access time, there is another timing factor associated with disk read-write operations. The *rotational delay time* is the time required for the disk to attain the desired position at the selected read-write head. The maximum revolution time for a disk is the time required for one full revolution. The average rotational delay time is one-half the disk revolution rate. For example, if the disk revolves at 2400 revolutions per minute (a typical speed) then the average rotational relay time would be slightly over 11 milliseconds.

Some disk units have removable and replaceable disk packs (Fig. 4-5). These disk units are used as input/output units as well as storage devices. The disk pack is popular because it allows a user to move the data stored in one disk unit conveniently to another place so that they can be processed on various computer systems. Replacement of one disk pack by another takes less than one minute.

There is one other type of disk unit. This unit, called a *fixed-head disk,* has a stationary read-write head for each track. These head-per-track devices are much faster than other disk

Courtesy NCR Corp.

Fig. 4-5. Operator removing a disk pack from a magnetic-disk unit.

units since there are no moving parts; only the rotational delay time determines the access time. In fact, access times of the fixed-head disks are similar to magnetic drums. Fixed-head disk units are, however, more expensive than other types of disks.

A new type of disk, recently introduced, has proved to be a strong competitor with the previously mentioned disk units. These disks, called *floppy disks,* are flexible, made of oxide-coated mylar, and are stored in paper or plastic envelopes. The entire envelope is inserted in the disk unit, effectively protecting the contents of the disk surfaces. The disk surfaces are rotated inside the protective covering. The disk head contacts the track positions through a slot in the covering.

The student in Fig. 1-6 is placing a floppy disk (or diskette) into the disk unit. Disk units such as these are relatively inexpensive, and the disks themselves are cheap. It is estimated that eventually a diskette will cost around 50 cents. Because of their low cost and high speed, the floppy-disk units are being widely used, especially in minicomputer and microcomputer systems.

Magnetic Drum

A *magnetic drum* is a metal cylinder coated with magnetically sensitive material on its outer surface. The drum rotates at a constant speed. The drum surface is divided into several *tracks* or *channels*. Each track has an associated read-write head mechanism that is used to read and write data on the drum surface. A read-write head is suspended a very slight distance from the drum surface. Whenever new data are recorded, the old data are automatically erased.

As the drum rotates, reading and writing occurs when the specified area of the track (on some drums, a track is subdivided into several *sectors*) passes under the read-write mechanism for that track. Writing results in magnetized spots on the drum surface. Reading involves only sensing the magnetized areas.

MAGNETIC-BUBBLE STORAGE

A few years ago, IBM announced a magnetic-bubble memory chip about an inch in diameter, with a 10-megabit storage capability. Using such a compact memory, one could store the whole Library of Congress in the cubic area taken up by the average size console tv set. Within the next five to ten years, the capability to store all the knowledge of mankind in the corner of a room should exist.

Bubble memories consist of a thin orthoferrite film in which each "bubble" generated is a cylindrical magnetic domain that carries a polarization opposite to that of the film. Such bubbles, each about three micrometers in size, are packed in densities up to millions of bubbles per square inch. Ways have been found to move the bubbles stepwise at the rate of at least one million steps a second, and in this fashion, a bubble memory can be used to store data and perform logical operations.

The trouble with bubble memory is that it is accessed serially. This means that each storage cell must be rotated in its entirety to get to any one point. A search through bubble memory is thus serial instead of parallel or random, making access a major stumbling block that must be solved for the full potential of this memory to be realized. The next stage in bubble memory will probably be the development of independent shifts with complex addressing systems, so the information can be accessed through specialized packets.

Presently, bubble memory cannot replace random-access memory as the main memory in a computer because of its slow, serial nature. What it will replace, in its current state, is magnetic disk and magnetic tape.

Disks and tape store data on thin magnetic film. In a disk or tape though, the film itself moves mechanically at high speed; in a bubble memory, the bubbles move at high speed through the film. In a disk or tape, the information is fixed in location and passes the read-write head in only one dimension. In a magnetic-bubble memory, the information travels in two dimensions anywhere in the film. Bubble memories have an additional advantage. They are able to perform logical operations on stored data without having to read the data back in storage again. Also, bubble memories are electronic and should be very reliable, since they have no moving parts.

LASER-HOLOGRAPHIC STORAGE

As computers continue to grow in size and complexity, storage will have to be increased significantly at no sacrifice in speed. This means the information will have to be packed much more densely in whatever storage device is used. Holography is a technique that can further the development of large storage devices. With recent advances in holography and laser-beam technology, computer developers are studying optical memories whose ultimate storage capacity may well be in excess of 100 million bits of data, and whose random-access time may be as short as one microsecond.

Holograms make use of a high-energy laser beam to store or display three-dimensional images. The image produced by a hologram can easily be read by a photodetector, and information can be stored redundantly.

A holographic memory is made on a special recording medium somewhat similar to conventional photographic film. The recording process starts with the construction of a data mask that represents the contents of a page. Each mask is basically an array of pinholes, blocked where *0*s are to be recorded and transparent where *1*s are needed. Each data mask is recorded holographically, one at a time, on the recording medium. Information is retrieved from the memory by projecting the data recorded on the hologram onto a light-sensitive detector. The detector converts the optical information into electronic signals that the computer can process.

Several experimental laser-holographic memory systems have been developed. IBM has developed a system that stores more than 100 million bits of information on a nine-square-inch holographic plate. A system developed by a Japanese firm is capable of accommodating a telephone directory of 3800 pages on 16 pieces of film, each measuring five square inches. It has a capacity much greater than present storage units and is considerably faster than conventional magnetic tapes or disks in information read out.

Another system has been developed that can record over 70,866 bits of information onto a single centimeter of eight-millimeter photographic film at a rate of over 10 million bits per second. Laser storage devices are still considered to be in the early experimental stages and will probably not become economically feasible in the near future.

THIN-FILM STORAGE

Thin-film storage, which utilizes concepts similar to those that magnetic-core storage is based on, has been used as internal storage for some recent computers. It is, however, more compact, more expensive, and faster in access time than is magnetic-core storage.

One form of thin-film memory consists of a series of metallic-alloy dots, a few millionths of an inch thick, deposited on a glass, ceramic, or plastic plate. The dots are connected by very fine wires and perform the same as magnetic cores. The dots can be magnetized in either of two stable preferred directions. Several thousand dots may be deposited on a one-inch-square plane. Because the thin films consist of so many small dots, the arrangement of circuits to perform reading and writing operations is difficult. A common method is to etch copper wires onto an insulating material. Then, by closely positioning these circuits, the dots can be magnetized and their direction of magnetization sensed.

VIRTUAL STORAGE

System designers and programmers have typically had to be concerned with internal memory capacity to make sure that they could fit their computer programs and working data into the available space. If the programs were too large for memory, the programmer would segment the program, putting the first part in internal storage and the other segments in auxiliary or secondary storage. When the first section was complete, the second section would be brought into internal storage (overlaid in the same memory area that contained the first section). The use of overlays can be limited to smaller sections, so that a main segment is kept intact and smaller portions are overlaid.

The concept of *virtual memory* is to have the hardware and software *automatically* segment the program and to move segments into storage when needed. The auxiliary storage, usually disk units, is, in effect, utilized as an "extension" of the internal memory of the computer. Virtual memory is the memory space defined by a range of addresses specified by the programmer and different from the addresses utilized by the memory system. A device is required for translating the addresses used

by the program into the correct memory location addresses. The size of virtual memory is consequently limited only by the addressing capability of the computer and not by the number of locations in its internal memory. With virtual memory, the programmer has the illusion that the memory of the computer is larger than it really is.

The basic element of a virtual memory is a program segment or *page*—a fixed-size unit of storage, usually 2048 or 4096 bytes. The pages of memory are swapped back and forth in such a way that the internal memory (real memory) of the computer is expanded to many times its actual capacity. The process of swapping programs or data back and forth is referred to as *page-in,* since the page goes from disk to internal memory, and *page-out* as a page leaves the internal memory and is stored on the disk unit.

The difficult part of any memory organization is keeping track of what part of the program is in internal storage and what part is stored on the disk. A technique called *dynamic memory allocation* is used in the management of memory resources. This technique divides a selected area of internal memory into pages. Any available page may be assigned for different purposes, depending on the requirements of the moment. A control routine keeps account of which pages are free so that the available memory space can be immediately assigned as needed. This is accomplished by a technique wherein available pages are linked together in the form of a chain. When a memory page becomes available, it is appropriately added to the chain. The control routine shuffles programs or data from auxiliary storage into available memory pages as required.

Virtual memory allows a programmer to write a program as if internal memory were limitless. With virtual memory, the computer takes care of the difficulty of scheduling the swapping of data and programs.

Chapter 5

Computer Input/Output Devices

Courtesy NCR Corp.

For a computer to be useful there must be convenient ways of putting the information to be processed into it, and getting the results out. This is the mission of the input/output devices. Input and output devices are the means by which the computer communicates with the outside world. Input units transfer data to the computer and output units receive data from it. When input or output units are connected directly to the computer, they are considered to be *on-line*. When they operate independently of the computer, they are called *off-line*.

The off-line concept involves separating the slow input/output equipment from the central processing unit by intermediate storage: magnetic tape or disk pack. This separation maximizes the usage of the central processing unit, since it allows input/output operations to occur at a higher rate.

A large computer system may involve many different types of off-line equipment: punched cards-to-magnetic tape, paper tape-to-magnetic tape, keyboard-to-magnetic tape, keyboard-to-disk pack, magnetic tape-to-printed form, magnetic tape-to-digital-plotted form, magnetic tape-to-microfilm, and printed document-to-paper tape.

From the early stages of computer development, input and output equipment have acted as restraining factors on the high speed of the computer. Since most of the data that a computer uses or produces must go through input/output equipment, it is understandable that there is much concern over the speed of these devices. The relatively slow speed of devices such as card readers and paper-tape readers is the reason many computer systems use magnetic tape and removable magnetic disks as the primary method of communicating with the computer. Data is then recorded on magnetic tape or magnetic disk prior to its use on the computer. This can be accomplished by using off-line data preparation equipment or even a small off-line computer system dedicated to this purpose. Likewise, computer output can be recorded on magnetic tape or disk packs and later transcribed to printed or other forms by off-line equipment.

Input/output devices operate under the control of the computer as directed by a stored computer program. For example, an instruction to read a card would cause the card reader to read a card and transmit the information to computer storage. An instruction to print a message would cause one or more lines of copy to be printed on a printing device such as a typewriter or line printer. Thus, instructions in the program select the required device, direct it to read or write, and indicate the location in computer storage where data will be inserted or retrieved.

In this chapter, we will look at some of the most common input/output devices. Fig. 5-1 shows some devices and identifies them as input, output, or both.

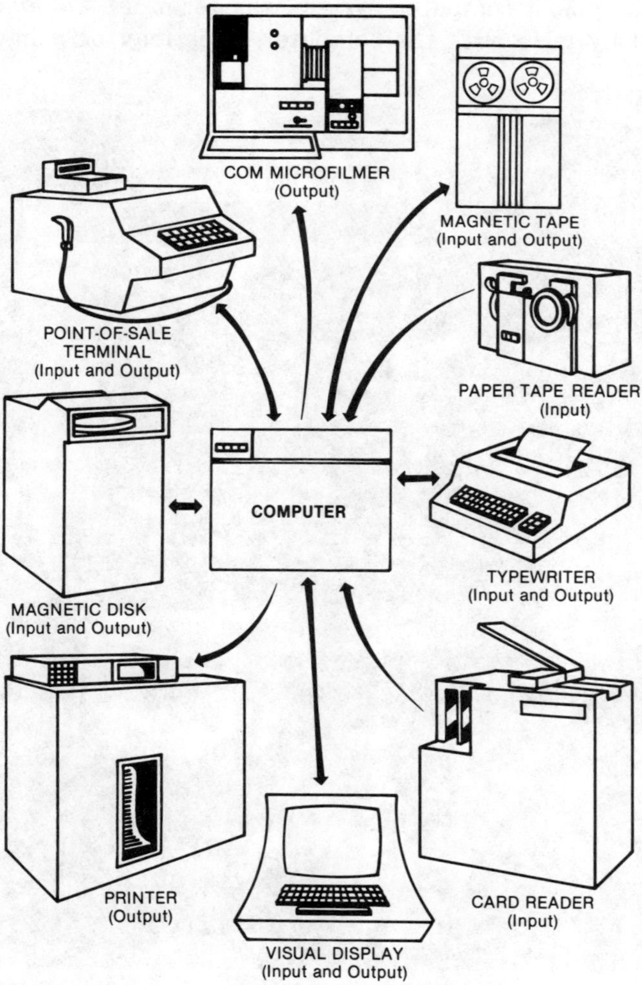

Fig. 5-1. Input and output devices.

VISUAL DISPLAY TERMINALS

The *cathode-ray-tube* (crt) terminal is used widely as a computer input/output device. A crt terminal looks like a cross between a typewriter and a tv set (Fig. 5-2). Information sent from the computer to the terminal is displayed on the screen. In most instances—though not always—the crt terminal is equipped with a keyboard to give it two-way communications capability.

In a typical computer system, the terminal would be connected by wire with the computer. This may be a hard-wire

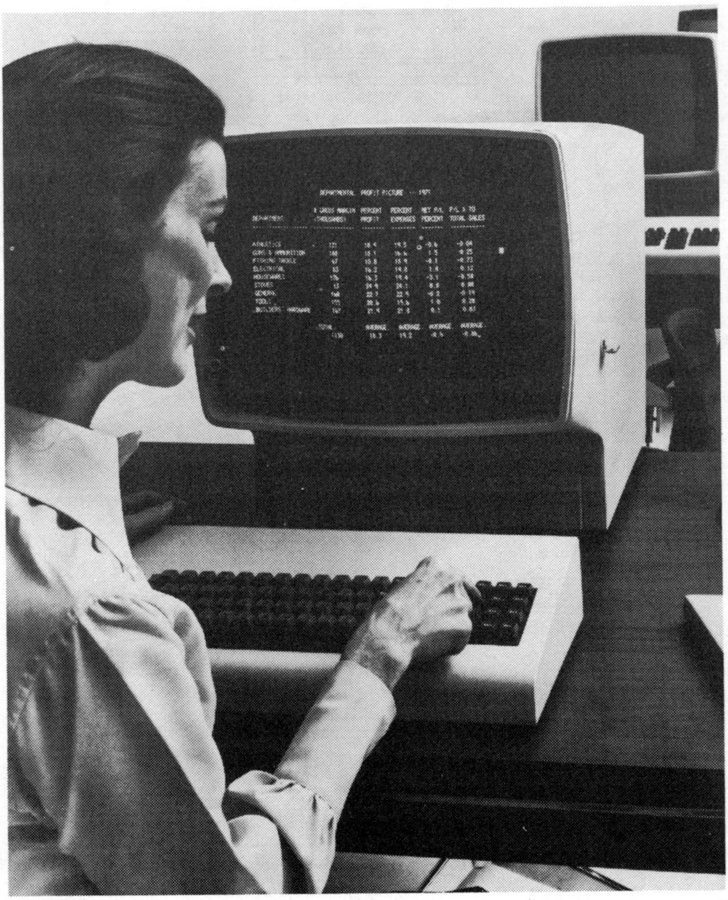

Courtesy IBM Corp.

Fig. 5-2. A crt terminal.

connection directly with the computer, or the terminal may be one of many in a system network, operating under the control of multiplexers or a communications control computer. If the crt terminal is at a remote location, its connection with the computer usually would be through telephone lines. Fig. 5-3 shows several crt terminals being used in a Japanese banking system.

Some crt terminals can only display text; others can also display drawings. Some terminals are equipped with a light pen (Fig. 5-4), which can be used to make drawings on the screen that are subsequently transmitted to the computer.

The visual display terminal is the most useful microcomputer output device. This is primarily because it is fast, quiet, and costs less than a printing device. The two most common types of terminals used in microcomputer systems are the video monitor and the tv receiver.

Courtesy NCR Corp.

Fig. 5-3. Crt terminals being used in a large-scale computer system located in Japan.

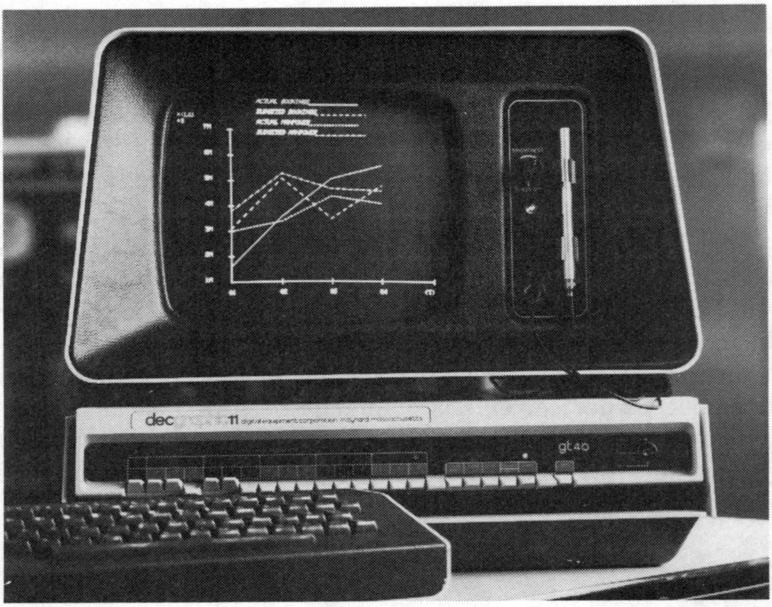

Courtesy Digital Equipment Corp.

Fig. 5-4. A crt terminal with a light pen.

A video monitor is made specifically for information display and is very similar to a home tv set, except that it does not include the electronics for receiving signals from a distant tv station. A tv receiver used with computers is simply a modified home tv set. Fig. 5-5 illustrates a tv receiver that is designed for use with many microcomputers.

Another type of visual display is called a *plasma panel.* Unlike other display systems, plasma panels do not use crt or tv tubes. They substitute etched glass plates separated by a gas which glows when excited by an electrical pulse. Plasma panels do not require constant reexitation; once a particular point on the display is turned on, it continues to glow a bright orange until it is turned off. The display consists of a series of bright dots that can be formatted into alphanumeric characters and diagrams.

PRINTING DEVICES

Printing devices provide permanent and readable records of information from the computer. The printing device receives

Courtesy The Digital Group

Fig. 5-5. A tv receiver designed for use with microcomputers.

Courtesy Interdata, a Unit of Perkin-Elmer Data Systems

Fig. 5-6. A typewriter designed for use with a computer as both a keyboard input device and an output printing device.

information in electronic form which activates printing elements in the printer, thus causing information to be printed. There are three main printing devices used with computers: the typewriter, the line printer, and the teletypewriter.

The *typewriter,* which may be used as a keyboard input device as well as an output printing device, provides a method for printing limited amounts of information. This device can print up to 200 characters per second. Typewriters, such as the one shown in Fig. 5-6, are commonly used as control devices in

Courtesy IBM Corp.

Fig. 5-7. A line printer.

medium- and large-scale computer systems, and as primary input/output devices in many small-scale computer systems.

The *line printer,* which is the most important hard-copy output device to be used with computers, prints a line at a time at a very fast rate. This device, shown in Fig. 5-7, is used to produce reports, summaries, and similar output on continuous paper forms. The paper may be blank, lined, or printed in any form.

There are two major categories of printing techniques. In *impact printing,* a type carrier contacts an inked ribbon and paper. In *electrostatic printing,* the paper is charged with line images and is passed through an ink fog. Ink adheres to the charged portions of the paper. Then heat is used to fix the line images. Electrostatic printing is faster than impact printing because of simpler mechanical construction, but impact printing is the more common method.

Many microcomputer and minicomputer systems use a typewriter-like device, called a *teletypewriter,* as the primary

Courtesy Teletype Corp.

Fig. 5-8. A teletypewriter.

method of getting information into or out of the computer. One model of the teletypewriter (see Fig. 5-8) includes a low-speed paper-tape reader and punch. Such a device provides two forms of input (keyboard and paper tape) and two forms of output (printed form and paper tape).

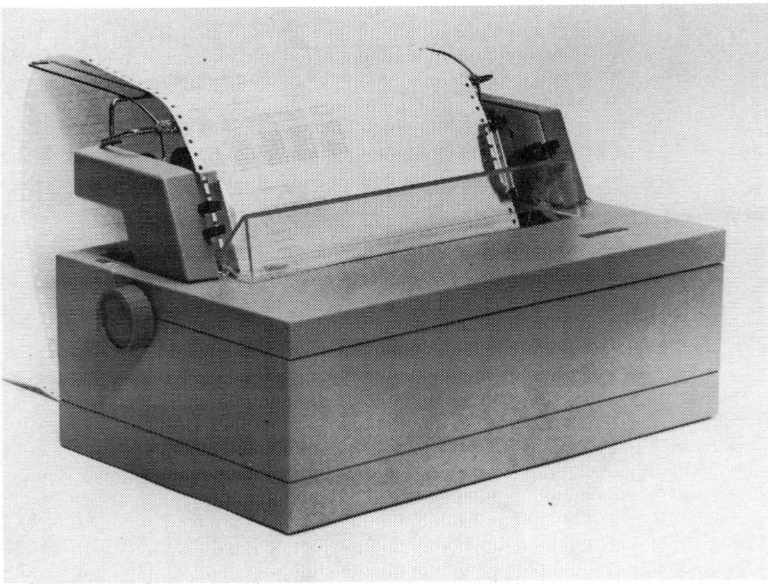

Courtesy IBM Corp.

Fig. 5-9. A printer designed for use with the IBM 5100 portable microcomputer.

Fig. 5-9 illustrates a printer designed specifically for use with a microcomputer system. Printing devices of this type give microcomputer users a low-cost method of satisfying moderate printing requirements.

CARD READER AND PUNCH

A *card reader* is a device which accepts punched cards and senses what is on each card (reads it). Then the information punched on the cards is transmitted to the memory of the computer. Fig. 5-10 shows two types of punched cards. The 80-column card at the top is the standard size card used with most data-processing equipment. The 96-column card at the bottom is used with some newer computer systems.

Card readers are of two basic types: mechanical and optical. Mechanical card readers use metal brushes, which feel for holes in the cards. Once the holes have been found, electrical circuits are established which enable the card reader to transmit data, in the form of characters, to computer memory. Optical card readers operate similarly to mechanical ones except that light beams detect the holes, electrical circuits are established, and information is transmitted. Mechanical card

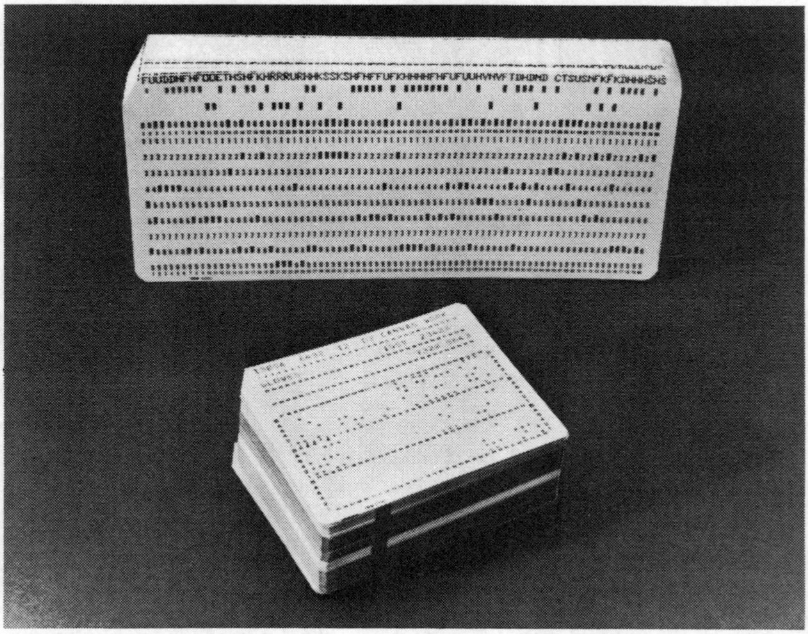

Courtesy IBM Corp.

Fig. 5-10. Two types of punched cards.

readers read cards at the rate of about 250 cards per minute. Optical card readers read cards at rates of up to 2000 cards per minute. At the fastest speeds, card readers supply information to computer memory at a rate of over 2500 characters per second. Fig. 5-11 shows a punched-card reader.

The *card punch* punches information from computer storage into blank cards. The card punch has a hopper that holds many blank cards. The blank cards are moved under the punch knives,

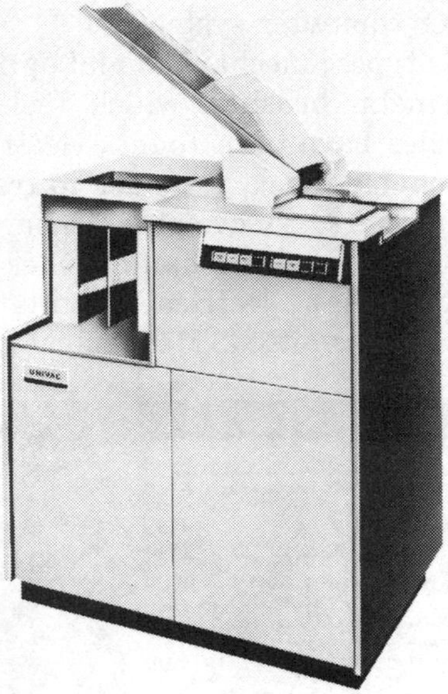

Fig. 5-11. A punched-card reader.

Courtesy Sperry Univac,
a Division of Sperry Rand Corp.

one at a time, where holes are punched in the card after the proper knives have been activated.

PAPER-TAPE READER AND PUNCH

Perforated paper tape with its *holes* and *no-holes* coding is used to input information into the computer and to record information from the computer in much the same manner as punched cards. Reading speeds vary from a few hundred characters per second up to a thousand characters per second. Punching speeds are somewhat slower, being in the range of several hundred characters per second.

There are numerous makes and models of *paper-tape readers* and *punches*. Fig. 5-12 shows a reader. Many paper-tape punches are attachments for adding machines, cash registers, typewriters, point-of-sale terminals, and bookkeeping machines. When punched with information, the tape may be used in a paper-tape reader for direct transmission to computer memory or for recording on magnetic disk or tape for faster computer input.

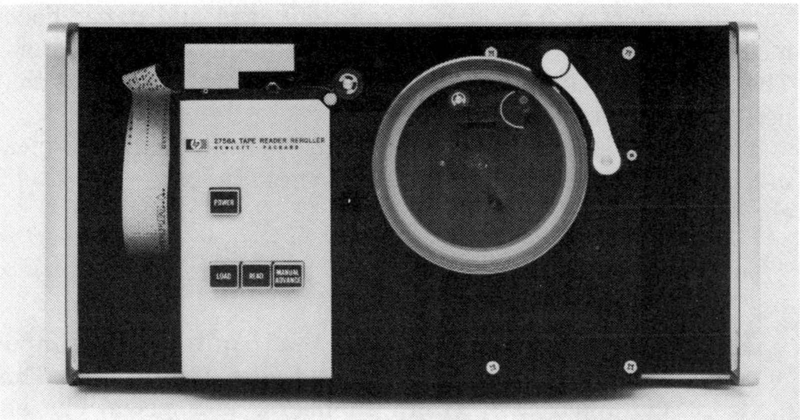

Courtesy Hewlett-Packard

Fig. 5-12. A paper-tape reader.

MAGNETIC-INK CHARACTER READER

The *magnetic-ink character reader* is a special-purpose input device that was designed as an aid to the automation of the

Courtesy IBM Corp.

Fig. 5-13. A magnetic-ink character reader used by banks to process checks.

banking industry. This device can read card and paper documents inscribed with a special magnetic-ink character font. The printed check is the most common form of document that uses these printed characters.

The device shown in Fig. 5-13 can read and sort a typical mixture of different sized checks at a speed in excess of 150,000 checks per hour.

OPTICAL CHARACTER READER

Another character-reading device that can be used as input to computers is the *optical character reader* (Fig. 5-14). This device reads upper-case letters, numbers, and special characters that are printed on paper documents. Documents to be read are placed in a hopper, and then transported in the reader past an optical scanning position where a powerful light and lens enable the machine to distinguish the letters, numbers, and special characters as patterns of light. These light patterns are converted into electrical pulses for use by the computer.

There are four general types of optical character readers: (1) page readers, which read 215.9×279.4 mm ($8\frac{1}{2} \times 11$ inch) documents; (2) document readers, which read a line or two from small documents about 101.6×203.2 mm (4×8 inches) or 50.8×101.6 mm (2×4 inches); (3) reader/punches, which read data printed on a card and punch the

Courtesy IBM Corp.

Fig. 5-14. An optical character reader.

data into the same card; and (4) journal tape readers, which read printed cash register or adding machine listing tapes.

Page readers tend to be large, expensive, multifont machines because of the flexibility required to scan the loose formats of varying pages. Document readers, journal tape readers, and reader/punches are somewhat smaller and less expensive because of a simpler transport mechanism and the smaller scanning areas required for their types of input.

Optical character readers are widely used by utility companies, oil companies, department stores, mail-order houses, and credit-card companies. The use of these readers simplifies the computer input process.

OPTICAL MARK AND MARK-SENSE READERS

In the last section, we discussed the optical character reader. Some optical character readers have the ability to read both alphabetic characters and marks. Optical mark and mark sensing is performed by detecting the presence or absence of pencil marks in specified positions on a form. Many areas of data collection are simplified by using preprinted forms that require

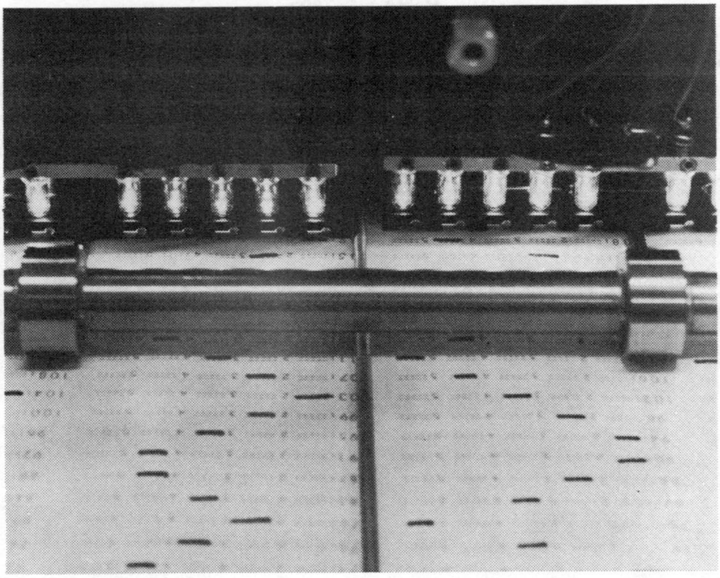

Courtesy IBM Corp.

Fig. 5-15. Closeup of the reading mechanism of a mark-sense reader.

only that the user fill in appropriate boxes with pencil marks. Such forms are commonly used for collecting inventory information, taking school attendance, conducing a census, recording a public opinion poll, or taking a test. Forms of this type may be read by *optical mark* and *mark-sense readers.*

The mark detection system of an optical mark reader generally consists of a light source, mirrors, and light-sensitive photocells. A mark is detected when a drop occurs in the amount of light arriving at the photocells after being reflected by the document being scanned. In contrast, the mark detection system of a mark-sense reader generally consists of sets of three brushes each of which make contact with marks. A voltage is applied to the outer two brushes of the sets and a mark is detected when a current passes through the graphite mark to the center brush.

Documents that are to be read by an optical mark reader can be marked with standard lead pencils. Documents read by mark-sense readers must be marked with special pencils containing soft and highly conductive leads. Fig. 5-15 shows a closeup of the reading mechanism of a mark-sense reader.

PLOTTERS

Automatic plotting devices are used with computers to produce pictorial or graphic representations of information. The

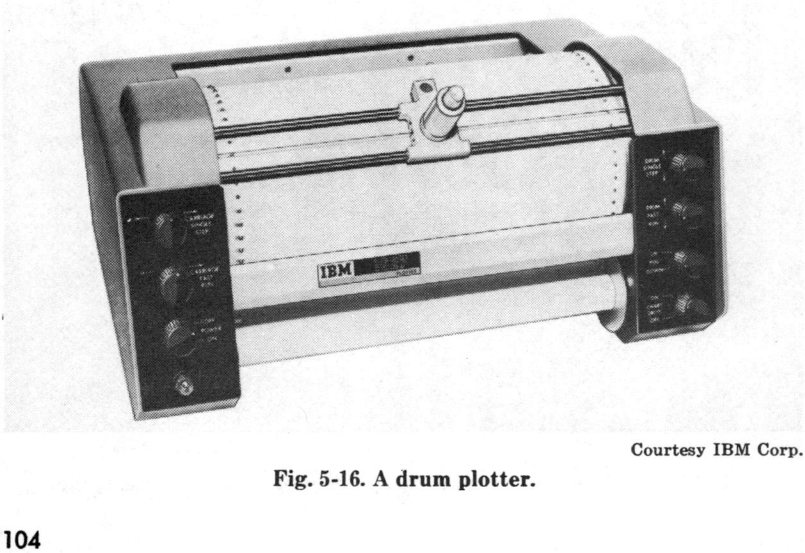

Courtesy IBM Corp.

Fig. 5-16. A drum plotter.

Courtesy California Computer Products, Inc.

Fig. 5-17. A flatbed plotter.

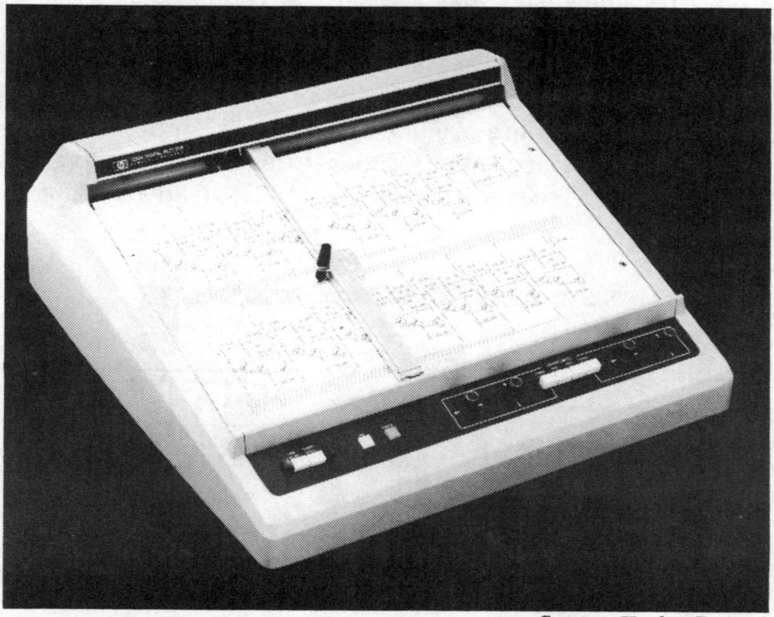

Courtesy Hewlett-Packard

Fig. 5-18. A digital plotter producing an electrical diagram.

digital plotter is a device that can draw under control of the computer. Typical applications might be the drawing of graphs, weather maps, land contour maps, subdivision maps, computerized art, or highway maps.

The two most common forms of plotters are the *drum* and *flatbed* types. The pen of a drum plotter (Fig. 5-16) is driven in one axis while the paper moves positively or negatively in the other axis. The flatbed plotter (Fig. 5-17) moves the pen in both the X and Y axes and the table is usually fixed. The computer provides pen movement and functional commands to the plotter in digital form, and these commands are then converted into pen motions.

Fig. 5-18 illustrates a digital plotter being used to draw an electrical diagram. The movement of the pen is under the control of the computer.

COMPUTER OUTPUT MICROFILM

With the increasing calculating speeds of computers, a growing problem is how to obtain output from the computer. Printers have become faster, but are slow in comparison with the speeds at which computers can generate output.

*C*omputer *O*utput *M*icrofilm (COM) has recently come of age. Although COM does not solve all problems associated with computer output, it does provide an additional option that system designers may consider. Fig. 5-19 shows how the COM microfilmer interfaces with a computer. Instead of printing

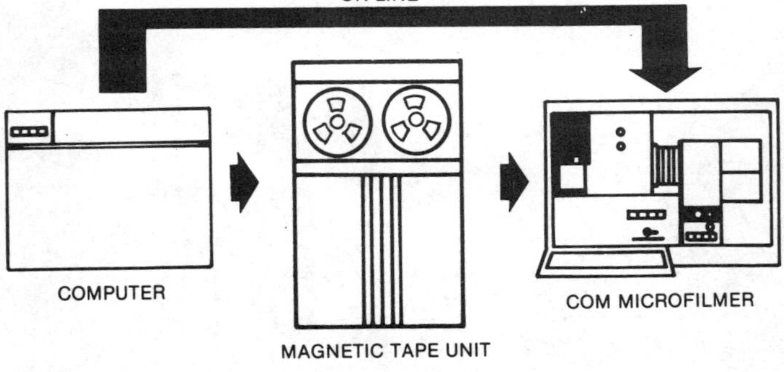

Fig. 5-19. Illustration of how a COM microfilmer interfaces with a computer.

pages on the printer, the computer generates an output magnetic tape. This magnetic tape is used as input to a COM unit. (An example of a COM unit is Kodak's KOM-90 shown in Fig. 5-20.) The COM unit reads data from the magnetic tape, displays it on the face of a cathode-ray tube, and photographs it onto 16-mm roll microfilm. Data recording is accomplished at a rate up to 120,000 characters per second or 26,000 lines per minute, approximately equal to 300 printout pages per minute. The Bell & Howell 3800 COM system is shown in Fig. 5-21.

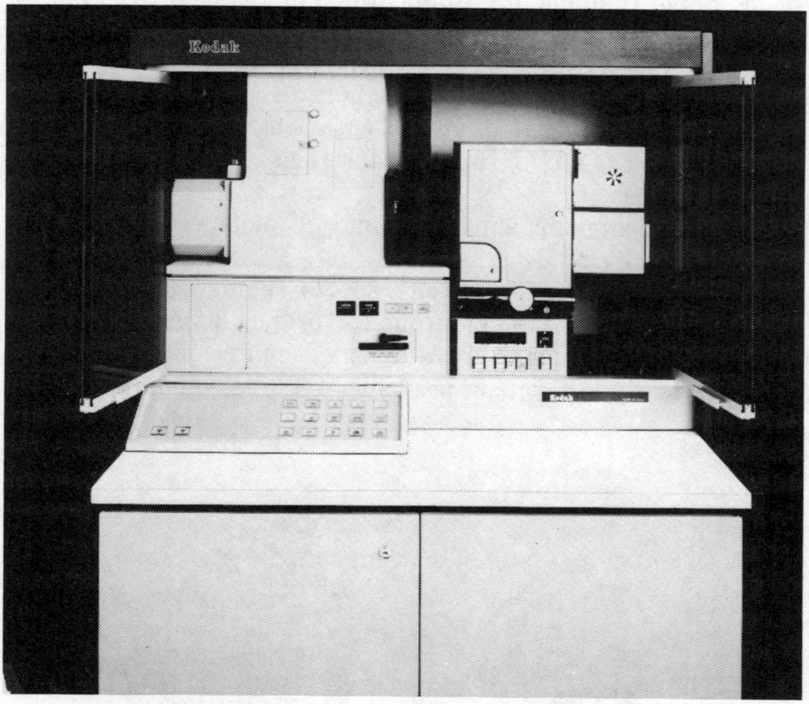

Courtesy Eastman Kodak Co.

Fig. 5-20. The Kodak KOM-90 microfilmer.

As shown in Fig. 5-19, the COM Microfilmer can be directly connected to the computer (on-line), thus eliminating the necessity of recording the data on magnetic tape.

Alternative to the reel of microfilm is *microfiche*, a 10.16- × 15.24-cm (4 × 6 inch) sheet of microfilm that contains 208 or more full pages of information (see Fig. 5-22). Microfiche films are simple to file and quick to retrieve. When placed in a microfiche viewer, the single page needed is shown in full size on the screen for easy reading; and, if desired, a full-size photocopy of the single page may be printed out in seconds. Typical output speeds of computer-stored data to microfiche is one microfiche per minute, or approximately 12,000 pages per hour.

The uses for computer output microfilm are probably limitless. Microfilm reduces a high volume of documentary data to manageable proportions and frees the user from time-consuming searches, and the computer from high-volume printing tasks. Some fundamental applications of COM are the following:

- Business-oriented listings with a low or high frequency of reference, but with an infrequent need for updating.
- Computer-generated data bases, such as catalogs, indexes, directories, bibliographies, abstracts, and financial data.
- Libraries.
- Engineering drawings, including plots, graphs, maps, charts, circuit designs, etc.
- Management information reports requiring both alphanumeric and graphic output for proper display of data.
- Insurance; examples are agents' commission statements, agents' digest system, positions' records, vendors' records, etc.

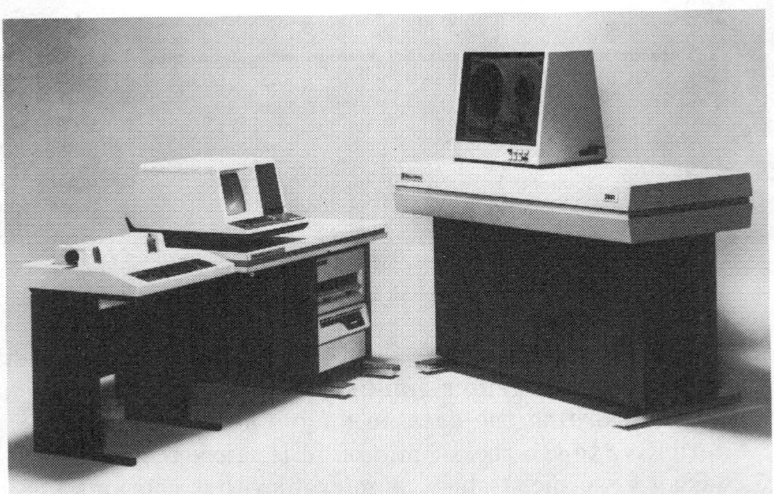

Courtesy Bell & Howell

Fig. 5-21. The Bell & Howell 3800 COM system.

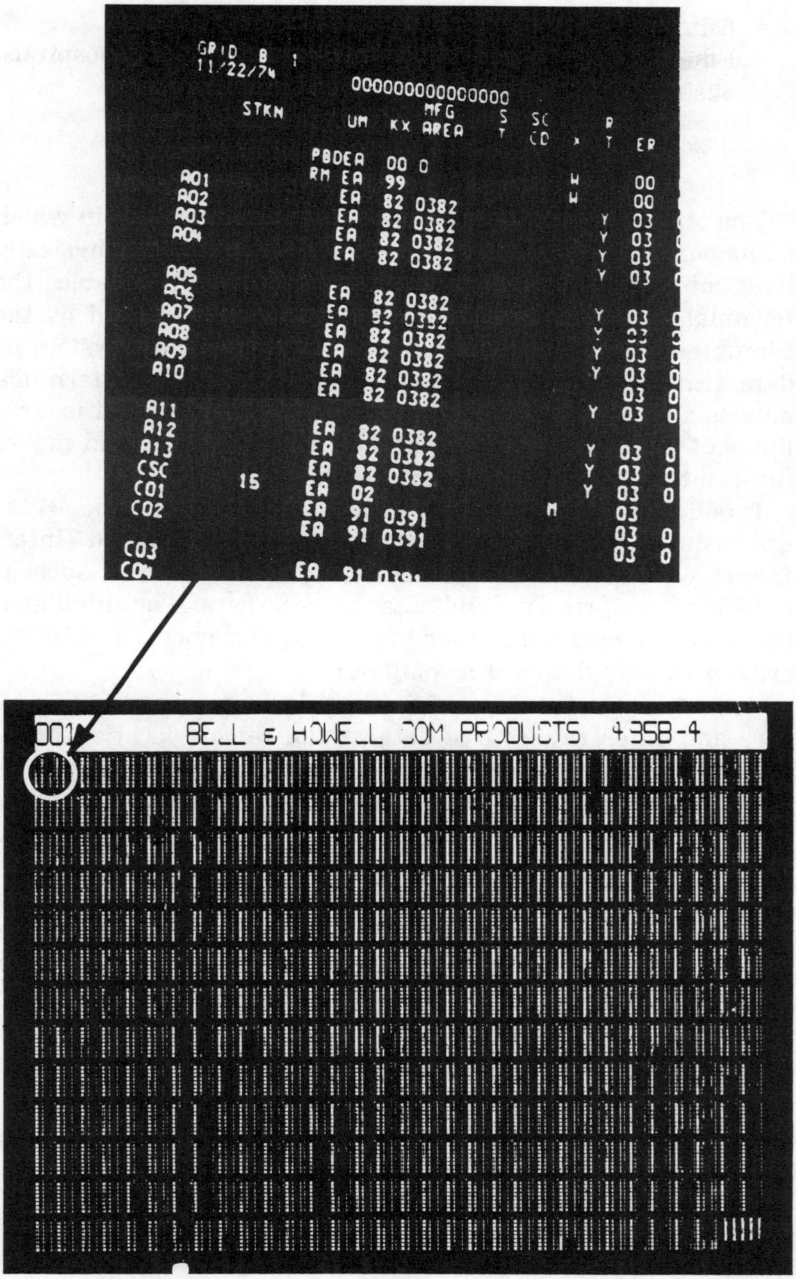

Courtesy Bell & Howell

Fig. 5-22. A typical microfiche film.

- Animated movies.
- Educational and training films for industry, hospitals, business, government, and schools.

INTELLIGENT TERMINALS

The term *intelligent terminal* designates a terminal in which a number of computer processing characteristics are physically built into, or attached to, the terminal unit. This enables the terminal to perform some functions normally handled by the computer, thus relieving the load on the computer system or data transmission lines. Specifically, the intelligent terminal detects and corrects certain operator errors, relieves the computer of some routine tasks, speeds up processing, and makes information available more easily and more quickly.

Intelligent terminals are usually cathode-ray-tube (crt) units equipped with a keyboard. They may be connected (interfaced) with a number of other input/output devices, such as card readers, printers, and cassette recorders. The intelligent terminal, coupled with other input/output devices, greatly increases the capability of a computer.

An important function of the intelligent terminal is to capture and enter raw source data at the remote location of its origin, such as a sales office, branch office, or mobile office. Since the terminal can be programmed for specific applications, this assures that entries are made in the proper places in fill-in blanks. Operators always know exactly what is being entered and where entries are to be made through visual verification with the crt display. Each entry is checked as it is made, and the operator can make corrections before committing data to the computer by simply rekeying the data.

Many of the intelligent terminals use microcomputers or microprocessors to control various functions. These micros can be programmed to perform many unique and special functions that may be required for a special application.

POINT-OF-SALE TERMINALS

Computer users are starting to realize the potential advantages of capturing data at the source. Some of the benefits of a good data collection system are: reduction of clerical costs;

increased accuracy of information because of the elimination of the manual handling and transcribing of data; more effective cost control; and sounder operating decisions by management, because they are getting timely management information, not history.

Useful data must have at least two characteristics: it must be accurate and it must be timely. Neither of these characteristics can be overlooked. The person who is capturing the data should do the fewest number possible of the simplest things possible.

Characteristics of point-of-sale systems are: the input device should be installed as close as possible to the point where the data are generated, the device should be easy to operate by the person at that location who is familiar with the characteristics of these data and with the important effect of errors in the data, precoded information should be used when possible, and a method of visual verification and correction is desirable.

For a number of years, some cash registers have been equipped with a paper-tape punching mechanism to record the facts of each sale when these facts are entered on the keyboard of the machine. For example, the sales clerk enters the amount of sale, tax, and other charges and credits, if any. The clerk may also enter the stock number and unit quantity of merchandise sold as well as any other data desired. While this is being done, the machine punches a paper tape with the amount and identification of each item. At the end of the day or period, the punched tape is removed from the cash register and placed in a device that records the data from the paper tape to magnetic tape to feed the day's sales to the computer, which updates the accounts receivable, cash on hand and stock records, and produces sales analysis reports for the store management.

This semiautomatic method of capturing data is certainly better than complete manual systems; however, there is still much more room for improvement. Today, several companies are producing systems that eliminate the manual keying of data (an excellent place for error to creep into a point-of-sale system). Fig. 5-23 shows a retail system that reads the magnetic strip on a price tag.

Today, computerized supermarkets throughout the country are becoming rather common. The key to these checkout systems is an optical scanning device which "reads" an identifica-

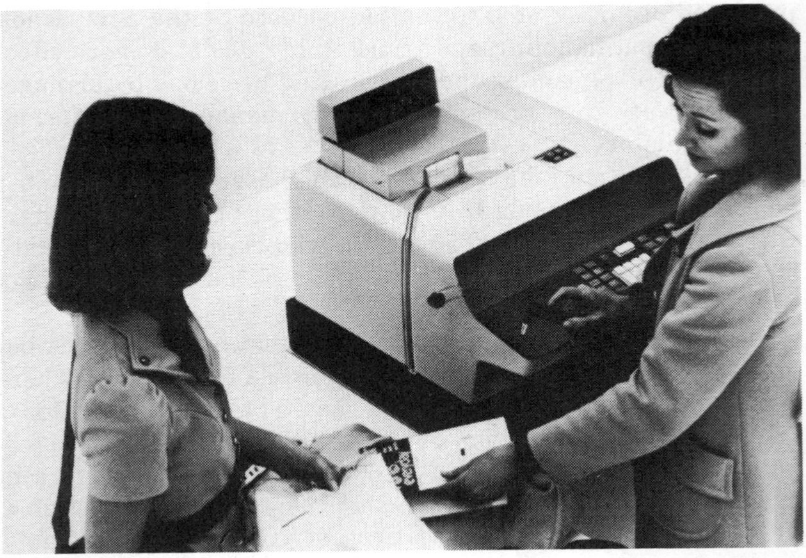

Courtesy IBM Corp.

Fig. 5-23. A point-of-sale terminal.

tion code placed on each item of merchandise and transmits this information to a computer. The computer uses this information to create a perpetual inventory control system.

The code used to identify products is the *U*niversal *P*roduct *C*ode (UPC), a 10-digit numbering system for identifying items sold by stores (Fig. 5-24). The first five digits in the code identify the manufacturer; the second five digits identify that manufacturer's product. This 10-digit code is expressed in a symbol as a series of vertical bars that can be understood by computer equipment. This symbol is printed on most of the 10,000 items sold in a typical supermarket. Upon receiving the code, the computer immediately matches it with product information such as price. It then relays this data to a cash register where it is visually displayed to both the customer and the checker. Simultaneously, the price is printed on the customer's receipt along with the product name.

Placing the price in computer memory eliminates the tedious job of price-marking items and also eliminates checkout errors that occur because of illegible price marks and ring-up mistakes. The store manager can also use the system to check the inventory of any product, to determine sales up to the moment at any checkstand or in any department, to know total sales, and to change prices of products.

We briefly discussed two areas (retail stores and supermarkets) where point-of-sale terminals are used. The capturing of

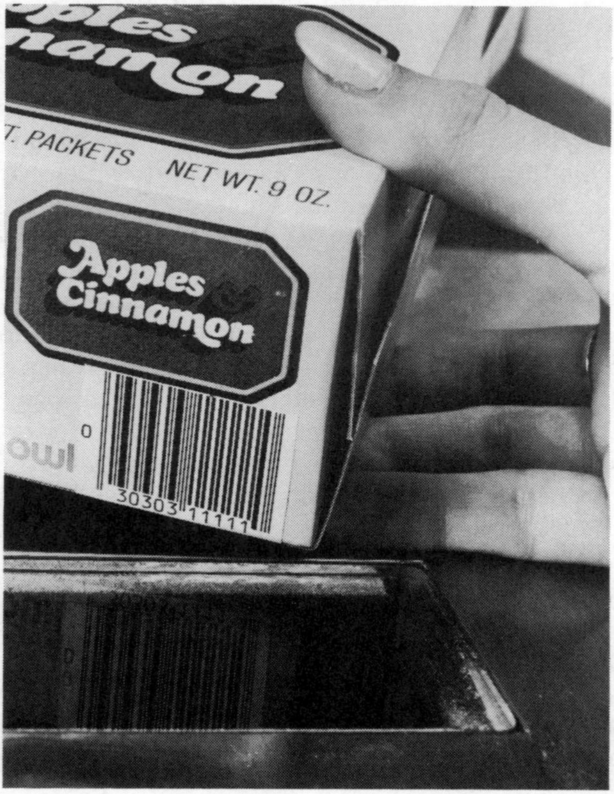

Courtesy IBM Corp.

Fig. 5-24. The *U*niversal *P*roduct *C*ode (UPC), an optical scanning system code for identifying products and their prices.

data at its source is commonly referred to as *source data automation.* No additional steps are needed to transcribe the data to computerized form. Point-of-sale terminals, magnetic-ink character reading devices (such as those used by banks), optical character reading devices (such as those used by utility companies), and other recognition devices offer the possibility of preparing data only once at the original source and sending this data directly to the computer. There are many application areas that could be drastically improved by using source data automation systems.

AUDIO RESPONSE TERMINALS

Computers can now talk! A program looks up words to be spoken in a dictionary, stored in a computer memory, and determines how they are to be pronounced and stressed. It then calculates how the human vocal track would move in speaking the words, in order to determine what sounds would be produced. This information is then passed on to an electronic device which actually produces the sound.

Audio response, or *voice response,* systems are used in a wide variety of businesses. The uses to which banks can apply voice response techniques are extensive. A teller's inquiry can get a response regarding the existence or nonexistence of an account, or whether the balance is sufficient to cover a check. A bank officer can be informed of the status of a loan, a trust account, or the details of a mortgage. In a retail store, audio response provides instant and private advice at the point of sale regarding a customer's credit and also provides credit-card verification. A long list of audio response uses could be made for such diverse businesses and industrial activities as real estate, transportation, manufacturing, insurance, wholesale, and many others.

Equipment which allows the computer to recognize spoken words is also under development, and some systems have actually gone into use. At present these are not so highly developed as the audio response device.

COMPUTER NETWORKS

Data communications involves the transmission of information from one point to another. A system for data communications consists of some type of terminal that is used to generate and receive electronic signals transmitted over communication lines. In addition, a *data set* is often required. This device converts digital signals for transmission over communications lines. Information to be transmitted is first converted by the terminal into an intermediate form acceptable to a data set. The data set converts the signals to a form which can be trans-

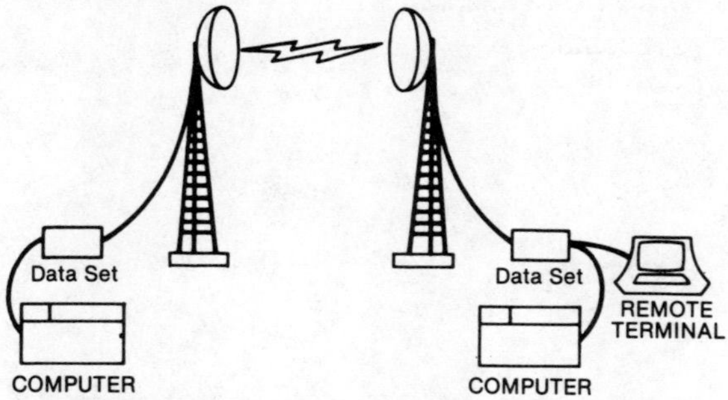

Fig. 5-25. Illustration of data transmission between two computers or between a computer and a remote terminal.

mitted over a common communications line (see Fig. 5-25). At the other end of the communications line is another data set and another terminal to perform the conversions in reverse order.

Remote terminals for data communications systems may be a variety of devices: point-of-sale terminals, digital plotters, minicomputer systems, microcomputer systems, card readers, line printers, teletypewriters, data collection equipment, push-button telephones, visual display systems, and others.

Chapter 6

Steps in Problem Solving

Courtesy IBM Corp.

Programming is the process by which a set of instructions is produced for a computer to make it perform some specified activity. The activity can be anything from the development of a chess playing program to the solution of a complex engineering problem. The set of instructions that control the computer is called a *program*.

Preparing a computer program and checking it out are both time-consuming and important operations. Since the computer does not do any thinking and cannot make unplanned decisions, every step of the problem has to be accounted for by the program. A problem that can be solved by a computer need not be described by an exact mathematical equation, but it does need a certain set of rules that the computer can follow. If a problem needs intuition or guessing, or is so badly defined that it is hard to put into words, the computer cannot solve it. A great deal of thought must be put into defining the problem and setting it up for the computer in such a way that every possible alternative is taken care of. A computer cannot be expected to perform any task adequately unless the problem it is required to solve has been specified correctly in every detail, and the instructions it is asked to obey define in complete detail each step of the solution.

It should always be remembered that computers are used to implement the solutions to problems. Computers do not solve problems—*people solve problems*. The computer carries out the solution as specified by people.

There are five main steps that have to be covered before a program is completed. These steps are illustrated in Fig. 6-1 and are as follows:

1. Understand the problem.
2. Develop a solution (algorithm).
3. Draw a flowchart.
4. Write a program.
5. Run the program on a computer.

The amount of time spent on each of these steps will largely depend on the type and complexity of the problem being programmed; however, some attempt to implement each of these steps is required for practically every program. Even though the steps are indicated as isolated and distinct, they are not this clearly defined. Actually, the steps interact, intertwine,

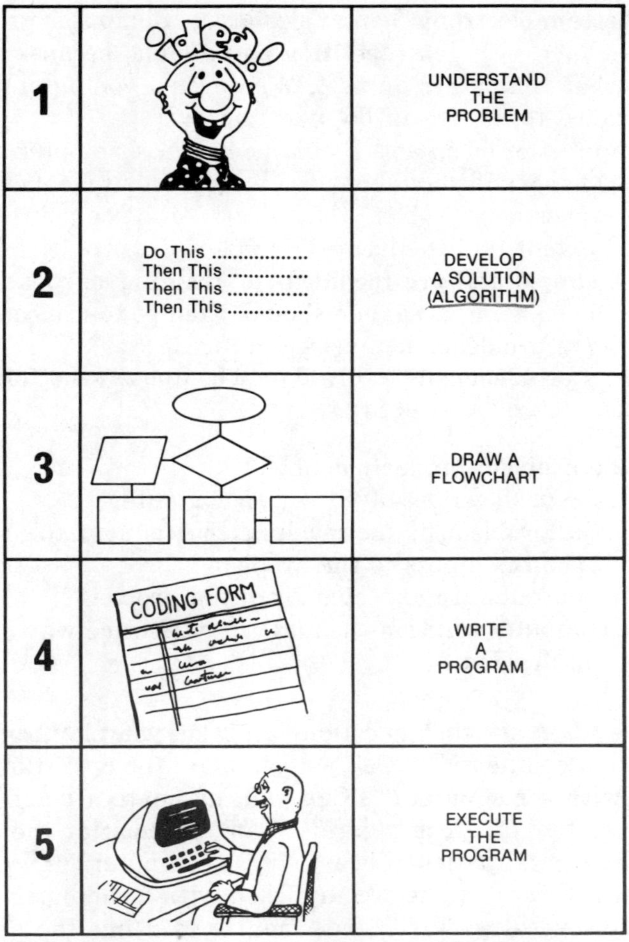

Fig. 6-1. The five main steps for solving a problem on a computer.

and recycle. Each of the steps is briefly described in this chapter.

UNDERSTAND THE PROBLEM

The first step in the solution of a problem is to understand the problem completely. You must be able to determine if it is feasible to solve the problem on a computer. Many problems are simply not computer problems.

Problems that are based on single formulas may very well be solved best on electronic hand calculators. Computer problems should involve as much repetition as possible, because repetition is what computers do best. Whatever a computer can be programmed to do, it can do over and over.

A computer problem also should be useful. Computer time is often expensive and should be used wisely. In a school environment, however, any problem that illustrates some point is useful to the extent that it educates. Many of the problems in this book are simple and are included for training purposes only. Outside the learning area, one should attempt to use computer time to solve problems of a useful nature.

Before a problem can be solved on a computer, the following questions must be answered:

- Is the problem properly defined?
- Can the problem be solved with a computer?
- Will the problem fit the machine that is available?
- What are the inputs to the problem?
- What outputs are expected from the problem?
- Is a computer solution the most cost-effective way of solving the problem?

People often ask such questions as, "Can you play backgammon with a computer?" "Can you simulate the operations of a missile with a computer?" "Can you automate a business inventory system on a computer?" "Can you monitor the operation of a hospital patient's heart with a computer?" Of course, all of these things can be accomplished with a computer, but it may take several weeks or even months to define the problem adequately. Although it may sound strange to say, we must know *exactly* what the problem is before we attempt to solve it.

DEVELOP A SOLUTION

When you fully understand the problem, you can proceed to develop a method for its solution. This method of solution is embodied in what we will call an *algorithm*. An algorithm is simply a precise, unambiguous procedure for the solution of a problem. It specifies a sequence of operations that provides the solution in a finite number of steps. Simply stated, an algorithm represents the logic involved in arriving at the solution to a problem.

DRAW A FLOWCHART

The English language is an unsatisfactory means of representing an algorithm. The language itself is inherently ambiguous, and the logical flow of complex problems is not easily explained in words. A technique widely used in computer problem-solving for representing algorithms is the flowchart (see Fig. 6-2). So, once the problem has been defined and an algorithm developed, a flowchart should be drawn to illustrate in symbolic figures the logic of the solution to the problem. Flowcharts are perhaps the best method available for expressing what you want computers to do. They are simple, easy to prepare and use, and eliminate ambiguities.

Courtesy IBM Corp.

Fig. 6-2. Flowcharts are a pictorial description of the procedures used by the computer to solve a problem.

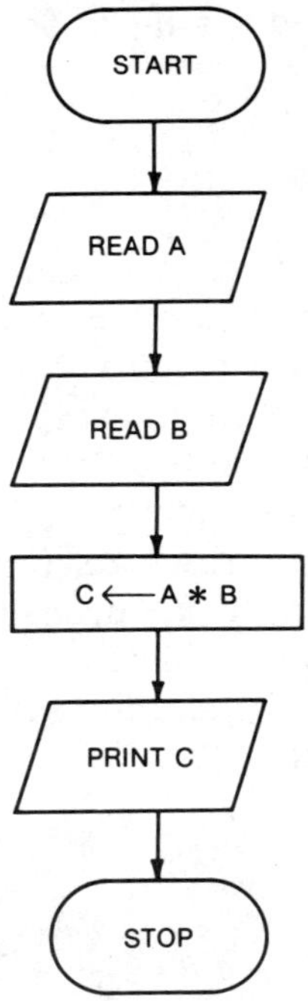

Fig. 6-3. A simple flowchart.

A simple example of a flowchart is shown in Fig. 6-3. (Chapter 7 will explain how to prepare flowcharts.) Observe that it is composed of several boxes, each representing some particular computer activity as described therein, and directional lines with arrows to designate the logical progression of the solution.

WRITE A PROGRAM

The flowchart is used as a guideline to the actual coding of the program in a *programming language.* The program, or list of computer instructions, will cause the computer to produce the solution to the problem.

```
10    LET N = 1
20    IF N > 100 THEN 60
30    PRINT N * N ;
40    LET N = N + 1
50    GO TO 20
60    END
```

Fig. 6-4. A program written in the BASIC programming language that calculates and prints the squares of all the whole numbers from 1 to 100.

An example of what a program looks like when written in an actual programming language is shown in Fig. 6-4. This program, written in the BASIC programming language, calculates and prints the squares of all the whole numbers from 1 to 100. An introduction to the BASIC language is found in Chapter 9.

" SAY SOMETHING IN BASIC!"

The more sophisticated and easier to use a language is, the less control a user will have over the final form of the program that is actually executed by the computer. Thus, some loss of efficiency in running time or an increase in the size of the program may occur. These penalties are counterbalanced by the speed of writing a program in an easy-to-use symbolic language and the likelihood of fewer mistakes.

Whatever programming language is used to write a program, the user's goal is to reproduce the logic of the program as described in a flowchart as simply, economically, and efficiently as possible.

EXECUTE THE PROGRAM

After the program has been written, you must input the program and data (if required) into the computer and instruct the machine to execute the program (see Fig. 6-5). If the program contains no mistakes, the computer will execute the program and output the desired results. If the program contains mistakes, you must find out why the program failed, make neces-

Courtesy MITS

Fig. 6-5. A user typing a program into an Altair 680 microcomputer system.

Courtesy IBM Corp.

Fig. 6-6. A programmer debugging a computer program.

sary corrections, and try again. This process is called *debugging* the program. You must keep in mind, however, that if the program executes, and answers are printed, there is no guarantee that these numbers are accurate. You must perform some check to see if the results are "correct" (Fig. 6-6).

Computer manufacturers often offer software to help test programs. Programs such as trace routines, memory-dump routines, and register-dump routines are often helpful in testing programs. Debugging systems are available on many computers. Such a system provides the user with a program designed specifically to help detect program errors. This system

Courtesy Data General Corp.

Fig. 6-7. A hand-held programmer's console designed to help debug programs written for microNOVA minicomputers.

allows the programmer to specify breakpoints, where the computer will stop. The programmer can then use the typewriter to enter data into the computer and to receive printouts. These debugging aids help in obtaining clues to the problem. Fig. 6-7 illustrates a hand-held programmer's console, a program-development tool designed for use with minicomputers.

Before coding a program, it helps to remember some of the so-called axioms of programming:

- Every computer program contains at least one bug.
- If there is a bug, the computer will find it.
- If anything can go wrong, it will.

With these axioms in mind, happy debugging!

Chapter 7

Flowcharting

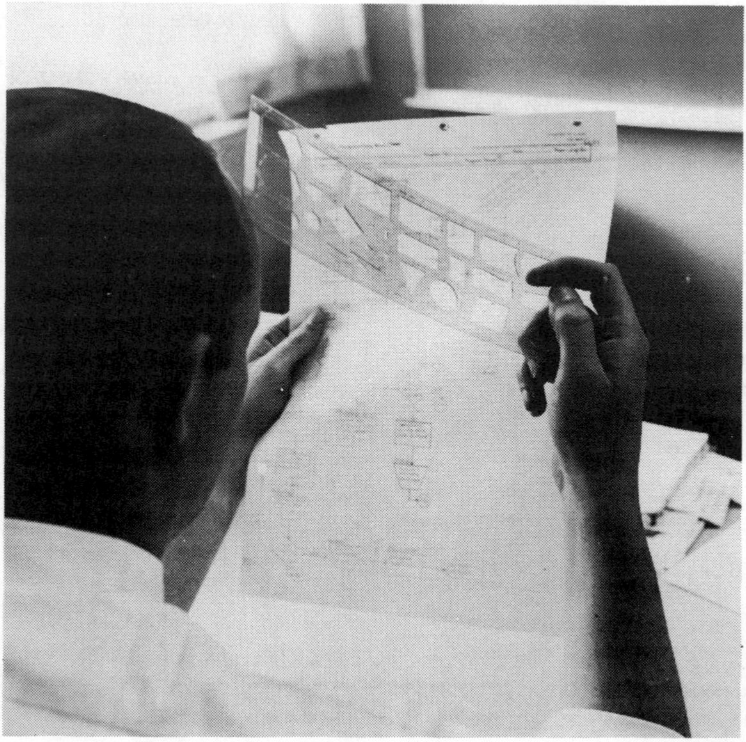

Courtesy IBM Corp.

As programming applications become more detailed and complex, it is increasingly difficult to state all the possible parts of a problem that must be coded. In order to minimize this problem, a system called *flowcharting* has been developed to represent the logical flow of processing.

A *flowchart* is a symbolic means of representing information about the information flow of a problem. There are two types of flowcharts: the *system flowchart,* which describes the data flow of a system, and the *program flowchart,* which graphically shows the flow of data of a computer program.

SYSTEM FLOWCHART

A system flowchart is a graphic representation of an entire system, or portion of a system, consisting of one or more computer operations. It is composed of interconnected flowcharting symbols arranged in the sequence in which the various system

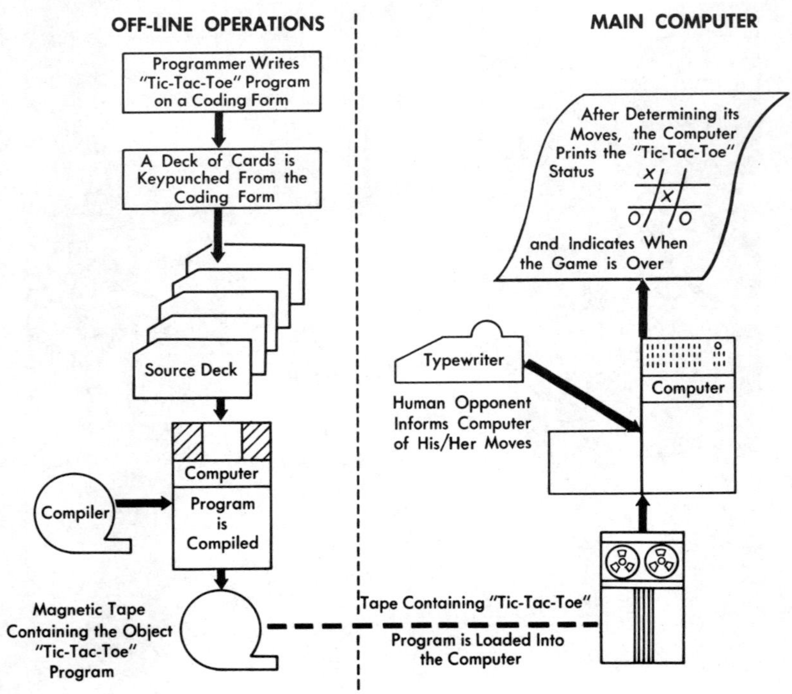

Fig. 7-1. System flowchart of the preparation and execution of a "tic-tac-toe" program.

operations are performed. The system flowchart is an overall planning, control, and operational description of a specific application. Other than this brief discussion and the illustration of a "tic-tac-toe" system flowchart in Fig. 7-1, we will not be concerned with this type of flowchart.

PROGRAM FLOWCHART

The program flowchart is a graphical or pictorial representation of a procedure that allows one to see the overall organization of the program. It is basically a diagram composed of directional lines, symbols, and information about the procedure. The program flowchart is sometimes called a flow diagram, a process flowchart, or a logical diagram. The term flowchart will be used throughout the remainder of this book and is meant to imply the program flowchart.

For each problem to be solved with a digital computer, it is necessary to plan in advance definite logical procedures, or *algorithms,* which the computer can follow without manual intervention. The step-by-step process that the computer uses to solve a problem is called a computer program, and one way to determine the steps of a program is through the use of a flowchart. The major uses of a flowchart are:

- To help in the development of a computer program.
- To illustrate in a graphical form how the logic of the program is laid out. This illustration aids in communication with other people about the logic of the program.
- To provide documentation for the program.
- To use as a reference worksheet while writing the program.

It is doubtful that any two people would prepare the same flowchart from a given problem description. To increase the probability that one person will be able to understand another's flowchart, certain conventional symbols are usually employed by computer users.

FLOWCHART SYMBOLS

Because flowcharts contain many different classes of operations, it is convenient to represent each class of operation by a uniquely shaped symbol. Table 7-1 illustrates a partial set of standard flowcharting symbols. These symbols are similar to the ones used by most computer users. The most frequently used symbols are discussed in the following paragraphs:

Table 7-1. Standard Flowcharting Symbols

Symbol	Symbol Name	Symbol Use
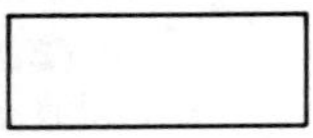	Process Symbol	Represents calculations, processing, or any function not covered by a specific symbol.
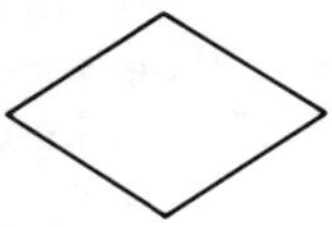	Decision Symbol	Represents a decision, question, or comparison.
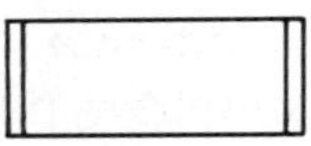	Predefined Process Symbol	Represents a subroutine.
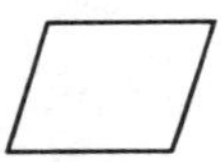	Input/Output Symbol	Represents any input/output function.
	Connector Symbol	Represents a junction in a line of flow, connects broken paths in the line of flow, and connects several pages of the same flowchart.
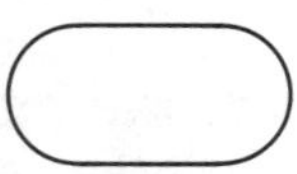	Terminal Symbol	Represents the start or end of a program.
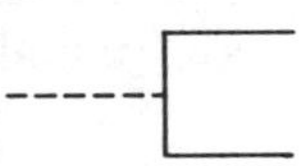	Annotation Symbol	Contains descriptive comments or clarifying notes about the program.
	Flow Symbol	Connects the symbols and indicates flow.

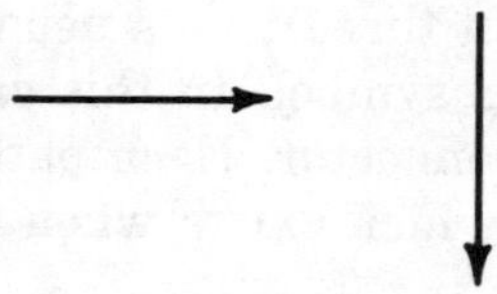

Flow Symbol

Lines with arrowheads are used to indicate the sequence in which the various actions described by a flowchart are to be performed.

Flowcharts should be constructed to conform to the natural tendency to read from left to right, top to bottom, although variations are sometimes desired in order to achieve symmetry and to emphasize certain points.

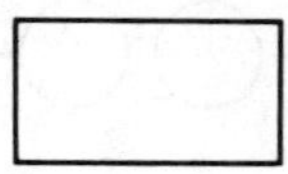

Process Symbol

The process symbol will contain the description of a process, an operation, memory assignments, or unexecutable information. Only one line can enter and one line can leave this symbol. The operation is indicated inside the symbol box by a concise description, or algorithm, defining the operation. This symbol is also used for all operations in a program that are not assigned to one of the other symbols.

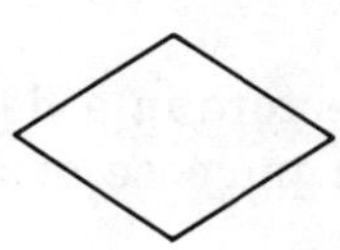

Decision Symbol

The decision symbol indicates those points in a program where a change in program control is to be made based on some type of decision. The symbol may be used for two-way decisions, three-way decisions, or multiple decisions. The decision box has a single entry and, depending on the way it is used, may have one, two, or three exits. For a three-way decision, three lines must leave the symbol. For a multiple decision path (greater than three), it is usually easier to read if only one line leaves the symbol. In this case the line must go directly to a variable connector. Each path must be labeled to indicate the condition which exists when the path is used.

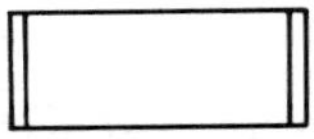

Predefined Symbol

The predefined symbol indicates a reference to a subroutine. The name (or explanation) of the subroutine is enclosed by a rectangle symbol. Only one entry and exit is allowed with this symbol.

Fixed-Connector Symbol

The fixed connector is used to connect two or more remote parts of a flowchart with one another. A remote connector indicates the junction where a computational path conveniently ends or starts (for example, at the end of a page). The connectors are identified by inserting either a numeric value or an alphabetic character in the representative circles. *Numeric tags* should be used to represent transfer of program control, *alphabetic* tags should be used to represent end-of-page connections, while *alphanumeric* tags should be reserved for use by variable connectors.

The use of fixed connectors in a flowchart should be kept to a minimum as the main purpose of a flowchart is to portray the logic of a program.

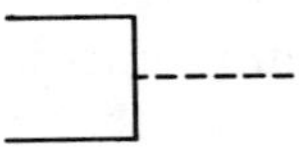

Annotation Symbol

The annotation symbol is used to supply descriptive information concerning the flowchart. This symbol may be used to indicate the existence of an indicated condition at some specific point in the flow path. The symbol is connected to the flow line by a dashed line.

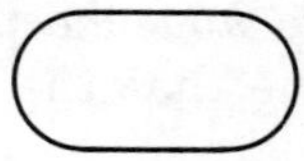

Terminal Symbol

A sausage-shaped symbol is used to represent where a program *begins* or *ends*.

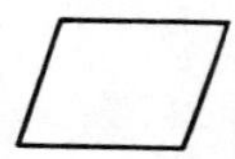

Input/Output Symbol

The input/output symbol is used for all input/output operations not covered by a specific symbol.

CONSTRUCTION OF THE FLOWCHART

Flowcharts can be prepared showing any degree of detail. It is customary to begin with very simple diagrams showing

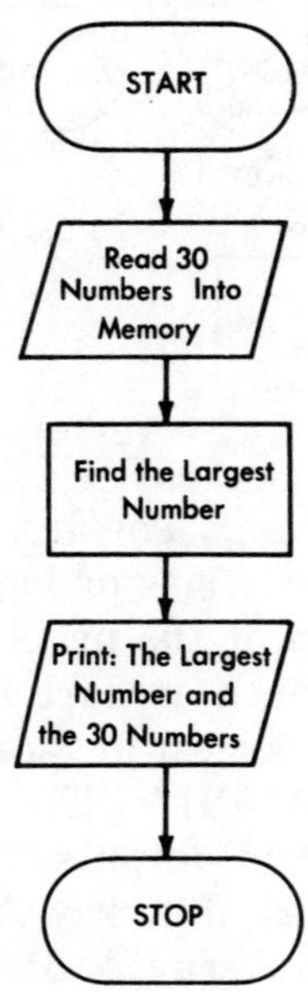

Fig. 7-2. General flowchart of the "Find Largest Number" program.

the gross logical structure and then gradually amplifying each of the boxes in successive redrawings of the same flowchart until the required amount of detail is obtained.

Since much of the detailed computer program in the solution of a problem is devoted to *housekeeping* functions, it is generally reasonable to assume that the first flowchart will omit

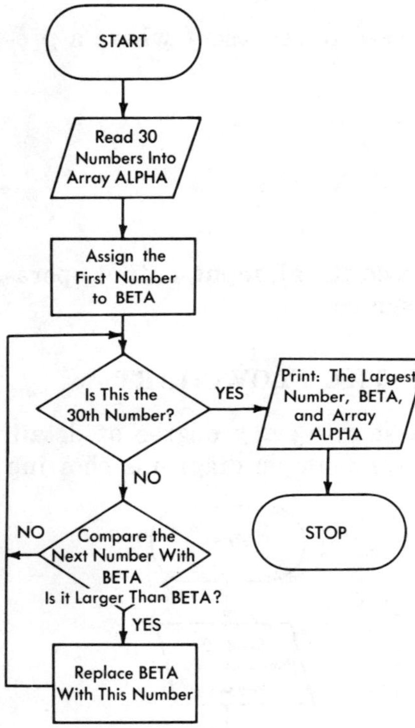

Fig. 7-3. Second draft of the "Find Largest Number" flowchart.

these functions. The first draft would most likely consist, then, of the basic series of logical operations necessary to perform the solution of the problem. Such a flowchart is illustrated in Fig. 7-2. This flowchart describes a procedure that may be used to find the largest of 30 numbers. The 30 numbers are located in Array ALPHA. The procedure places the largest number in BETA and outputs to the printer the value of BETA and all 30 values of Array ALPHA. If the following values were assigned to Array ALPHA:

9	32	17	27	4	3
6	2	16	7	31	14
34	6	22	12	1	20
21	47	28	4	9	12
8	13	30	49	10	16

the procedure would then determine that 49 was the largest number.

The second draft of the *Find Largest Number* flowchart would include a few more details of the problem and the program logic would be described in more detail (Fig. 7-3).

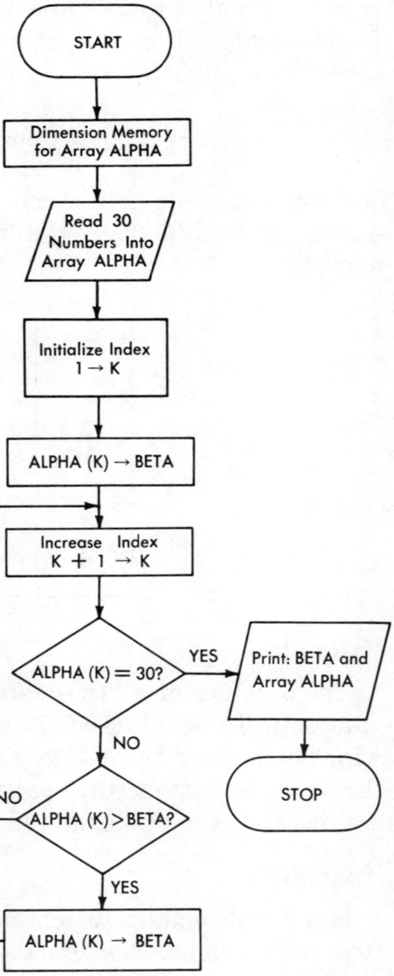

Fig. 7-4. Final flowchart of the "Find Largest Number" program.

The final draft of the *Find Largest Number* flowchart includes a detailed description of the program logic and all housekeeping functions. This flowchart is shown in Fig. 7-4.

The hierarchy of flowcharts tends to force the user to think in a logical manner, from a general solution of a problem to a detailed description of the computer program logic.

FLOWCHARTING TEMPLATE

A flowcharting template (Fig. 7-5) provides the programmer with a simple means of drawing the various shaped symbols of a flowchart. These templates are usually obtainable from a computer manufacturer, a college bookstore, or a computer book publisher.

FLOWCHARTING EXAMPLES

Several sample flowcharts are presented in the following examples to illustrate the proper use of the flowcharting symbols:

1	0	1
0	1	0
1	0	0

Example 1

The 9 values of a "tic-tac-toe" board are represented by the values in Table ITIC. This table is indexed by the index K, which will vary from 1 to 9. Count the number of "ones" in the table and store this value in the variable named IONE. A flowchart for this example is shown in Fig. 7-6.

Example 2

Make a flowchart which can be used to count the value of twenty-five coins. The coins are located in Array COIN. Store

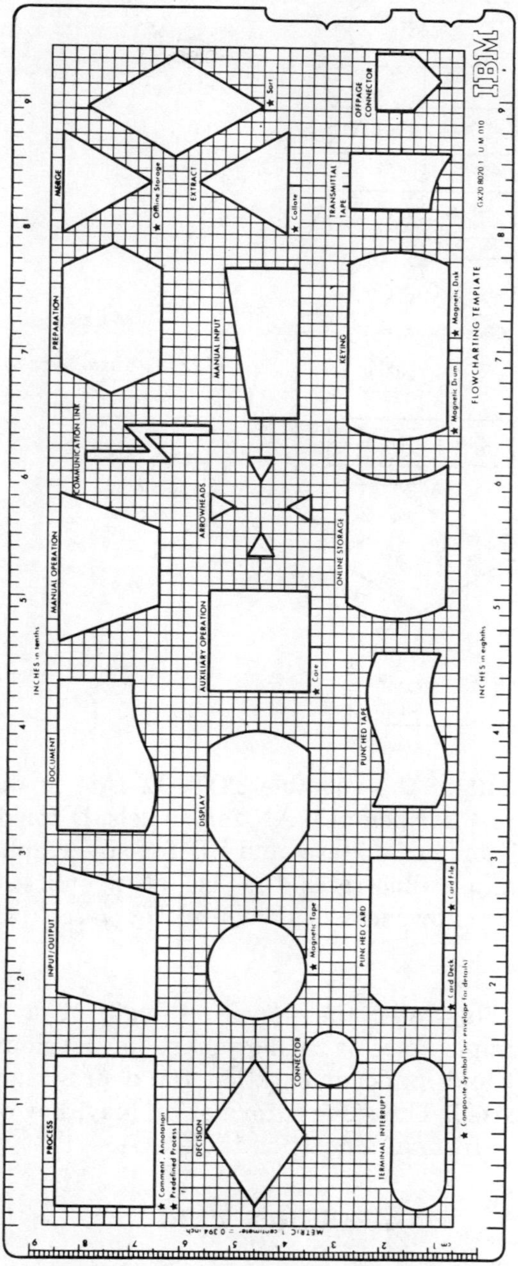

Fig. 7-5. A flowcharting template.

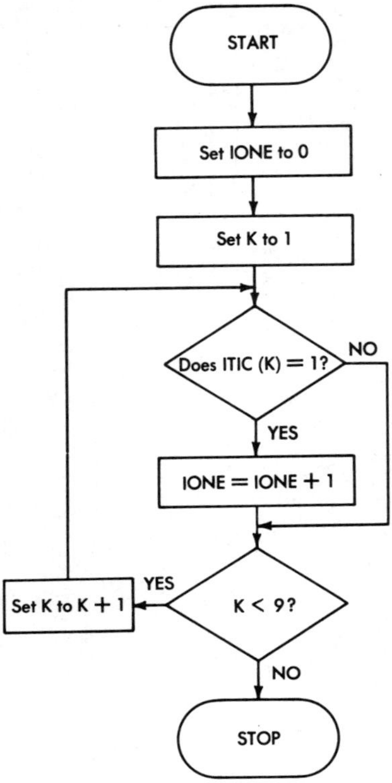

Fig. 7-6. Flowchart for Example 1.

the final count in the variable TOTAL. Intermediate storage variables are P for pennies, AN for nickels, D for dimes, Q for quarters, H for half-dollars, and SD for silver dollars.

This example illustrates the use of a subroutine named DCOINV. The flowchart is shown in Fig. 7-7.

Example 3

Fig. 7-8 illustrates the flowchart logic of a "tic-tac-toe" game. The importance of the flowchart for developing the program logic, and as documentation for a program, cannot be overemphasized. The same information may, however, be presented in the form of a decision table.

DECISION TABLES

Decision tables are a valuable aid in describing a problem, and provide a different view of problems and their solutions

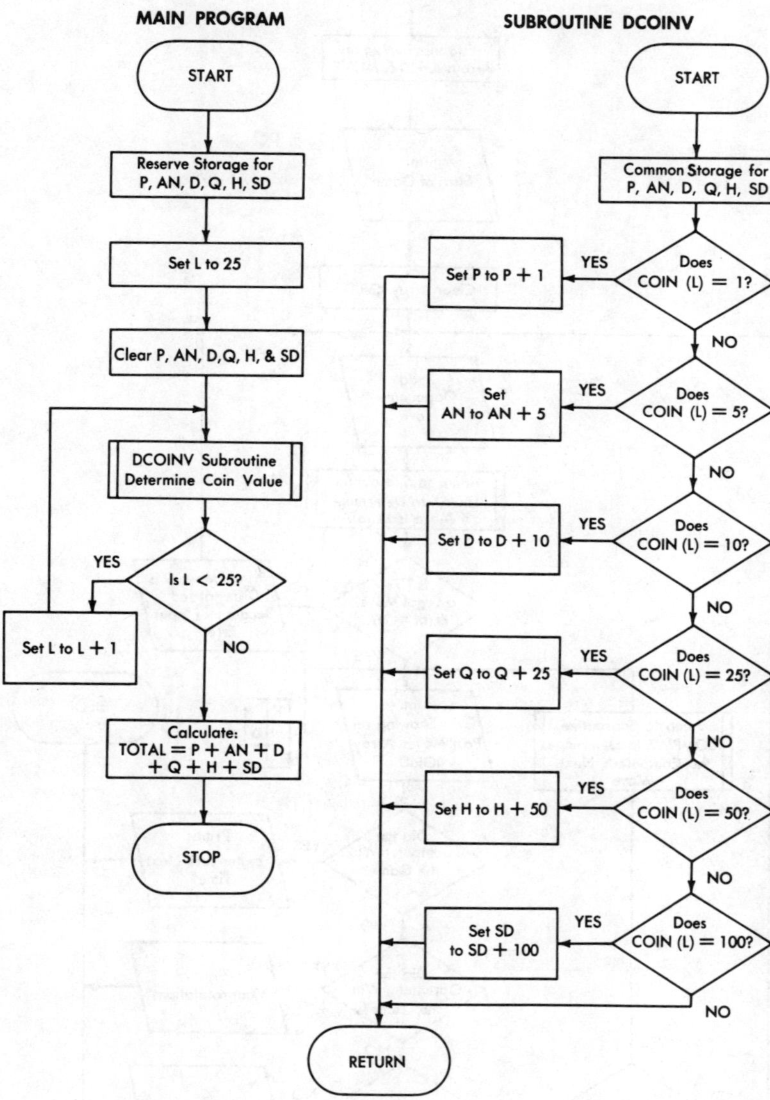

Fig. 7-7. Flowchart for Example 2.

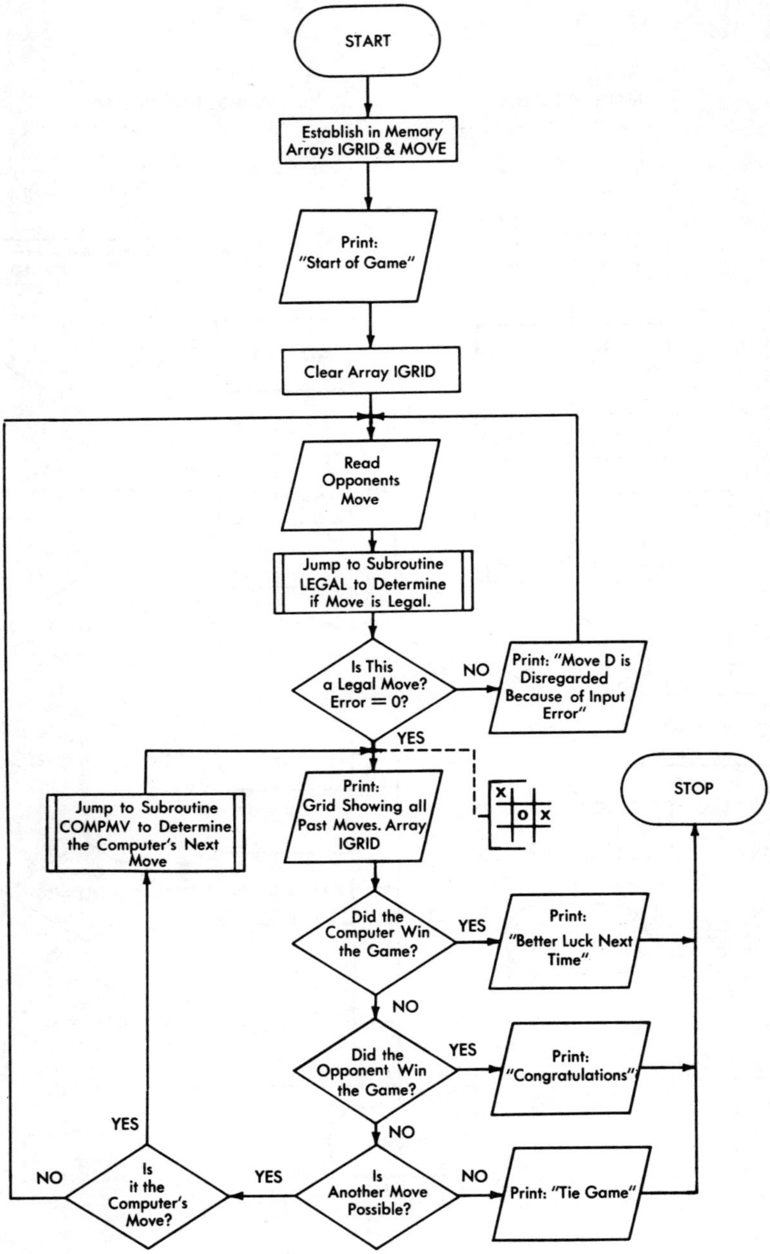

Fig. 7-8. Flowchart for Example 3.

than do flowcharts. Decision tables do not introduce any radical new concepts, but simply describe the logical flow of a problem in tabular form. They are extremely useful when the decision logic of a program becomes excessively complicated. Decision tables were initially intended to replace flowcharts for certain classes of problems. However, the decision-table format is now being used as a man-to-machine communication method and a compiler is used to read and interpret a tabular language program.

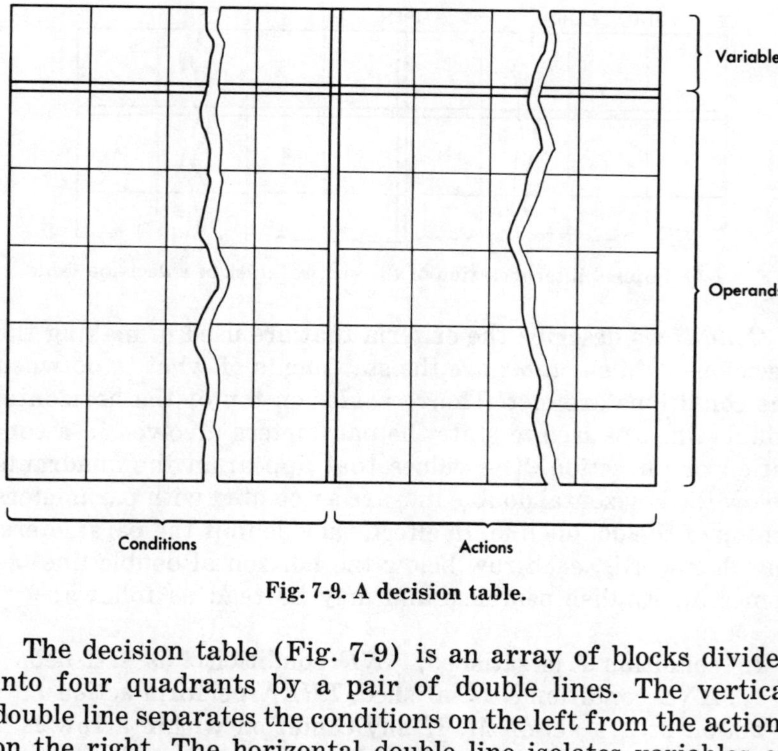

Fig. 7-9. A decision table.

The decision table (Fig. 7-9) is an array of blocks divided into four quadrants by a pair of double lines. The vertical double line separates the conditions on the left from the actions on the right. The horizontal double line isolates variables on the top from the associated operands which appear in the quadrants below the double line.

The decision table provides for one or more *conditions* to be tested for, and one or more *actions* that are to be performed if those conditions are satisfied. Consider giving the following interpretations to the vertical lines of the decision table of Fig. 7-9:

Left-most line . . . . IF
Lines left of vertical double line . . . . AND
Vertical double line . . . . THEN
Lines right of vertical double line . . . . ; (semicolon)
Right-most line . . . . (period)

The preceding English interpretations are illustrated in Fig. 7-10.

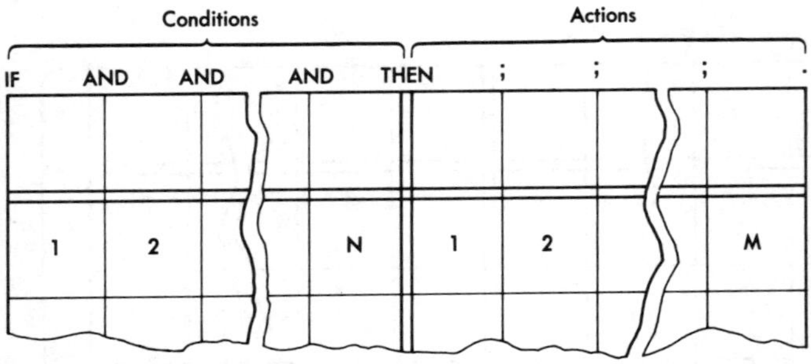

Fig. 7-10. Implied interpretation of the vertical lines of a decision table.

Conditions describe the criteria that are used in making the decisions, while *actions* are the statements of what to do when the conditions are met. The *variables* on top of the horizontal double line are used to state the parameters involved in a condition or an action. The values that appear in the quadrants below the horizontal double line are associated with parameters on top of the double line. In effect, they delimit the parameters. In other words, each row below the horizontal double line becomes an English sentence and may be read as follows:

> *IF* condition *1* is satisfied, *AND* condition *2* is satisfied, . . . *AND* condition *N* is satisfied, *THEN* perform action *1;* action *2;* . . . action *M*. If any condition within a row is not satisfied, the row is said to have *no solution.* The table is considered *solved* when all the conditions of any row are satisfied and their associated actions performed.

The importance of the horizontal and vertical double lines in the decision table must not be overlooked. Fig. 7-11 describes an exploded illustration of the decision table with emphasis on the quadrants determined by these double lines.

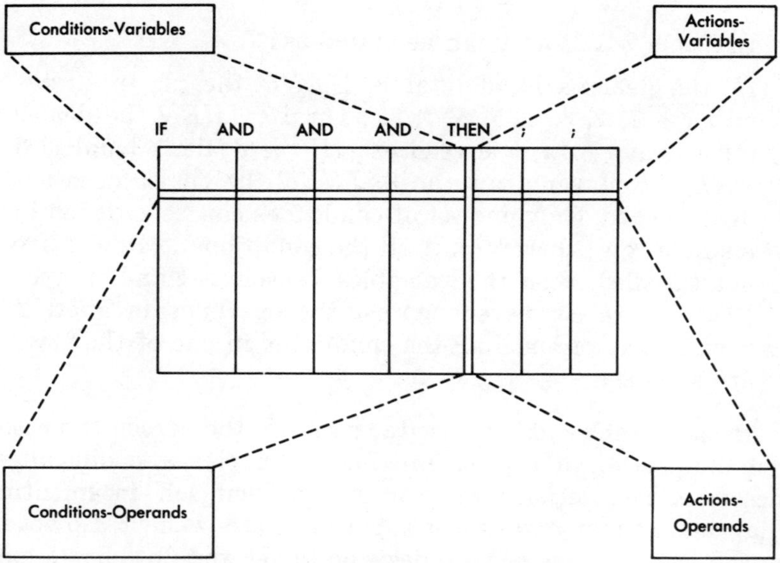

Fig. 7-11. Exploded view of a decision table.

To illustrate the use of a decision table, and the way it is read, let us consider a simple case of describing the dealer's strategy in the gambling game of *Baccarat* (Table 7-2). The count of the dealer's hand and the card dealt the player are used as criteria for determining what action the dealer is to perform.

Table 7-2. A Decision Table for the Game of Baccarat

IF Dealer's Hand	AND Player Draws	THEN Dealer
1	1-10	Draws
2	1-10	Draws
3	1-7; 9-10	Draws
3	8	Does not draw
4	2-7	Draws
4	1; 8-10	Does not draw
5	4-7	Draws
5	1-3; 8-10	Does not draw
6	6-7	Draws
6	1-5; 8-10	Does not draw
7	1-10	Stands
8	1-10	Turn cards over
9	1-10	Turn cards over
10	1-10	Draws

In Table 7-2, Row 1 can be stated as:

IF the dealer's hand total is 1 *AND* the player draws either a 1, 2, 3, 4, 5, 6, 7, 8, 9, or 10, *THEN* the dealer must draw. Row 4 is read as: *IF* the dealer's hand is 3 *AND* the player draws an 8, *THEN* the dealer does not draw a card. Only one set of conditions can be satisfied in a single row; therefore, if all the conditions in Row 1 are not satisfied, then the variables (Dealer's Hand, Player Draws) are compared against the operands in another row, and so on until all the conditions in one of the rows are satisfied.

Decision tables may be used to simplify the person-to-person communication of a program that is complex and difficult to describe. The decision table is an excellent self-documenting diagram. In many ways it is superior to a flowchart. However, a well-balanced use of both decision tables and flowcharts may yield a more complete description of the logic of a complex problem. The two techniques are complementary and not exclusive.

Chapter 8

Writing the Program

Courtesy NCR Corp.

The key to the succesful use of a computer is programming. The computer cannot add two numbers unless it has been directed to do so. In fact, the simplest task is a major problem for the computer, although, paradoxically, the most complex problem is a simple task when it has been properly programmed.

Problem definition, problem analysis, determining the method of solution, and flowcharting are the first steps in program preparation. They are normally carried out independently of the computer.

Programming involves writing a set of instructions in a sequence that will produce a desired result when the sequence is executed on the computer. These instructions will be stored in the internal memory of the computer. The data, or information upon which these operations are performed, are also stored in the internal memory of the computer.

Writing sequences of instructions is called *coding*. Coding can take place at various levels, ranging from machine language (basic language of the computer) to problem-oriented language (symbolic language in problem terminology). These different levels are:

- Machine language.
- Assembly language.
- Higher-level language.

All forms except machine language are symbolic in nature and must be translated into machine-language instructions. The computer operates at the level of machine coding and, therefore, all other codes must eventually be translated into that form.

MACHINE-LANGUAGE CODING

When computers were relatively new, programmers wrote computer programs in the basic language of the computer. This consisted of writing instructions as long strings of numbers. Needless to say, this was a tedious process and required a programmer with much patience and training in mathematics.

A typical machine-language instruction might be, for example, the number 6340217, where 63 is the computer code for addition and 40217 is the memory location where the number to be added is located. A machine-language program would consist of many such numerical instructions.

SYMBOLIC LANGUAGES

Symbolic languages were developed to overcome the many inconveniences of machine language. Symbolic coding involves programming a computer to recognize instructions in a language more easily understood by the user, and then translating these expressions into machine language. This concept has led to the development of a large number of different symbolic programming languages that are easy to use and understand.

Before examining the various types of symbolic languages, let us define several terms. As stated earlier, a *program* is a meaningful sequence of *statements*. Statements, in turn, are strings of symbols from a given alphabet composed of letters, digits, and special characters. The form of each statement obeys a set of rules (*syntax*) and possesses an operational meaning (*semantics*). Collectively, the alphabet, syntax, and semantics are termed a *language*.

A *source program* is a computer program written in a symbolic language. The instructions or statements of a source program are processed in the computer to produce a program that can eventually be executed on the machine. This processing function is called *translating,* and the processor program is called a *translator*. Thus, the translator converts a program written in a symbolic source language into machine language. This machine-language program is called an *object program.* A translator, then, converts a source program into an object program. The object program is the program that is run on the computer to produce the desired results.

Symbolic languages are more suitable for human use than are machine languages. They are designed to facilitate computer programming, and they tend to be associated in some sense with the problems under consideration. One of the features that hastened the widespread acceptance of programming languages is that computer programs written in this more convenient form could be translated to machine language by another computer program running on the same or possibly a different computer. One of the significant aspects of the philosophy behind the use of symbolic languages and translator programs is that the same computer may process programs written in many different languages, provided that a translator program has been written for each language.

ASSEMBLY-LANGUAGE CODING

An *assembly language* is a *low-level* symbolic language used for developing computer programs which must go through an *assembly* in order to be converted into a machine code required for operation on a computer. It is called a low-level language because it closely resembles the machine code of a computer rather than the language of a problem.

Programming in an assembly language offers a number of important advantages over programming in machine code. In assembly language, all operation codes of the computer are given *mnemonic* designations. For instance, the actual operation code for the instruction *Add* may be 100110. In the assembly language, one need only write the mnemonic operation code ADD.

Most computer users never learn the actual machine codes. All data and machine addresses in the commands are written using symbolic notation. The user is thereby relieved of potential problems in the effective allocation of computer storage. The use of symbolic addresses reduces the clerical aspect of programming and eliminates many programming mistakes. Because the symbols are chosen to be meaningful, the program is also much easier to read and understand than if it were written with numerical addresses.

An assembly-language program cannot be directly executed by a computer. The mnemonic operation codes and symbolic addresses must be translated into a form the machine can use. This is the function of the *assembler*.

The assembly process begins with a source program written by the user. Ordinarily, a special coding form is used, such as that shown in Fig. 8-1 (we shall examine this program later). The user must then input the assembler into the internal storage of the computer.

Next, the user inputs (via a keyboard terminal, card reader, etc.) the source-language program into the computer where it is processed by the assembler. The assembler, which is simply

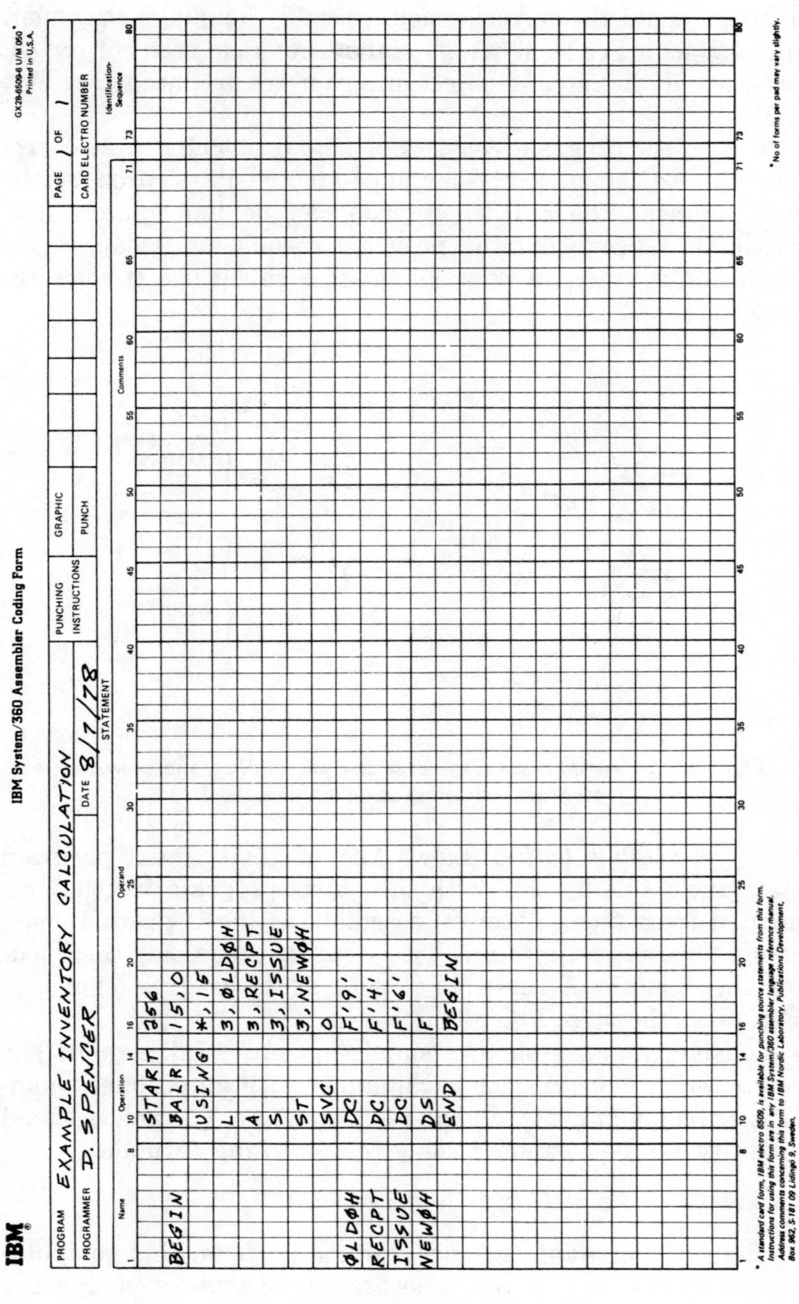

Fig. 8-1. A program written in assembly language.

a program itself, converts each assembly-language statement into a machine code. When all statements have been converted, an *assembly listing* and object program are produced (see Fig. 8-2).

The object program consists of actual machine code corresponding to the assembly-language statements written by the programmer. The object program can be immediately executed, thus producing the program results, or it can be recorded on magnetic disk or magnetic tape for use at some future time.

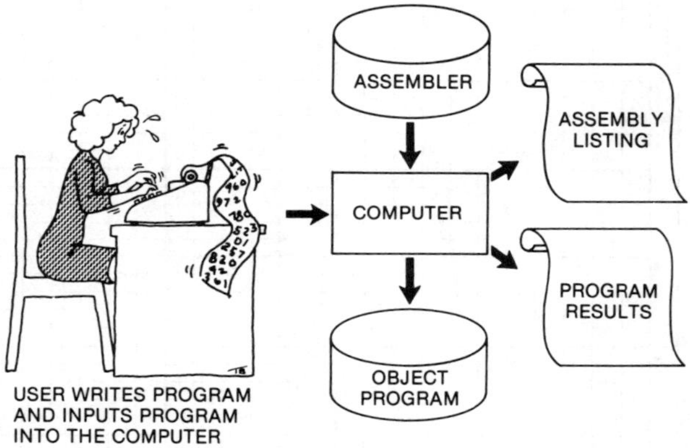

Fig. 8-2. The assembly process—creating, assembling, and executing a program written in assembly language.

The *assembly listing* shows the original source-program statements side by side with the object-program instructions created from them. After an assembly listing is printed, most computer users refer to this listing rather than using their coding sheets again. An assembly listing of the program shown in Fig. 8-1 is shown in Fig. 8-3.

Consider an example of a simple inventory calculation. The computer user begins the calculations with an on-hand quantity, a receipt quantity, and an issue quantity. The new on-hand quantity can be computed using the following formula:

NEW OH = OLD OH + RECPT − ISSUE

The assembly-language program to perform this computation is shown in Fig. 8-3. The first three lines of coding are housekeeping instructions. The processing instructions start with the mnemonic operation code for *Load.* This L is converted by the assembler into the actual machine code for *Load* —hexadecimal 58 (binary 0101 1000). The 3 is the number of the computer register in which a word from storage is to be loaded. OLDOH is the symbolic address of the word in storage to be stored into computer register 3. The assembly listing for this program, shown in Fig. 8-3, shows both the source-language statement and the associated machine code. The translation of the other processing instructions—A for *Add,* S for

```
                                          START  256
000100  05 F0                      BEGIN  BALR   15,0
                          000102          USING  *,15
000102  58  30  F 012                     L      3,OLDOH
000106  5A  30  F 016                     A      3,RECPT
00010A  5B  30  F 01A                     S      3,ISSUE
00010E  50  30  F 01E                     ST     3,NEWOH
000112  0A  00                            SVC    0
000114  00000009                   OLDOH  DC     F'9'
000118  00000004                   RECPT  DC     F'4'
00011C  00000006                   ISSUE  DC     F'6'
000120                             NEWOH  DS     F
                                          END    BEGIN
```

Fig. 8-3. Assembly listing for the program shown in Fig. 8-1.

Subtract, and ST for *Store*—can be examined in Fig. 8-3. The SVC instruction is used to inform the computer that there are no more computations in this program. The three DC instructions are used to establish numerical values for OLDOH, RECPT, and ISSUE. The DS instruction is used to identify NEWOH, where the computer result will be stored. The END instruction informs the assembler that the termination of the program has been reached.

The assembly language presented in the previous example was for use on the IBM System/360 computer. Assembly languages for other computers are different and, therefore, prevent a program written in the assembler language of one machine from being used on another machine.

Some assembly languages include instructions that are equivalent to a specific set of one or more ordinary instructions in the same language. These instructions are called *macroinstructions,* or simply *macros;* and, when assembled, they are expanded into a predefined set of fundamental instructions. The assembler that processes macros is often called a *macroassembler,* and the language that contains these macros is called a *macroassembly language.*

An example of a macro would be a *Move* instruction. This instruction is assembled into two machine-code instructions: MOVE A, B, would cause the macroassembler to generate *Load A* and *Store A at B* instructions.

HIGHER-LEVEL LANGUAGES

In contrast to assembly languages and machine languages, in which the source language is still highly dependent upon a particular hardware system, higher-level languages relate to the procedures being coded and are thus relatively machine independent. Therefore, a program coded in a higher-level language can be executed on any computer system that has a translator available for that programming language.

"I ADORE COMPUTER USERS—THEY ALWAYS KNOW SO MANY FOREIGN LANGUAGES!"

Essentially, higher-level languages are completely general in application, although among the contemporary systems several are clearly better adapted to numeric-type problems and others are better adapted to nonnumeric-type problems. Three of the more popular numeric-type languages are FORTRAN, BASIC, and APL; while popular languages for nonnumeric-type applications are COBOL and RPG. A higher-level language designed for multipurpose use is PL/1.

Many higher-level programming languages have been introduced in recent years, primarily because this type of language simplifies the programming task. The use of a higher-level language reduces the requirement that the user have a detailed knowledge of computers. This, in turn, allows the user to concentrate more deeply on steps that are more closely related to the problem. Higher-level programming languages are widely accepted and used by people not having a strong background in computer programming.

A program can be written in a much shorter time when a higher-level language is used, primarily because the language includes a set of very powerful instructions. A higher-level language instruction may accomplish the same operation as several lower-level machine instructions.

Both the coding and debugging tasks are simplified when one uses a higher-level language. Many of these languages are self-documenting; i.e., a listing of the program will suffice for documentation purposes. However, this usually applies only to very small computer programs. A *compiler* is used to translate a program written in a higher-level language into the basic language of the computer.

As in the assembly process, the process of carrying out a particular computation consists of two stages. First, the source-language program is translated, or compiled, into the equivalent object program; second, the object program is executed (see Fig. 8-4). The two stages are kept separate. Compilation is completed before any actual computation begins;

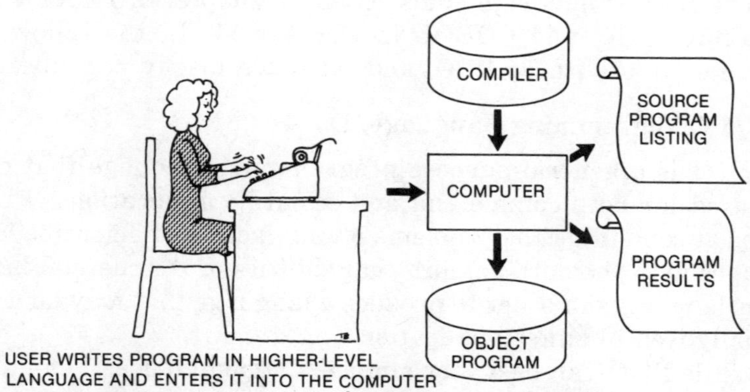

Fig. 8-4. Creating, compiling, and executing a program written in a higher-level language.

and, in fact, the entire object program is stored away before any part of it is executed.

At the completion of the compilations, one of two things may happen. The object program may be immediately executed, or it may be recorded on some suitable medium, such as magnetic disk or magnetic tape, for use later. The compile-and-immediately-execute process is often called the *compile-and-go* process.

Both assemblers and compilers provide auxiliary functions that assist the user in documenting and correcting the instructions written. These functions include program listings and error indications that are detected during the translating process. The errors detected by the assembler or compiler are called *diagnostics*. The process of correcting errors is commonly referred to as *program debugging*.

The major higher-level programming languages are BASIC, FORTRAN, COBOL, and, to a lesser extent, PL/1, RPG, and APL. These languages were developed by computer manufacturers and by committees consisting of representatives from manufacturers and users to make the computer available directly without having to work through an intermediary symbolic or machine-language programmer. The ease of learning and the ease of coding make it possible for a computer user to learn programming in a short time. Through the use of a terminal, or by coding the program on the proper coding form, the user can run the programs and produce the answer with little effort.

The BASIC language is discussed in Chapter 9, FORTRAN in Chapter 10, and COBOL in Chapter 11. In the following three sections, PL/1, RPG, and APL are briefly described.

PL/1 (*P*rogramming *L*anguage/*1*)

PL/1 is a general-purpose programming language that can be used for both commercial and scientific applications. PL/1 aims at combining the problem-solving facility of scientific languages with the data-handling capabilities of commercial business languages in order to produce a language that may be used equally well in either application.

While PL/1 can be a very simple language to use, it can also be employed to handle extremely complex computing problems. One of its most important characteristics is its modularity;

that is, the presence of different subsets of the language for different applications at different levels of complexity. The language has a block structure which allows program segmentation into blocks of language statements or subroutines of a total program.

PL/1 is versatile enough to process a wide variety of data types, such as fixed and floating-point numbers, and character and bit strings. The language structure is *free form.* No special forms are needed for coding, since the significance of each statement depends on its own format and not on its position within a fixed framework. Each PL/1 statement terminates with a semicolon (;). Because the PL/1 compiler recognizes the semicolon as a terminator, part of a statement, or many statements, can be written on one coding line.

PL/1 has the best debugging capability of all existing programming languages. A *default* feature, by which every error or unspecified option is given a valid interpretation, minimizes the effect of programming errors. For example, a PL/1 compiler, when confronted with an unmatched left parenthesis, will automatically insert a right one in the proper place.

```
WEATHER: PROCEDURE;
        DECLARE MAXDAY(7), MINDAY(7), AVERAGE(7);
        READ LIST ((MAXDAY(I), MINDAY(I)) I = 1 TO 7);
        AVERAGE = (MAXDAY + MINDAY) / 2;
        WRITE ((MAXDAY(I), MINDAY(I), AVERAGE(I))
        I = 1 TO 7) (2F(5), F(8, 1), SPACE);
END WEATHER;
```

Fig. 8-5. A PL/1 program to compute average daily temperature.

Fig. 8-5 shows a PL/1 program that will read the maximum and minimum temperature for every day of the week, and calculate and print the average daily temperature.

RPG (*R*eport *P*rogram *G*enerator)

RPG is a language that provides a simple method for writing instructions for a computer to accomplish a variety of commercial data-processing jobs. The purpose of RPG is simply to generate a report program. This program, in turn, is used to write the desired report.

In small-scale computer systems, RPG is used extensively and is even finding acceptance in larger computer installations where there is a need for the production of business reports. There are two common versions of RPG: RPG I and RPG II. The languages are so similar that differences between them are more of an academic than an operational interest.

An easy language to learn and use, RPG is capable of handling several input files, selecting certain records from the files, performing limited mathematical computations, and producing the desired report from the records. During the process, it can also update records from the master file.

The use of RPG is restricted to situations where a simple report is desired from the computer rather than some complex processing or multiple output. It is a highly formalized language with very rigid specifications. Unlike other compiler languages where instructions are given, in RPG the programmer need only furnish data, specifying conditions and processing desired on special specification forms. Generally, four different types of specification sheets are used in writing RPG programs. They specify:

1. The form of input data.
2. The input/output devices to be used in executing the program.
3. The calculations that are required.
4. The form of output data.

A program specified on these special forms is translated by RPG into machine-code instructions.

APL (*A Programming Language*)

APL is a language for describing procedures in the processing of information. It can be used to describe mathematical procedures having nothing to do with computers, or to describe (to a human being) how a computer works. Most commonly, however, it is used for programming in the ordinary sense of directing computers how to process numeric or alphabetic data. The language was invented by Dr. Kenneth E. Iverson and described in a book entitled *A Programming Language*, published by John Wiley & Sons, Inc., 1962.

APL is one of the most concise, consistent, and powerful programming languages ever devised. Operations on single items extend simply and naturally to arrays of any size and shape. Thus, for instance, a matrix addition that in other higher-level languages might require two loops and a half-dozen statements, becomes simply A + B in APL.

The language is very mathematically oriented. It is, however, finding widespread acceptance among a variety of users, many of them in business and education. Fig. 8-6 shows an APL program that computes the total sales of five salesmen, each of whom sells the same three products.

```
      ∇SALES1
 [1]  'ENTER P'
 [2]  P←⎕
 [3]  'ENTER S'
 [4]  S←3 5⍴⎕
 [5]  J←1
 [6]  TOTAL←+/P×S[;J]
 [7]  'TOTAL SALES FOR SALESMAN ';J;' IS ';TOTAL
 [8]  →6×⍳5≥J←J+1
      ∇

      SALES1
ENTER P
⎕:
      1.25 4.30 2.50
ENTER S
⎕:
      40 20 37 29 42 10 16 3 21 8 35 47 29 16 33
TOTAL SALES FOR SALESMAN 1 IS 180.5
TOTAL SALES FOR SALESMAN 2 IS 211.3
TOTAL SALES FOR SALESMAN 3 IS 131.65
TOTAL SALES FOR SALESMAN 4 IS 166.55
TOTAL SALES FOR SALESMAN 5 IS 169.4
```

Fig. 8-6. An APL program.

INTERPRETIVE-LANGUAGE CODING

Interpretive coding permits programming in a language that is easier to learn than machine language. Many of the earlier interpretive languages were similar to machine language; however, they provide features and operations that were not inherent in the computer used for executing the program.

Interpretive systems are used primarily on computers that are too slow to permit efficient use of algorithmic languages, and on small computers (especially minicomputers and microcomputers) that have implemented higher-level programming systems such as BASIC, FORTRAN, or APL. They are also commonly used on small computers to provide a language that resembles machine language but is actually much easier to learn and use.

A program written in such a language is ordinarily executed one statement at a time by a translator called an *interpreter*. The interpreter is a computer program that must be entered into the memory of the computer and remain there during the execution of a program written in interpretive language. They are usually lengthy programs that can occupy several thousand bytes of internal memory. Hence, an interpreter may occupy a major portion of the memory of a small computer.

Many of the newer microcomputers are including BASIC interpreters in ROM (*R*ead-*O*nly *M*emory). For example, the Radio Shack TRS-80 microcomputer includes ROM BASIC in its basic machine configuration. To use the BASIC language, one merely has to turn the computer on and it is immediately available for use.

Chapter 9

BASIC Programming

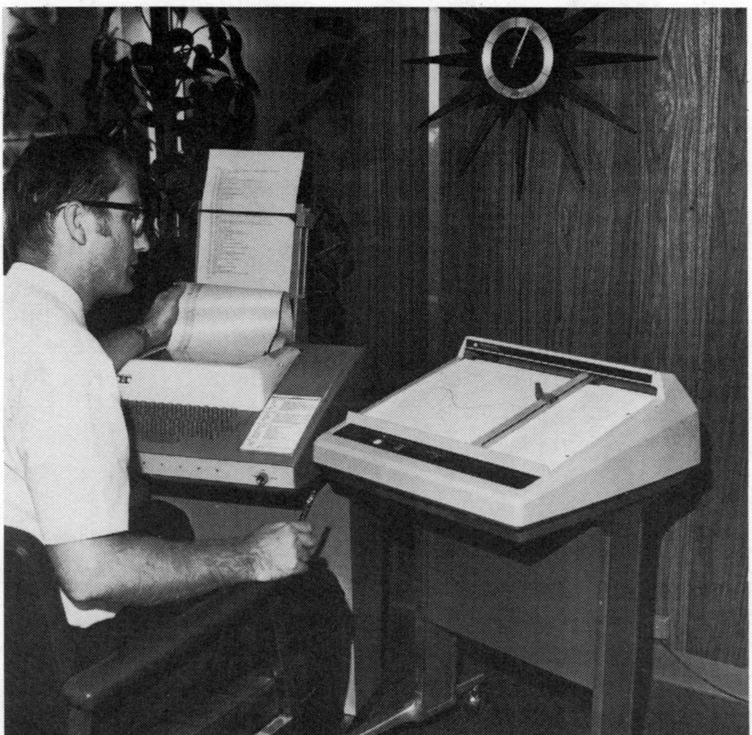

Courtesy Hewlett-Packard

BASIC, an acronym for *B*eginner's *A*ll-purpose *S*ymbolic *I*nstruction *C*ode, is a language suitable for solving a wide variety of problems: business, scientific, games, engineering, etc. Since BASIC has a relatively small set of instructions and few rules for correct coding, it is an easy language to learn and use.

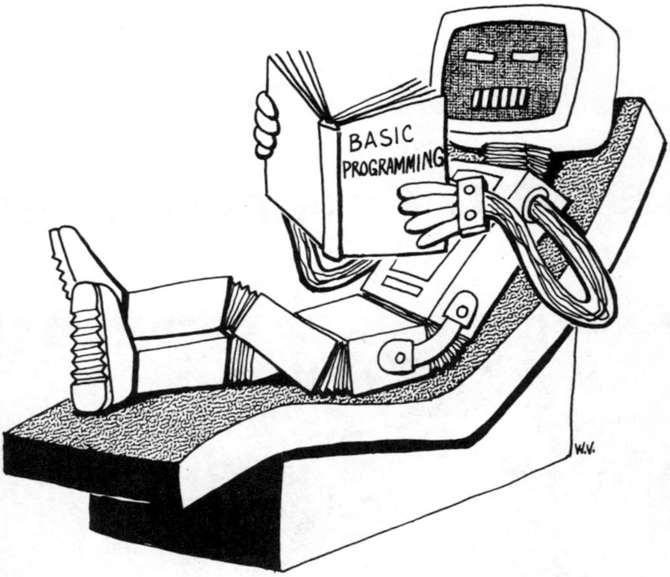

BASIC is available on most computer systems including microcomputers and minicomputers. The primary purpose of this chapter is to provide you with an elementary knowledge of BASIC so that you can write programs to instruct the computer to solve simple problems.

WRITING A PROGRAM IN BASIC

A BASIC program consists of a set of directions (program statements) that provides a solution to some specific problem. Each statement in a BASIC program has a line number. Fig. 9-1 illustrates a simple BASIC program that has seven statements. Note that each statement in the program has a line number and that the numbers are arranged in increasing order. The computer will execute these statements in sequence unless a program instruction directs otherwise.

```
10    REM BASIC PROGRAM FOR DETERMINING THE
20    REM SQUARE ROOT OF A↑2 + B↑2
30    READ A, B
40    LET R = SQR (A↑2 + B↑2)
50    PRINT "SQUARE ROOT OF", A, "PLUS", B, "IS", R
60    DATA 10, 20
70    END
```

Fig. 9-1. BASIC program to compute the square root of $a^2 + b^2$.

Let us now examine how a person would prepare a program to compute the squares and cubes of the first fifteen integers. A BASIC program to accomplish this is as follows:

```
100 FOR I = 1 TO 15
200 LET J = I * I
300 LET K = I * I * I
400 PRINT I, J, K,
500 NEXT I
600 END
```

Let us examine each statement in this program:

```
100 FOR I = 1 TO 15
```

The first statement in the program instructs the computer to repeat statements with line numbers 200, 300, and 400 fifteen times increasing the value of I by 1 each time the set of statements is executed. I would be assigned the value of 1 the first time the statement set is executed, 2 the next time, 3 the next, and so on.

```
200 LET J = I * I
```

This instruction is used to compute the square of the current value of I. If I is 1, then J would be equal to 1×1, or 1. If I is 2, then J would be equal to 2×2, or 4. If I is 3, then J would be equal to 3×3, or 9, and so forth.

```
300 LET K = I * I * I
```

This statement is similar to the last statement with the exception that the cube of the current value of I is computed instead of the square. If I is 4, then K would be equal to $4 \times 4 \times 4$, or 64.

```
400 PRINT I, J, K,
```

This statement directs the computer to print the values of I, J, and K.

```
500 NEXT I
```

This statement is used as a terminating statement for statement number 100.

```
600 END
```

This statement identifies the end of the program.

This program may be executed by typing RUN. The results of the program execution are printed as follows:

```
1       1       1       2       4
8       3       9       27      4
16      64      5       25      125
6       36      216     7       49
343     8       64      512     9
81      729     10      100     1000
11      121     1331    12      144
1728    13      169     2197    14
196     2744    15      225     3375
```

Suppose at this point that we wish to have the computer print the value of I in one column, the value of J in another column, and the value of K in another column. We can do so by changing statement number 400 to the following:

```
400 PRINT I, J, K
```

After the new statement is typed, we can obtain a new listing of the program by typing LIST. The program now appears as follows:

```
100 FOR I = 1 TO 15
200 LET J = I * I
300 LET K = I * I * I
400 PRINT I, J, K
500 NEXT I
600 END
```

Again, we execute the program by typing RUN and the following output is printed on the terminal:

```
1       1       1
2       4       8
3       9       27
4       16      64
5       25      125
6       36      216
7       49      343
```

8	64	512
9	81	729
10	100	1000
11	121	1331
12	144	1728
13	169	2197
14	196	2744
15	225	3375

The previous printout is not bad; however, it could be improved if a column heading was printed at the top of each column. This may be accomplished by adding a new statement:

```
50 PRINT "NUMBER", "SQUARE", "CUBE"
```

This statement causes the computer to type the word NUMBER at the top of column 1, SQUARE at the top of column 2, and CUBE at the top of column 3.

The LIST command again causes the program to be printed as follows:

```
50 PRINT "NUMBER", "SQUARE", "CUBE"
100 FOR I = 1 TO 15
200 LET J = I * I
300 LET K = I * I * I
400 PRINT I, J, K
500 NEXT I
600 END
```

The reader should note that the statement numbered 50 was automatically inserted above line number 100. By typing RUN, the following printout would be obtained:

NUMBER	SQUARE	CUBE
1	1	1
2	4	8
3	9	27
4	16	64
5	25	125
6	36	216
7	49	343
8	64	512
9	81	729
10	100	1000
11	121	1331
12	144	1728
13	169	2197
14	196	2744
15	225	3375

A BRIEF SUMMARY OF THE BASIC LANGUAGE

The BASIC language in this section is not complete, but it does include enough BASIC statements to enable the reader to write simple programs.

Line Numbers

Each statement in a BASIC program must have a line number between 1 and 99999. It is a good idea to start numbering with 10 or 100 and leave gaps of 10 numbers (10, 20, 30, 40, 50, 60, etc., or 100, 110, 120, 130, etc.) in the event that you subsequently wanted to insert new statements in the program.

Constants

A constant or number in BASIC may contain a decimal point, a minus sign, and up to six digits. Commas may not be included and a positive number need not be preceded by a plus sign. Several valid numbers are:

```
  72.3
   3.46
643210
    .02
  -.107
```

A constant may also be represented with a power of ten, such as 23×10^2. In BASIC this number, which represents 2300, would be written as 23E2.

Variables

A variable represents values, usually ones that are not known at the time the program was prepared, or quantities that will take on changing values. A variable is represented by a one-letter name such as A, B, C, . . . , Z, or a two-character name such as A1, A2, A3, . . . , Z9.

A variable may be subscripted; i.e., a variable containing a pointer to some specific location in a list or table. Some legal subscripted variables are:

A(4)—fourth item of a list called A
R(27)—twenty-seventh item of a list called R

D(2, 3)—item of a table named D that is located in row 2 and column 3.

Operators

There are five basic operators in BASIC:

+ addition	Example: X + Y
– subtraction	Example: X – Y
* multiplication	Example: X * Y
/ division	Example: X / Y
↑ exponentiation	Example: X ↑ Y

Expressions and Functions

A BASIC expression is a sequence of variables, constants, and functions separated by operating symbols and/or parentheses to form a meaningful mathematical expression. Parentheses are used to group several items together. The items contained inside a parentheses pair are computed before the parenthesized quantity is used in further computations. For example, in the expression:

```
X * (A * B — C) + 43,
```

the computations would be performed in the following order:

A * B — C	first
X * (A * B — C)	second
X * (A * B — C) + 43	last

The following expression contains a BASIC library function that computes the square root of a value:

```
A + SQR(X) — 36
```

In addition to the square-root function, BASIC includes nine other functions:

SIN (X)	sine of X
COS (X)	cosine of X
TAN (X)	tangent of X
ATN (X)	arctangent of X
EXP (X)	natural exponential e^x
ABS (X)	absolute value of X
RND (X)	random number
INT (X)	integer part of X

Remarks

A comment or remark may be included in a BASIC program by using the REM statement. A remark is used to provide supplementary information in a program. A remark in BASIC is the word REM followed by whatever remark you choose. Several remarks follow:

```
100 REM THIS IS A REMARK
100 REM JOHN P. PROGRAMMER
260 REM CIVIL ENGINEERING PROGRAM
```

Sequence of Program Statements

The computer will execute statements in sequential order (top of the page to the bottom) unless directed to do otherwise.

Spaces

Spaces may be inserted in a program statement to clarify reading. These spaces have no effect on the execution of the statement. For example, the statement:

```
10 LET R = R + 1
```

could also be written as

```
10 LET R     =     R+     1
```

without changing the meaning of the statement.

STATEMENTS

The following is a brief discussion of some of the more important statements in the BASIC language.

LET variable = expression

The LET statement is used when one wants the computer to perform a computation, alteration, or initiation. For example:

```
20 LET A = A + B - 36
```

GO TO line number

The GO TO statement is used to transfer program control to a specified location in the program. For example:

```
40 GO TO 200
```

READ variable, variable, variable, . . .

The READ statement causes the variable listed in it to be given, in order, the next available numbers in the *data block*. For example:

```
100 READ A7, D, R6
```

DATA number, number, number, . . .

The DATA statement is used to store numbers in a *data block* (a section of computer memory that is used to hold numbers for READ operations). For example:

```
210 DATA 26, 7, 10
```

INPUT variable, variable, variable, . . .

The INPUT statement allows the user of the terminal to assign data values at program execution time. When this statement is executed, it causes the computer to print a "?". The user responds by typing in the desired values for the variables, separated by commas if more than one, followed by a carriage return. For example:

```
65 INPUT A, Z3, R
```

DIM letter (constant)

This statement reserves computer memory for tables and lists. For example:

```
10 DIM A(23), Z(10, 15)
```

END

The END statement must be the last statement in the program. It, therefore, must have the highest line number of any statement in the program. For example:

```
400 END
```

PRINT label and/or expression

The PRINT statement is used to print data on the terminal. For example:

```
120 PRINT A, B2, C6, Z7
```

DEF FN (letter) (variable) = expression

This statement allows one to define a function other than a standard library function. For example:

```
40 DEF FNX(Z) = ABS(X) — 273
```

GOSUB line number

This statement is used to call a subroutine. For example:

```
100 GOSUB 263
```

RETURN

The RETURN statement is used in a subroutine to return control to the main program. For example:

```
200 RETURN
```

IF expression, relation THEN line number

This statement is a "conditional transfer of control" statement that provides for a selection of two alternate paths. The following relations may be used:

less than	<
less than or equal	<=
greater than	>
greater than or equal	>=
equal	=
not equal	<>

For example:

```
100 IF X = 26 THEN 200
```

STOP

This statement transfers program control to the END statement. For example:

```
677 STOP
```

FOR variable = expression TO expression STEP expression

This statement sets the specified conditions of a *program loop* and causes the loop to be executed. For example:

```
100 FOR A = 1 TO 30 STEP 3
```

NEXT

The NEXT statement is used to identify the end of a *program loop.* There is a NEXT statement associated with every FOR statement.

RESTORE

This statement restores the *data bank* pointer to the first number in the data bank. A subsequent READ statement will then start reading data at the beginning of the data bank again. For example:

```
10 RESTORE
```

EXAMPLE PROGRAMS

χ^2 Program

Let us consider the construction of a BASIC program that will compute statistical decisions about populations on the basis of sample information. Suppose that in a particular sample, a set of possible events $E_1, E_2, E_3, \ldots, E_k$ are observed to occur with frequencies $f_1, f_2, f_3, \ldots, f_k$ called *observed frequencies,* and that according to probability rules they are expected to occur with frequencies $e_1, e_2, e_3, \ldots, e_k$ called *expected frequencies.* Often we wish to know whether observed frequencies differ significantly from expected frequencies. A measure of the discrepancy existing between observed and expected frequencies is supplied by the statistic χ^2 (read *"chi square"*) given by:

$$\chi^2 = \frac{(f_1 - e_1)^2}{e_1} + \frac{(f_2 - e_2)^2}{e_2} + \frac{(f_3 - e_3)^2}{e^2} + \ldots + \frac{(f_k - e_k)^2}{e_k}$$

Table 9-1 illustrates a random number table of 250 digits showing a distribution of the digits 0, 1, 2, 3, . . . , 9. Let us

Table 9-1. A Random Number Table

Digit	0	1	2	3	4	5	6	7	8	9
Observed Frequency	17	31	29	18	14	20	35	30	20	36
Expected Frequency	25	25	25	25	25	25	25	25	25	25

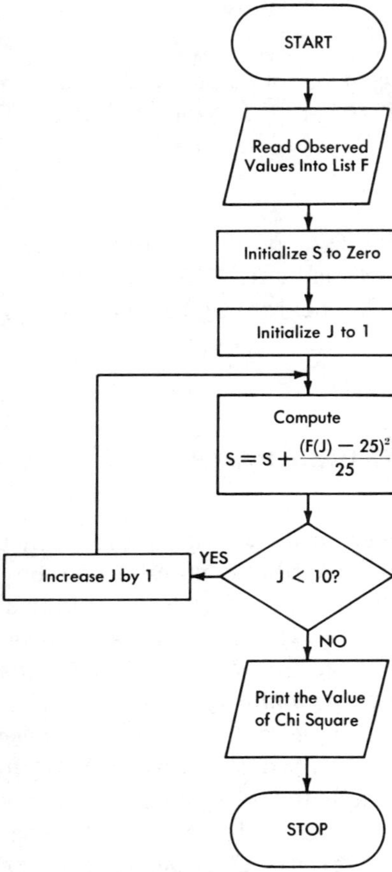

Fig. 9-2. Flowchart of the χ^2 program.

examine this distribution and determine if the observed distribution differs significantly from the expected distribution. In other words, compute χ^2 and if it is larger than 21.7, we can conclude that the observed distribution differs significantly from the expected distribution.

A flowchart of a procedure to perform this analysis is shown in Fig. 9-2 and a BASIC program follows:

```
010 REM CHI SQUARE PROGRAM
020 FOR I = 1  TO 10
030         READ F(I)
040 NEXT I
050 LET S = 0
060 FOR J = 1 TO 10
070       LET S = S + (F(J) — 25) ↑ 2/25
```

```
080 NEXT J
090 PRINT "CHI SQUARE IS"; S
100 DATA 17, 31, 29, 18, 14, 20, 35, 30, 20, 36
100 END
```

The following line of output is printed whenever the program is executed on the computer:

```
CHI SQUARE IS 23.28
```

Since the program computed a chi square of 23.28, which is larger than 21.7, it follows that some suspicion is cast upon the table of random numbers.

Number Sum Program

The BASIC program in Fig. 9-3 determines the sum of all numbers between 100 and 1000 that are divisible by 13.

```
10    REM NUMBER SUM PROGRAM
20    LET S = 0
30    FOR N = 100 TO 1000 STEP 13
40    LET S = S + N
50    NEXT N
60    PRINT "NUMBER  SUM = "; S
70    END
RUN
NUMBER SUM = 38395.
```

Fig. 9-3. Number sum program.

Dice Program

The BASIC program shown in Fig. 9-4 simulates rolling a pair of dice. The output shows how the dice fell for 15 rolls.

Money Program

Queen Laura, leader of a wealthy Caribbean island, was distributing her wealth to the one million natives who lived on the island. She gave $1 to the first native. The next two natives got $2 each. The next three natives each got $3, and so on. The BASIC program shown in Fig. 9-5 determines what the millionth native received.

Armstrong Number Program

One hundred fifty three is an interesting number because

$$153 = 1^3 + 5^3 + 3^3$$

```
10    REM DICE PROGRAM
20    PRINT "TYPE NUMBER OF ROLLS TO BE MADE";
30    INPUT N
40    PRINT "FIRST DIE", "SECOND DIE", "TOTAL"
50    PRINT
60    FOR A = 1 TO N
70    LET D1 = INT (6 * RND (1) + 1)
80    LET D2 = INT (6 * RND (1) + 1)
90    LET T = D1 + D2
100   PRINT D1, D2, T
110   NEXT A
120   END
RUN
TYPE NUMBER OF ROLLS TO BE MADE? 15
   FIRST DIE        SECOND DIE        TOTAL
      4                 1               5
      6                 2               8
      6                 3               9
      2                 5               7
      2                 4               6
      2                 3               5
      2                 5               7
      3                 3               6
      3                 1               4
      3                 3               6
      3                 4               7
      3                 2               5
      4                 2               6
      4                 4               8
      3                 4               7
```

Fig. 9-4. Dice program.

```
10    REM MONEY PROGRAM
20    LET A = 0
30    LET B = 1
40    LET A = A + B
50    IF A > = 1. E + 06 THEN 80
60    LET B = B + 1
70    GO TO 40
80    PRINT "THE MILLIONTH NATIVE GOT $ " ; B
90    END
RUN
THE MILLIONTH NATIVE GOT $1414
```

Fig. 9-5. Money program.

```
100    REM ARMSTRONG NUMBER PROGRAM
110    FOR N = 100 TO 999
120    LET A = INT(N/100)
130    LET B = INT(N/10) — 10*A
140    LET C = N — 100*A — 10*B
150    IF N < > A ↑ 3+B ↑ 3+C ↑ 3 THEN 190
160    PRINT "ARMSTRONG NUMBER"; N
170    PRINT "EQUALS "; A ↑ 3; "+"; B ↑ 3; "+"; C ↑ 3
180    PRINT
190    NEXT N
200    END
RUN
ARMSTRONG NUMBER 153
EQUALS  1     +  125     +  27
ARMSTRONG NUMBER 370
EQUALS  27    +  343     +  0
ARMSTRONG NUMBER 371
EQUALS  27    +  343     +  1
ARMSTRONG NUMBER 407
EQUALS  64    +  0     +  343
```

Fig. 9-6. Armstrong number program.

Numbers such as this are called *Armstrong* numbers. Any *n*-digit number is an Armstrong number if the sum of the *n*th power of the digits is equal to the original number. The BASIC program in Fig. 9-6 determines three other Armstrong numbers.

Coin Tossing Program

The BASIC program shown in Fig. 9-7 uses the RND (random number) library function to simulate heads and tails (heads if the random number is less than 0.5; tails if the random number is 0.5 or greater). The program simulates the flipping of 15 coins and prints out the number of heads and tails obtained.

SUMMARY

The dialogue between the terminal user and the computer is a powerful tool for the user. Conversational programming is an easy way for nonprogramming personnel to prepare computer programs. Using a conversational programming language such as BASIC, a user can learn to prepare programs after as little as two to four hours of instruction.

```
10    REM COIN TOSSING PROGRAM
20    LET T = 0
30    LET H = 0
40    FOR N = 1 TO 15
50    LET R = RND (1)
60    IF R < .5 THEN 100
70    PRINT "TAIL"
80    LET T = T + 1
90    GO TO 120
100   PRINT "HEAD"
110   LET H = H + 1
120   NEXT N
130   PRINT "NUMBER OF TAILS = " ; T
140   PRINT "NUMBER OF HEADS = " ; H
150   END
RUN
TAIL
HEAD
TAIL
TAIL
HEAD
HEAD
TAIL
HEAD
HEAD
TAIL
HEAD
TAIL
HEAD
HEAD
TAIL
NUMBER OF TAILS = 7
NUMBER OF HEADS = 8
```

Fig. 9-7. Coin tossing program.

The BASIC language contains the capability of developing solutions to many problems. BASIC has an easy method of inputting data to the computer and printing out results. It is for these reasons that BASIC has become a very popular programming language.

It was not the purpose of this chapter to present a complete description of the BASIC language. Many statements were briefly discussed, however, and the reader will find that these should suffice for developing many BASIC programs.

Chapter 10

FORTRAN Programming

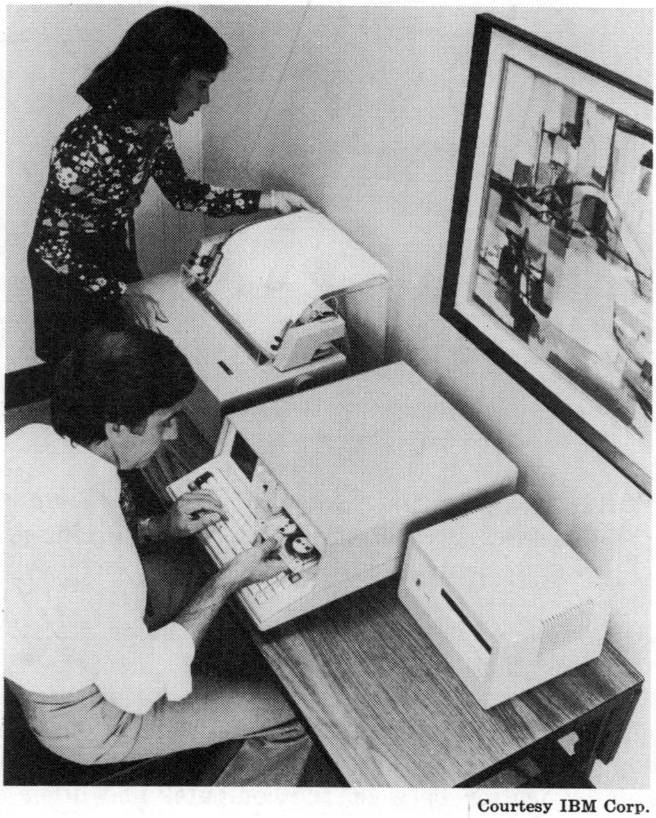

Courtesy IBM Corp.

As stated in Chapter 8, FORTRAN (acronym for *FOR*mula *TRAN*slation) is a higher-level language that was originally designed as a scientific and mathematical language to allow scientists, engineers, and mathematicians to use the computer to solve their problems. However, for the past decade, management scientists and business programmers have found FORTRAN to be extremely valuable for solving a wide variety of business problems: queuing models, statistical studies, inventory management, sales forecasting, class scheduling, etc. This chapter contains a brief introduction to the FORTRAN language.

"YOU'LL JUST LOVE MS. LOONA. SHE SPEAKS ENGLISH, SPANISH, GERMAN, FORTRAN, AND COBOL FLUENTLY!"

OVERVIEW OF FORTRAN

A FORTRAN program consists of a series of *statements*. These statements represent the solution to a specific problem. FORTRAN statements may be classified into four types:

1. *Arithmetic Statements*—These statements describe computations that are to be performed.
2. *Control Statements*—These statements specify the sequence in which other statements are to be executed.
3. *Input/Output Statements*—These statements provide communication between the computer and other system

equipment such as card readers, printers, magnetic-tape units, etc.

4. *Specification Statements*—These statements provide information to the FORTRAN compiler.

In order to aid the computer user in the use of the various statements, there is a standard FORTRAN coding form (Fig. 10-1). FORTRAN statements are written one to a line in the spaces marked 7–72. Spaces are numbered to correspond to the columns in a standard punched card (Fig. 10-2). Columns 1–5 may be used to write numbers by which the statements may be subsequently referenced. Comments may be included in a program by placing a C in column 1 and the comment in columns 2 through 72. Each line of the coding form is used to prepare a punched card.

A FORTRAN PROGRAM

Let us consider the construction of a FORTRAN program with a simple example to convert Fahrenheit temperature

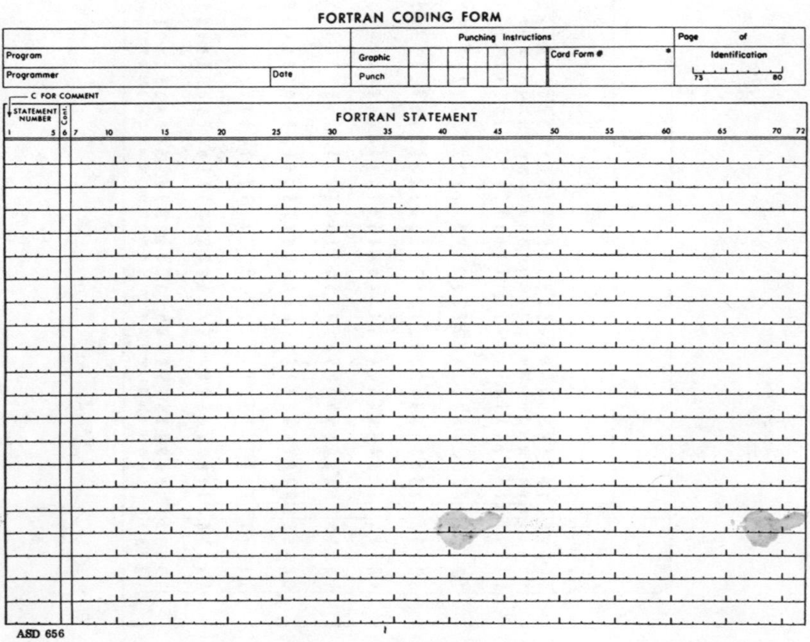

Fig. 10-1. A FORTRAN coding form.

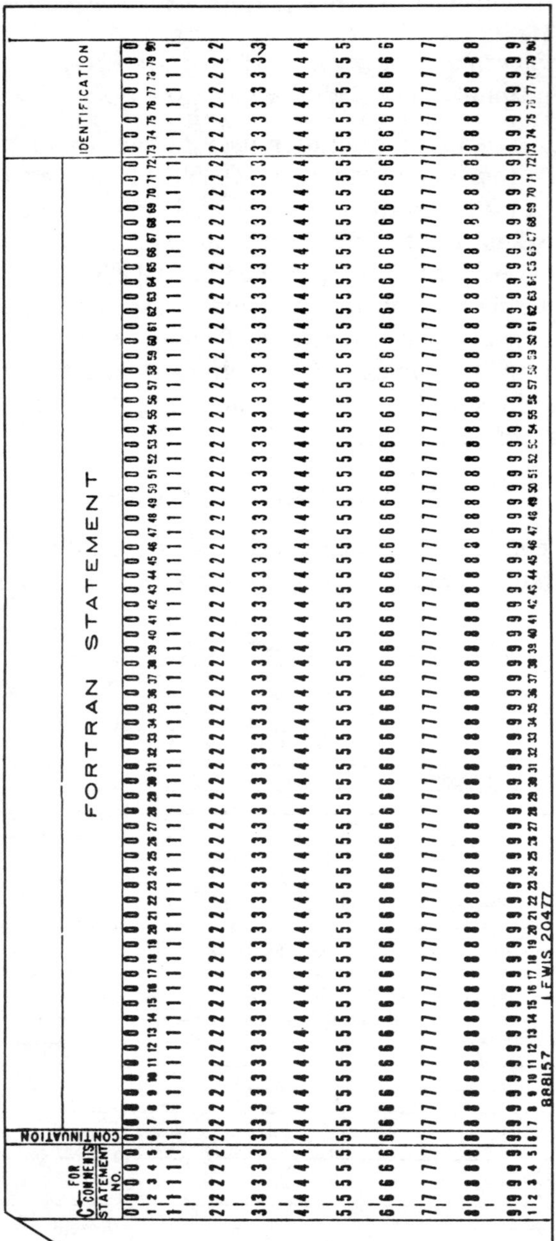

Fig. 10-2. A punched card for FORTRAN statements.

readings to equivalent readings in Celsius, Kelvin, and Rankine.

Fahrenheit temperature values may be converted to Celsius values by subtracting 32° from the Fahrenheit temperature reading and then multiplying the difference by 5/9 (Reference Equation 1).

$$C = 5/9(F - 32°) \tag{1}$$

Kelvin temperature may be obtained by adding 273° to a Celsius value (Reference Equation 2).

$$K = C + 273° \tag{2}$$

A Rankine measurement can be obtained by adding 460° to a Fahrenheit value (Reference Equation 3).

$$R = F + 460° \tag{3}$$

Figs. 10-3 and 10-4, respectively, illustrate a flowchart and FORTRAN program for converting 10 Fahrenheit values to their equivalent values in Celsius, Kelvin, and Rankine. This FORTRAN program reads a data card that contains the 10 values of Fahrenheit temperatures. The program then performs the conversions for all values and causes the following values to be printed:

FAHRENHEIT	CELSIUS	KELVIN	RANKINE
144	62.2222	335.222	604
36	2.2222	275.222	496
110	43.3333	316.333	570
98	36.6667	309.667	558
63	17.2222	290.222	523
26	—3.3333	269.667	486
14	—10.0000	263.000	474
78	25.5556	298.556	538
66	18.8889	291.889	526
51	10.5556	283.556	511
107	41.6667	314.667	567
2	—16.6667	256.333	462

The FORTRAN language discussed in this section is by no means complete, but it does include enough FORTRAN statements to enable the reader to start writing simple programs.

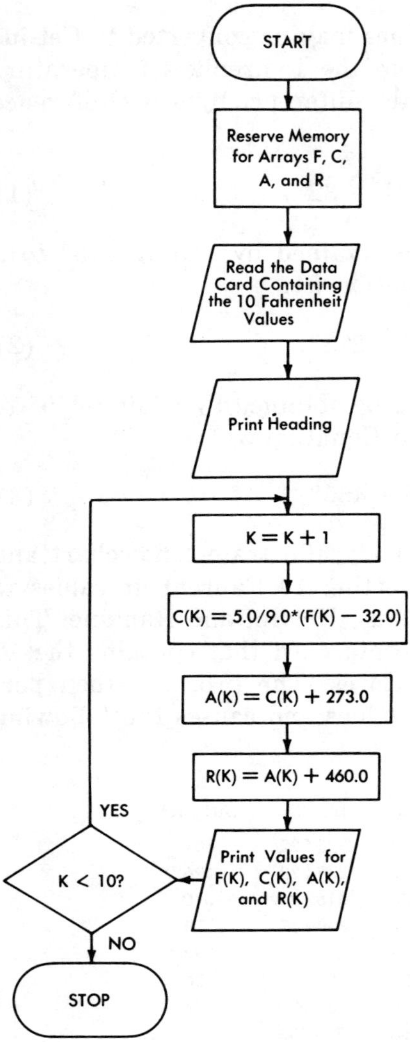

Fig. 10-3. Flowchart for the temperature conversion program.

CONSTANTS AND VARIABLES

In FORTRAN, there are two types of constants and variables: *fixed-point* and *real.* Fixed-point numbers (sometimes called *integers*) and the associated variables contain no decimal point; e.g., 364, 17, or 1000. A fixed-point variable is iden-

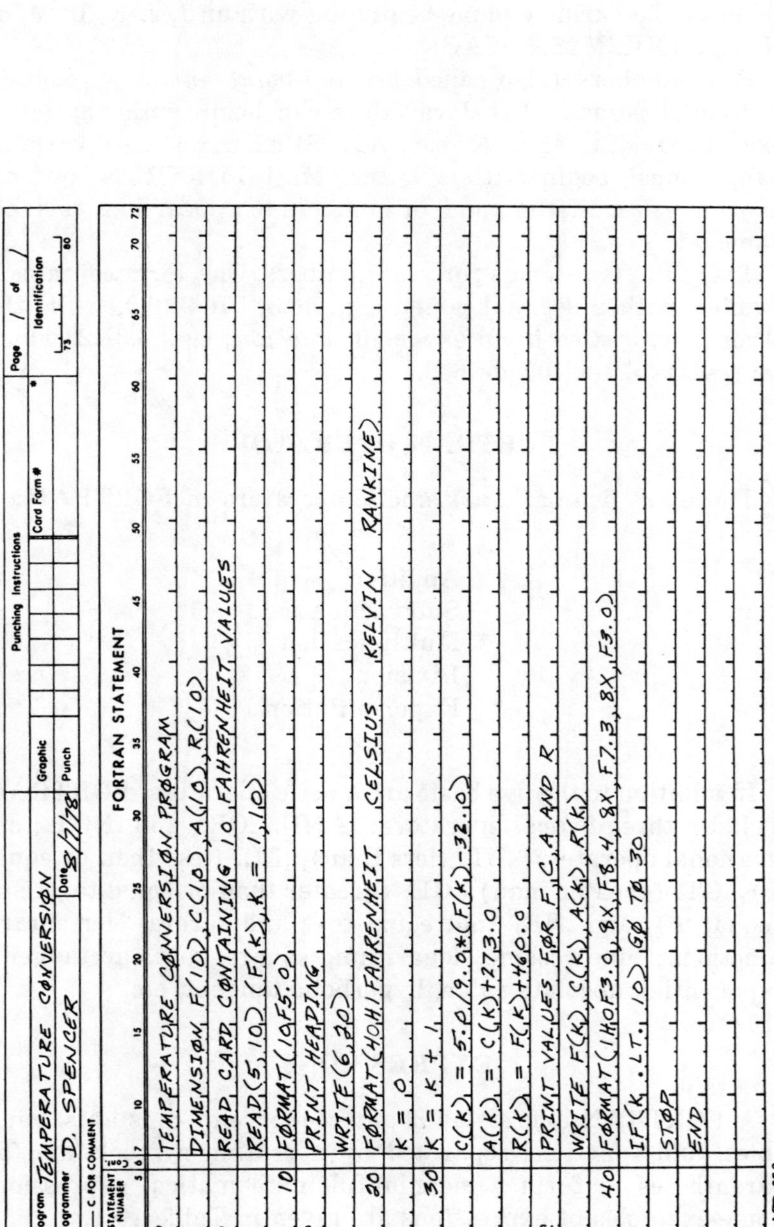


```
C     TEMPERATURE CØNVERSIØN PRØGRAM
      DIMENSIØN F(10),C(10),A(10),R(10)
C     READ CARD CØNTAINING 10 FAHRENHEIT VALUES
      READ(5,10)(F(K),K=1,10)
   10 FØRMAT(10F5.0)
C     PRINT HEADING
      WRITE(6,20)
   20 FØRMAT(40H1FAHRENHEIT   CELSIUS   KELVIN   RANKINE)
      K = 0
   30 K = K + 1
      C(K) = 5.0/9.0*(F(K)-32.0)
      A(K) = C(K)+273.0
      R(K) = F(K)+460.0
C     PRINT VALUES FØR F, C, A AND R
      WRITE F(K), C(K), A(K), R(K)
   40 FØRMAT(1H0F3.0,8X,F8.4,8X,F7.3,8X,F3.0)
      IF(K .LT. 10) GØ TØ 30
      STØP
      END
```

Fig. 10-4. FORTRAN program for the temperature conversion program.

tified by the variable name beginning with an I, J, K, L, M, or N; e.g., INK, M26, or JACK.

Real numbers (also called *floating-point numbers*) contain a decimal point and real variables can begin with any letter except I, J, K, L, M, or N; e.g., A27, SPEED, or T. All variable names must begin with a letter. Most FORTRAN systems allow five or six letters and/or numbers to appear in a variable name.

There are two forms for real numbers. One form contains a number with a decimal point; e.g., 46.3, 176.9, 2.0, while the other is expressed in an exponent notation; e.g., 6.3E2, which represents 6.3×10^2, or 630.

FORTRAN OPERATORS

There are five basic arithmetic operators in FORTRAN:

- + Addition
- − Subtraction
- * Multiplication
- / Division
- ** Exponentiation

In addition to the five basic arithmetic operators, FORTRAN includes three *logical* operators: .AND., .OR., and .NOT.; six relational operators; .LT. (less than), .LE. (less than or equal to), .GT. (greater than), .GE. (greater than or equal to), .EQ. (equal to), and .NE. (not equal to); and several elementary functions; sine, cosine, logarithm, square root, arctangent, exponential, absolute value, hyperbolic tangent, etc.

EXPRESSIONS

A FORTRAN *expression* is any sequence of constants, variables, and functions separated by operating symbols and/or parentheses to form a meaningful mathematical expression. Some examples of expressions are given in Table 10-1.

Parentheses can be freely used within FORTRAN expressions and should be used whenever any question as to the precise meaning of the statement might arise. Spaces may be used almost anywhere within an expression to make an expression easier to understand.

Table 10-1. Some Mathematical Expressions and Their FORTRAN Equivalents

Mathematical Expression	FORTRAN Expression
$ab - c + 6$	A*B — C + 6.0
$\frac{a+b}{c-d}$	(A + B)/(C — D)
$(x + y)^4$	(X + Y)**4
x^{k+3}	X**(K + 3)
sine a	SIN(A)
$\sqrt{b^2 - 4ac}$	SQRT(B**2 — 4.0*A*C)
$a > b$	A .GT. B
$A \leq b \cup c = d$	A .LE. B .OR. C .EQ. D

STATEMENTS

A statement is the FORTRAN way of representing an algebraic formula. The right side of a FORTRAN statement contains a FORTRAN expression, while the left side consists of a variable. The two sides are separated by an *"is replaced by"* sign (=).

The *"is replaced by"* symbol has a different meaning than the normal mathematical symbol has. For example, the statement—A = Y + 3—means that the value 3 is to be added to the quantity represented by Y and the sum is to replace the old value of the quantity represented by A.

Several other examples of FORTRAN statements follow:

```
   X = A + B + C
  AZ = SQRT(B*2+327.6)
 ANS = ((A + B)/(C  —  D))**2
   Y = Y  + 1
  L4 = A .LT. R2 .AND. S36 .GT. 20.0
   R = 364.7
```

Unconditional GO TO

The unconditional branching statement is of the form—GO TO *n*—where *n* is the number of some other statement in the program. The GO TO statement causes program control to be transferred to statement *n*, thus providing a way of breaking the linear sequence of commands.

Arithmetic IF

The arithmetic IF statement has the form—IF (*e*) *a*, *b*, *c*—where *e* is an expression, and *a*, *b*, *c* are statement numbers where program control will be transferred to, depending on whether the expression is negative, zero, or positive. If the expression is negative, control is transferred to statement number *a*, if the expression is zero, control is transferred to statement number *b*, and if the expression is positive, control is transferred to statement number *c*. The statement numbers *a*, *b*, and *c* may be the same or they may all be different.

Logical IF

The logical IF statement has the form—IF (*e*) *a*—where *e* is a logical expression, such as A .GT. B .OR. 63.0, and *a* is an executable statement, such as K = K + 4. If the value of the logical expression is *true*, statement *a* will be executed. If the value of the expression is *false*, the statement following the IF will be executed next.

DO

The DO statement is the most powerful statement in the FORTRAN language and has the form—DO n $i = m_1, m_2, m_3$—where n is a statement number, i is a nonsubscripted variable, and m_1, m_2, and m_3 are unsigned fixed-point constants or nonsubscripted fixed-point variables.

We can illustrate the operation of the DO statement by using the following example: DO 100 K = 4, 10, 2. When this statement is encountered in a program, the fixed-point variable K is set equal to the initial value of 4. This initial value has to exceed 1 or be 1. All statements following the DO statement are executed until statement number 100 is reached. At this point, the DO variable K is increased by 2 and control returns to the statement following the DO statement. The program keeps repeating this loop until the variable K is greater than 10, at which point control is directed to the statement following the DO loop terminating statement.

CONTINUE

The CONTINUE statement is a "do-nothing" statement and is often used as the terminating statement in a DO loop.

The DIMENSION Statement and Arrays

Consider the arrangement of a tic-tac-toe board:

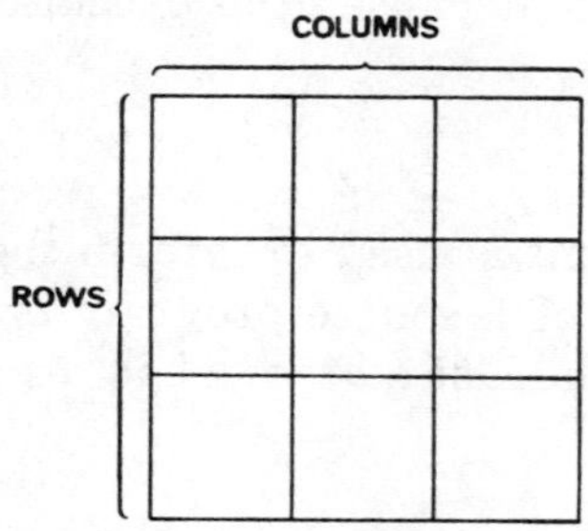

The board is divided into nine cells consisting of three rows and three columns. In FORTRAN, we can give the board a variable name such as BOARD, and can designate an arbitrary location on the board by—BOARD (I, J)—where I and J are fixed-point variables which assume the values 1, 2, and 3. I and J are called *subscripts* and BOARD (I, J) is called a *subscripted variable.* I in the above expression represents a row and J represents a column. A variable of this type is called an *array* in FORTRAN. If I represented 2 and J represented 3, then BOARD (I, J) refers to the array item in the second row and third column of Array BOARD. Subscripts need not be fixed-point variables—they may also be fixed-point numbers. Thus, BOARD (2, 1) would refer to the item in the second row and first column of Array BOARD.

Before arrays can be used in FORTRAN programs, the storage requirements must be specified. This is accomplished by using a statement of the form—DIMENSION BOARD (3, 3)—where the DIMENSION statement contains the name of the array, the maximum number of rows in the array, and the maximum number of columns in the array. Any number of array storage specifications may be contained in one statement by simply separating the variables by a comma. Thus, the statement—DIMENSION A(2, 3), B(16, 6), C(27)—would cause the FORTRAN compiler to reserve storage for a

2 by 3 array named A, a 16 by 6 array named B, and an array named C which has 27 items. This last array is called a *one-dimensional* array and has only one subscript. This type of array is often called a *list*. Arrays with two subscripts are *two-dimensional* and are often called *tables* or *matrices*.

STOP

The STOP statement causes the execution of the program to halt.

END

The END statement is used to inform the FORTRAN compiler where the end of a source program is located. The END statement must be the last statement in a program.

READ

The READ statement is of the form—READ (*i, n*) *list*—where *i* is a fixed-point constant or variable that identifies the input device (card reader, typewriter, paper-tape reader, etc.), *n* is the statement number of an associated FORMAT statement, and *list* is the names of the variables whose values are to be transmitted. The READ statement provides us with a way of getting information into the computer.

WRITE

The WRITE statement is of the form—WRITE (*i, n*) *list*—where *i* is a fixed-point constant or variable that represents the output device (printer, typewriter, card punch, etc.), *n* is the statement number of an associated FORMAT statement, and *list* is the names of the variables whose values are to be transmitted. The WRITE statement provides us with a way of getting information out of the computer.

FORMAT

The FORMAT statement specifies the arrangement of data on the input or output medium and also the type of conversion that is to be made between the internal and the external format.

The form of the FORMAT statement is—FORMAT (field specifications)—where several field specifications are used to describe the data structure which may take any of the following forms:

Alphanumeric Data—Alphanumeric messages may be read or printed by using the letter H, preceded by the number of characters in the message itself. Some FORTRAN compilers allow the use of *quotes* to specify a message.

Floating-Point Data—The specification F*w.d* is used for floating-point data transfer, where *w* is the entire length of the number, including decimal point and sign, and *d* specifies the number of figures to the right of the decimal point. If a data value contains a decimal point upon input, the F specification is overridden.

The floating-point exponential notation can be specified by using the form E*w.d*, where *w* and *d* have meanings that are similar to their F specification meanings.

Fixed-Point Data—The format I*w* is used for fixed-point values, where *w* is the number of places needed.

Slash—A slash (/) is used to inform the computer to return the carriage on the typewriter, to go to the next line on the printer, or to read the next card on the card reader.

Skip Spaces—To skip spaces between data on a card or printout, one can use the X specification. The general form of this specification is *w*X where *w* is the number of spaces that are to be skipped.

ROOTS PROGRAM

The roots of a quadratic equation of the form:

$$\mathrm{A}x^2 + \mathrm{B}x + C = 0$$

are given by the quadratic formula:

$$\text{root} = \frac{-\mathrm{B} \pm \sqrt{\mathrm{B}^2 - 4\mathrm{AC}}}{2\mathrm{A}}$$

For example, the equation $x^2 + 5x + 6 = 0$ can be factored as $(x + 2)\ (x + 3) = 0$, and the roots are $x = -2$ and $x = -3$. The FORTRAN program given in Fig. 10-5 uses the quadratic formula to solve a quadratic equation.

The first statement in the program is a comment statement. Statement 10 reads the values for the coefficients A, B, and C.

```
C       ROOTS PROGRAM
   10   READ(2,20)A,B,C
   20   FORMAT(3F5.1)
        IF(A .EQ. 0.0)GO TO 40
        ROOT1 = (—B+SQRT(B**2—4.0*A*C))/(2.0*A)
        ROOT2 = (—B—SQRT(B**2—4.0*A*C))/(2.0*A)
        WRITE(3,30)A,B,C,ROOT1,ROOT2
   30   FORMAT(4H A = , F5.1 , 3HB = , F5.1 , 3HC = ,
      2 F5.1 , 7HROOT1 = , F5.1 , 7HROOT2 = , F5.1)
        GO TO 10
   40   STOP
        END
```

Fig. 10-5. FORTRAN program for computing the roots of the quadratic equations: $x^2 + 5x + 6 = 0$, $x^2 + x - 2 = 0$, and $x^2 + x - 6 = 0$.

The fourth statement checks to see if the last data card (A = 0.0) has been read and, if so, terminates the execution of the program. The fifth and sixth statements use the quadratic formula to compute values for ROOT1 and ROOT2. These statements use the SQRT library function to find the square root. The next statement prints the values for the three coefficients and two roots. The program then loops back to statement 10 to read the next set of coefficients. The example shown in Fig. 10-6 includes data cards for the three equations $x^2 + 5x + 6 = 0$, $x^2 + x - 2 = 0$, and $x^2 + x - 6 = 0$ and the terminating card. A flowchart of the Roots program is shown in Fig. 10-7.

FIBONACCI NUMBER PROGRAM

Leonardo Fibonacci, a wealthy Italian merchant of the thirteenth century, introduced a set of numbers now known as *Fibonacci Numbers*. The first 16 of them are: 1, 1, 2, 3, 5, 8, 13, 21, 34, 55, 89, 144, 233, 377, 610. Each number of a Fibonacci number sequence is the sum of the two numbers immediately preceding it. That is:

$1 + 1 = 2$

$1 + 2 = 3$

$2 + 3 = 5$

$3 + 5 = 8$

$5 + 8 = 13$

$8 + 13 = 21$, etc.

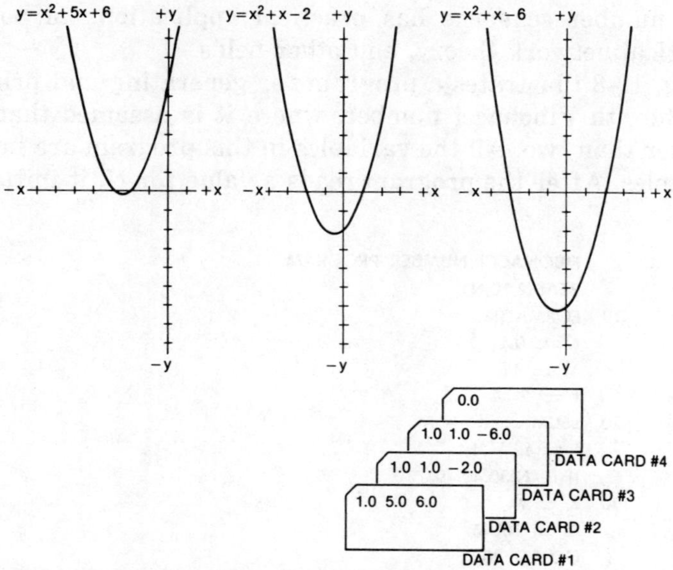

Fig. 10-6. Data cards for finding the roots of the three quadratic equations illustrated when $y = 0$.

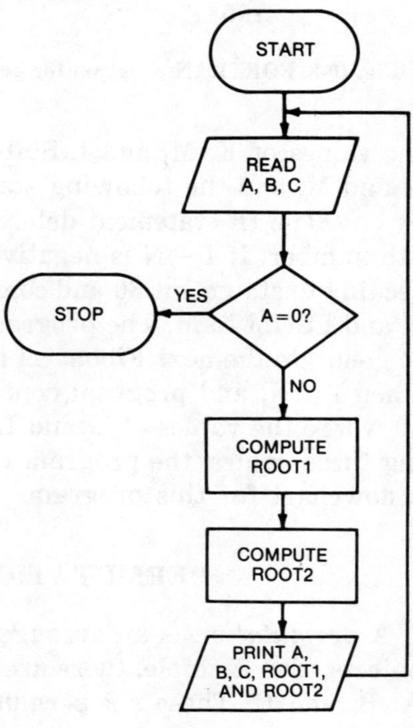

Fig. 10-7. Flowchart for the roots program of Fig. 10-5.

This number sequence has practical applications in botany, electrical network theory, and other fields.

Fig. 10-8 illustrates a program for generating and printing out the *n*th Fibonacci number, where it is assumed that *n* is greater than two. All the variables in this program are integer variables. After the program reads a value for N, it initializes

```
C     FIBONACCI NUMBER PROGRAM
      READ(2,10)N
   10 FORMAT(I3)
      K = 0
      M = 1
      I = 2
   20 LSUM = K + M
      I = I + 1
      IF(I—N)30,40,40
   30 K = M
      M = LSUM
      GO TO 20
   40 WRITE(3,50)N,LSUM
   50 FORMAT(1H0 , I5 , 24H —TH FIBONACCI NUMBER IS , I5)
      STOP
      END
```

Fig. 10-8. FORTRAN program for generating the *n*th Fibonacci number.

the values of K, M, and I. Statement 20 computes the sum of K and M, and the following statement advances the counter I by one. The IF statement determines if we have generated the *n*th number. If I − N is negative, the loop is continued by proceeding to statement 30 and completing the assignment of M to K and LSUM to M. The program then returns to statement 20 to generate the next Fibonacci number. The loop is terminated when I = N, and program control is transferred to statement 40 where the values of N and LSUM are printed. After printing these values, the program terminates. Fig. 10-9 illustrates a flowchart for this program.

PERMUTATION PROGRAM

A *permutation* is an arrangement or a sequence of a set of objects. For example, there are six permutations of the letters A, B, and C. These six permutations are: ABC, ACB, BAC,

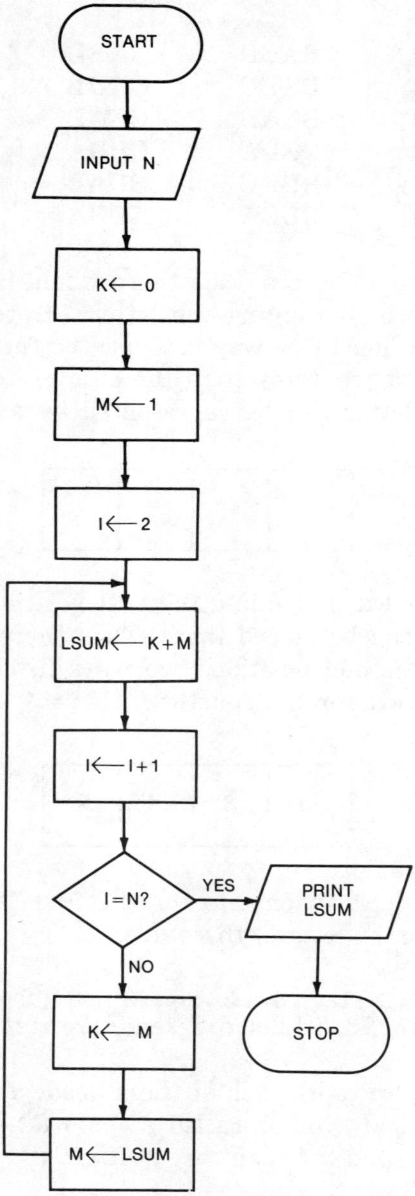

Fig. 10-9. Flowchart for the Fibonacci number program.

BCA, CAB, and CBA. There are 24 permutations of the letters A, B, C, and D. They are as follows:

ABCD	BACD	CABD	DABC
ABDC	BADC	CADB	DACB
ACBD	BCAD	CBAD	DBAC
ACDB	BCDA	CBDA	DBCA
ADBC	BDAC	CDAB	DCAB
ADCB	BDCA	CDBA	DCBA

If there were 14 letters, then there would be 87,178,291,200 different ways of arranging the letters. How was this large number determined? One way is to use the fundamental counting principle. If we apply it to the case of four letters, each position of a letter can be represented by a box as follows:

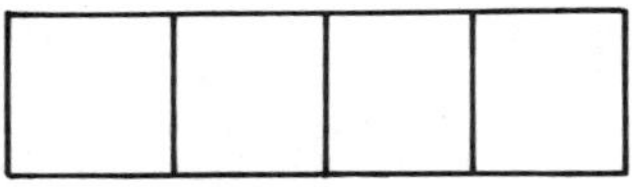

There are four ways of filling the first position, since any one of the letters can be placed there. Then there are three ways left to fill the second position, two ways to fill the third, and only one way left for the fourth:

4	3	2	1

The number of arrangements for the four letters is $4 \times 3 \times 2 \times 1 = 24$. For 14 letters, there are:

$$14 \times 13 \times 12 \times 11 \times 10 \times 9 \times 8 \times 7 \times 6 \times 5 \times 4 \times 3 \times 2 \times 1$$
$$= 87{,}178{,}291{,}200 \text{ different arrangements.}$$

A short way to write each of these products is to use a special mathematical symbol, called a *factorial* symbol (!). For example, $4 \times 3 \times 2 \times 1$ can be written as 4! (read *"four factorial"*). Thus,

$$14! = 14 \times 13 \times 12 \times 11 \times 10 \times 9 \times 8 \times 7 \times 6 \times 5 \times 4 \times 3 \times 2 \times 1.$$

In general, the number of permutations of n objects is:

$$n(n-1)(n-2)\ldots 3 \times 2 \times 1,$$

or, written in factorial form as:

$$n! = n \ldots 4 \times 3 \times 2 \times 1.$$

With this notation, we can write the formula for the number of permutations of n objects:

$${}_nP_n = n!$$

where the notation on the left means "the number of permutations of n objects taken n at a time." For example, the number of permutations of the letters COMPUTER is:

$$\begin{aligned}{}_8P_8 &= 8! = 8 \times 7 \times 6 \times 5 \times 4 \times 3 \times 2 \times 1 \\ &= 40{,}320\end{aligned}$$

Now let us discuss a formula for the number of permutations of n objects taken r at a time. As an example, consider a certain club of 10 boys and 12 girls. They wish to elect officers in such a way that the president and treasurer are boys and the vice-president and secretary are girls. In how many ways can this be done? The number of different ways of selecting the president and treasurer is ${}_{10}P_2$. The number of ways of selecting the vice-president and secretary is ${}_{12}P_2$. The total number of ways of choosing officers is:

$${}_{10}P_2 \times {}_{12}P_2 = (10 \times 9) \times (12 \times 11) = 11{,}880.$$

In general, the formula:

$${}_nP_r = \frac{n!}{(n-r)!}$$

gives the number of different ways of arranging r elements selected from a set of n elements; that is, the permutation of n things taken r at a time.

The previous formula can be rewritten as:

$${}_nP_r = n(n-1)(n-2)(n-3)\ldots(n-r+1),$$

which is a computational algorithm for ${}_nP_r$. The FORTRAN program shown in Fig. 10-10 computes the number of permutations of n things taken r at a time using the latter formula.

```
C       PERMUTATION PROGRAM
        INTEGER R,P
   10   READ(5,20)N,R
   20   FORMAT(2I3)
        IF(N .EQ. 0)GO TO 50
        P = 1
        L = N - R + 1
        DO 30 K = L,N
        P = P * K
   30   CONTINUE
        WRITE(3,40)N,R,P
   40   FORMAT(1H ,I3,12H THINGS TAKEN,I3,
      2 12H AT A TIME =,I8)
        GO TO 10
   50   STOP
        END
```

Fig. 10-10. FORTRAN program that computes the number of permutations of *n* things taken *r* at a time.

The program reads the following data cards:

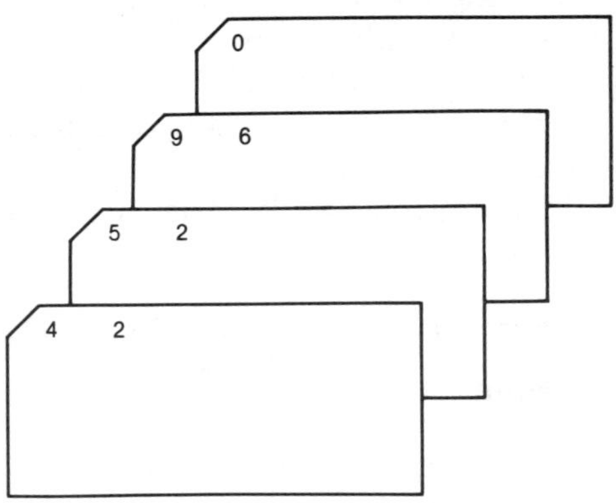

and produces the following printed output:

```
4 THINGS TAKEN 2 AT A TIME = 12
5 THINGS TAKEN 2 AT A TIME = 20
9 THINGS TAKEN 6 AT A TIME = 60,480
```

The INTEGER statement in this program is a special statement that allows the variables R and P to be treated as integer variables so that all computations could be performed in integer arithmetic. A flowchart of this program is shown in Fig. 10-11.

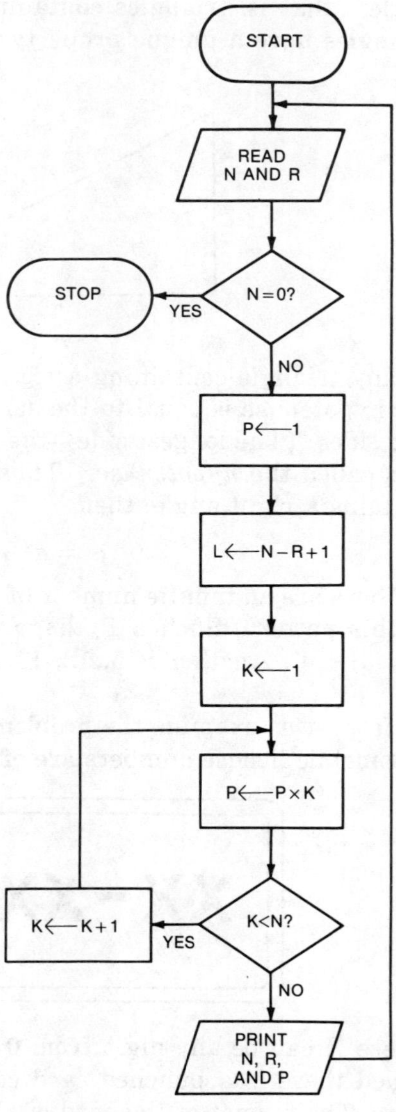

Fig. 10-11. Flowchart for the permutation program.

ROBBERY PROGRAM

This problem involves a knowledge of the Pythagorean theorem. Let us first review the elementary trigonometry involved. The Pythagorean theorem is one of the most basic theorems in trigonometry. It concerns, in particular, right triangles; that is, triangles containing a 90° angle. These right triangles have a unique property:

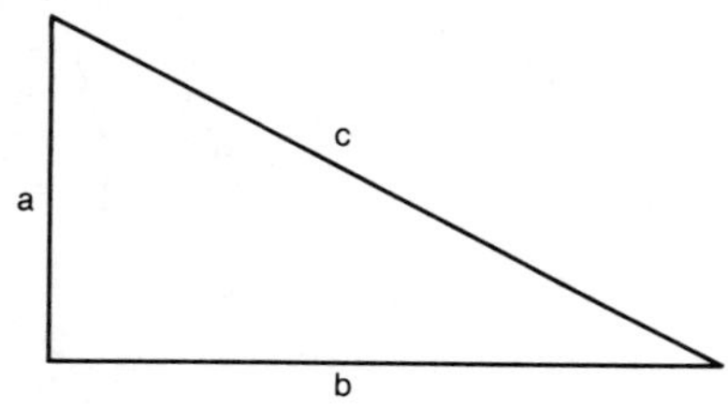

In any triangle containing a right (90°) angle, the square of the hypotenuse is equal to the sum of the squares of the other two sides. (The longest side—the side opposite the right angle—is called the *hypotenuse.*) Thus, if the triangle shown, *abc,* contains a right angle, then

$$c^2 = a^2 + b^2$$

There are an infinite number of integer triplets that conform to this pattern. Such a Pythagorean triplet is 3, 4, 5, where $5^2 = 3^2 + 4^2$. Another is 5, 12, 13, where $13^2 = 5^2 + 12^2$, and so on.

Now let us examine the problem. In a midwestern state, the automobile license numbers are of the form:

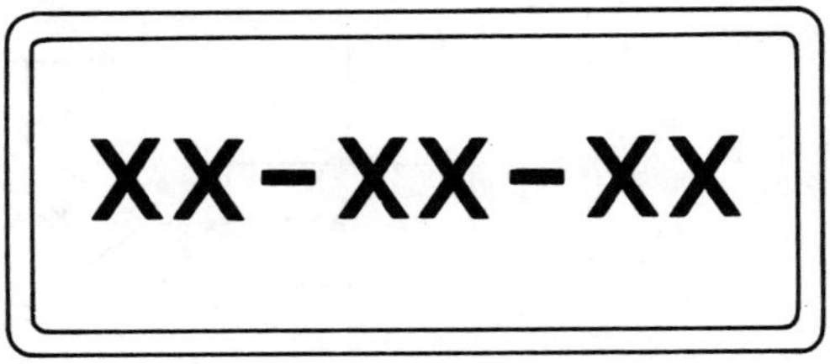

where X can be any digit from 0 to 9. For every license plate issued there is a punched card containing the number of the plate. The format of the card is (I2, 1X, I2, 1X, I2). A typical batch of such cards would look something like those in Fig. 10-12. The exact number of cards is not known, but a special card (called a *trailer card*) with −6 punched in columns 1 and 2 is placed behind the last card.

Subsequent to a robbery of his gas station, the owner, a former mathematics teacher, gave chase while the robbers were making their getaway in a truck. As he approached the truck, the owner was shot just as he managed to catch a glimpse of the license plate. The sheriff soon came on the scene and immediately questioned the gravely wounded owner about the license plate number. His last words were: ". . . *the sides of a right triangle.*"

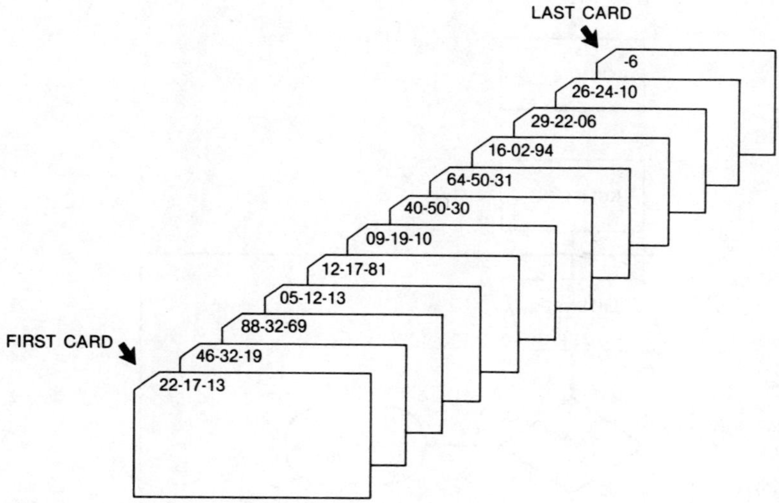

Fig. 10-12. Punched cards for the robbery program.

```
C     ROBBERY PROGRAM
      KOUNT = 0
      KULP = 0
   10 READ(2,20)I,J,K
   20 FORMAT(I2,1X,I2,1X,I2)
      IF(I)80,30,30
   30 KOUNT = KOUNT + 1
      IF(I**2 — J**2 — K**2)40,60,40
   40 IF(J**2 — K**2 — I**2)50,60,50
   50 IF(K**2 — I**2 — J**2)10,60,10
   60 KULP = KULP + 1
      WRITE(3,70)KOUNT,KULP,I,J,K
   70 FORMAT(9H CARD NO.,I4,16H IS SUSPECT NO.
     2 I2,/,11X,I2,1H—,I2,1H—,I2,//)
      GO TO 10
   80 STOP
      END
```

Fig. 10-13. FORTRAN program for the robbery program.

The sheriff, who had been using computers for years, quickly wrote the FORTRAN program shown in Fig. 10-13. This program examines all the license plate numbers in the state and

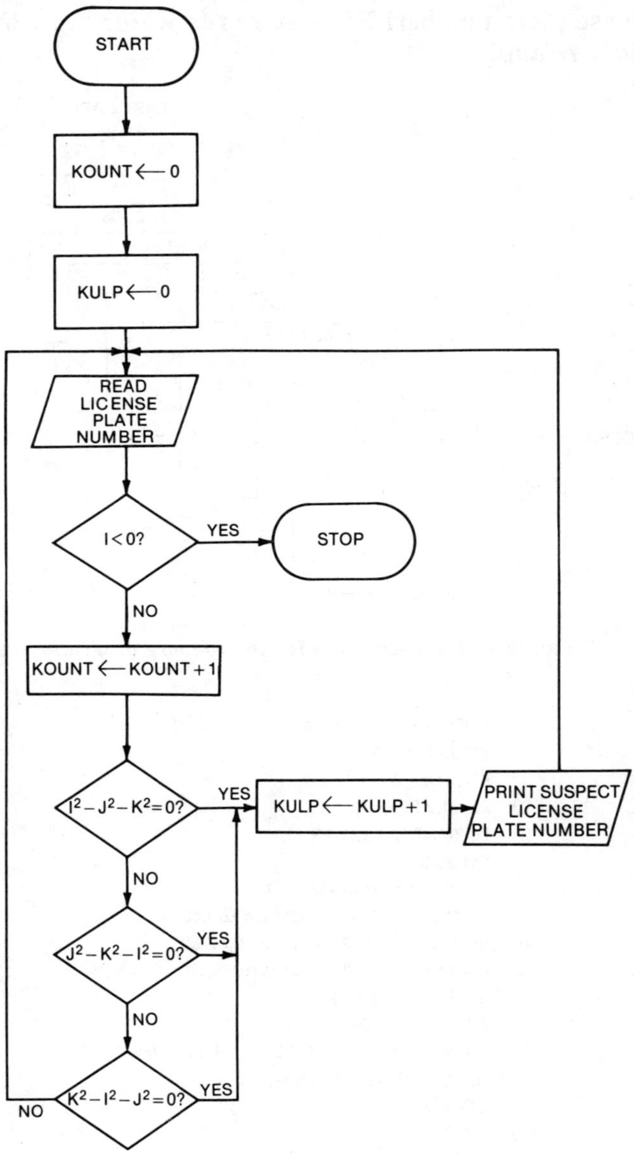

Fig. 10-14. Flowchart for the robbery program.

determines what automobiles are possible "suspects." The program output produced the following license plate numbers:

05–12–13   40–50–30   26–24–10

A short while after watching the owners of the automobiles with these license plates, the sheriff caught the men who committed the robbery and murder. The murderers are now spending time in the penitentiary, thanks to a modern-day sheriff. A flowchart of this program is shown in Fig. 10-14.

SUMMARY

FORTRAN is a powerful system for developing solutions to scientific, business, and general problems. The advantage to a language like FORTRAN is the ease with which the system can be learned. It is not unusual for a person to learn to write FORTRAN programs after only eight hours of instruction.

A complete coverage of FORTRAN was not possible in this chapter; however, several of the most used statements were discussed and the reader will find that these statements will suffice for developing many simple FORTRAN programs.

Chapter 11

COBOL Programming

Courtesy Burroughs Corp.

COBOL is an acronym for *CO*mmon *B*usiness-*O*riented *L*anguage. It is a procedure-oriented programming language which has been implemented on a large number of medium- and large-scale computer systems. It is designed for use in the solution of business data-processing problems. The language itself and the techniques for using it are, for the most part, conceived in terms of the problem to be solved and the results to be obtained rather than in terms of the specific features of the computer. The distinguishing features of the language are:

1. It aims at a realistic approach to the attainment of complete compatibility of programs written for different computers.
2. It is a subset of English, and, as such, readable by the uninitiated.
3. It caters to data structures of the sort found in typical office records, whether financial, personal, stores, etc.

COBOL CHARACTERS AND WORDS

The complete character set for COBOL consists of the 51 characters shown in Fig. 11-1. Some COBOL implementations

Alphabetical Characters

A B C D E F G H I J K L M N
O P Q R S T U V W X Y Z

Numerals

1 2 3 4 5 6 7 8 9 0

Special Characters

$ * , . " ( ) ; > <

= + − / and space

Fig. 11-1. The COBOL character set.

allow the use of other characters not shown in Fig. 11-1. For example, some systems allow the following 11 characters:

@] [& \ ← ↑ : % # '

A COBOL word is composed of a combination of not more than 30 characters chosen from the COBOL character set. The word cannot begin nor end with a hyphen. The space is not an allowable character in a word. There are two types of COBOL words: *programmer-supplied words,* and *reserved words* (or *names*). Programmer-supplied words or names such as EMPLOYEE-NUMBER, PART-NUM, LAST-NAME, VENDOR, GRADE-CARDS, and SALES-FILE are assigned by the programmer. Reserved words such as RANDOM, ACCEPT, MULTIPLY, and TALLYING have special meaning to the COBOL compiler and must be used according to COBOL language rules. These words are an inherent part of the COBOL system and users should avoid using these words for data or procedure names. A complete list of COBOL reserved words follows:

ACCEPT
ACCESS
ADD
ADVANCING
AFTER
ALL
ALPHABETIC
ALSO
ALTER
ALTERNATE
AND
ARE
AREA
AREAS
ASCENDING
ASSIGN
AT
AUTHOR

BEFORE
BLANK
BLOCK
BOTTOM
BY

CALL
CANCEL
CD
CF
CH
CHARACTER
CHARACTERS
CLOCK-UNITS
CLOSE
COBOL
CODE
CODE-SET
COLLATING
COLUMN
COMMA
COMMUNICATION
COMP
COMPUTATIONAL
COMPUTE
CONFIGURATION
CONTAINS
CONTROL
CONTROLS
COPY
CORR
CORRESPONDING
COUNT
CURRENCY

DATA
DATE
DATE-COMPILED
DATE-WRITTEN
DAY
DE
DEBUG-CONTENTS
DEBUG-ITEM
DEBUG-LINE
DEBUG-NAME
DEBUG-SUB-1
DEBUG-SUB-2
DEBUG-SUB-3
DEBUGGING
DECIMAL-POINT
DECLARATIVES
DELETE
DELIMITED
DELIMITER
DEPENDING
DESCENDING
DESTINATION
DETAIL
DISABLE
DISPLAY
DIVIDE
DIVISION
DOWN
DUPLICATES
DYNAMIC

EGI
ELSE
EMI
ENABLE
END
END-OF-PAGE
ENTER
ENVIRONMENT
EOP
EQUAL
ERROR
ESI
EVERY
EXCEPTION
EXIT
EXTEND

FD
FILE
FILE-CONTROL
FILLER
FINAL
FIRST
FOOTING
FOR
FROM

GENERATE
GIVING
GO
GREATER
GROUP

HEADING
HIGH-VALUE
HIGH-VALUES

I-O
I-O-CONTROL
IDENTIFICATION
IF
IN
INDEX
INDEXED
INDICATE
INITIAL
INITIATE
INPUT
INPUT-OUTPUT
INSPECT
INSTALLATION
INTO
INVALID
IS

JUST
JUSTIFIED

KEY

LABEL
LAST
LEADING
LEFT
LENGTH
LESS
LIMIT
LIMITS
LINAGE
LINAGE-COUNTER
LINE
LINE-COUNTER
LINES
LINKAGE
LOCK
LOW-VALUE
LOW-VALUES

MEMORY
MERGE
MESSAGE
MODE
MODULES
MOVE
MULTIPLE
MULTIPLY

NATIVE
NEGATIVE
NEXT
NO
NOT
NUMBER
NUMERIC

OBJECT-
COMPUTER
OCCURS
OF
OFF
OMITTED
ON
OPEN
OPTIONAL
OR
ORGANIZATION
OUTPUT
OVERFLOW

PAGE
PAGE-COUNTER
PERFORM
PF
PH
PIC
PICTURE
PLUS
POINTER
POSITION
POSITIVE
PRINTING
PROCEDURE
PROCEDURES
PROCEED
PROGRAM
PROGRAM-ID

QUEUE
QUOTE
QUOTES

RANDOM
RD
READ
RECEIVE
RECORD
RECORDS
REDEFINES
REEL
REFERENCES
RELATIVE
RELEASE
REMAINDER
REMOVAL
RENAMES
REPLACING
REPORT
REPORTING
REPORTS
RERUN
RESERVE
RESET
RETURN
REVERSED
REWIND
REWRITE
RF
RH
RIGHT
ROUNDED
RUN

SAME
SD
SEARCH
SECTION
SECURITY
SEGMENT
SEGMENT-LIMIT
SELECT
SEND
SENTENCE
SEPARATE
SEQUENCE
SEQUENTIAL
SET
SIGN
SIZE
SORT
SORT-MERGE
SOURCE
SOURCE-
COMPUTER
SPACE
SPACES
SPECIAL-NAMES
STANDARD
STANDARD-1
START
STATUS
STOP
STRING
SUB-QUEUE-1
SUB-QUEUE-2
SUB-QUEUE-3
SUBTRACT
SUM
SUPPRESS
SYMBOLIC
SYNC
SYNCHRONIZED

TABLE
TALLYING
TAPE
TERMINAL
TERMINATE
TEXT
THAN
THROUGH
THRU
TIME
TIMES
TO
TOP
TRAILING
TYPE

UNIT	VARYING	ZEROS
UNSTRING		
UNTIL	WHEN	+
UP	WITH	−
UPON	WORDS	*
USAGE	WORKING-	/
USE	STORAGE	**
USING	WRITE	>
		<
VALUE	ZERO	=
VALUES	ZEROES	

In Chapters 9 and 10, we learned that BASIC and FORTRAN had about 20 and 40 reserved words (or statement names), respectively. In contrast to these languages, COBOL has around 300 reserved words.

COBOL CODING FORM

To write programs in COBOL, the programmer must pay attention to punctuation, spacing, and indentations. A special COBOL coding form is usually used as an aid to the programmer. Although not absolutely necessary, its use simplifies writing the format required by COBOL. Fig. 11-2 illustrates a sample COBOL coding form. In compiling, only columns 7 to 72 are used, while columns 1 to 6 and 73 to 80 are for identification and reference purposes. The positions on the coding form have the following meaning:

COLUMN	USE
1-3	Recording the page number.
4-6	Recording the line number.
7	Signaling the continuation of a command, indicated by a hyphen. Also signaling a comment, indicated by an asterisk.
8-72	Program coding. Column 8 is also called the A margin and column 12 the B margin.
73-80	Program identification.

Each line on the coding form corresponds to a single punched card. Division, section, and paragraph names begin at the A margin (column 8) while paragraph contents are written starting at the B margin (column 12). Most of the program coding, except significant names, starts at the B margin.

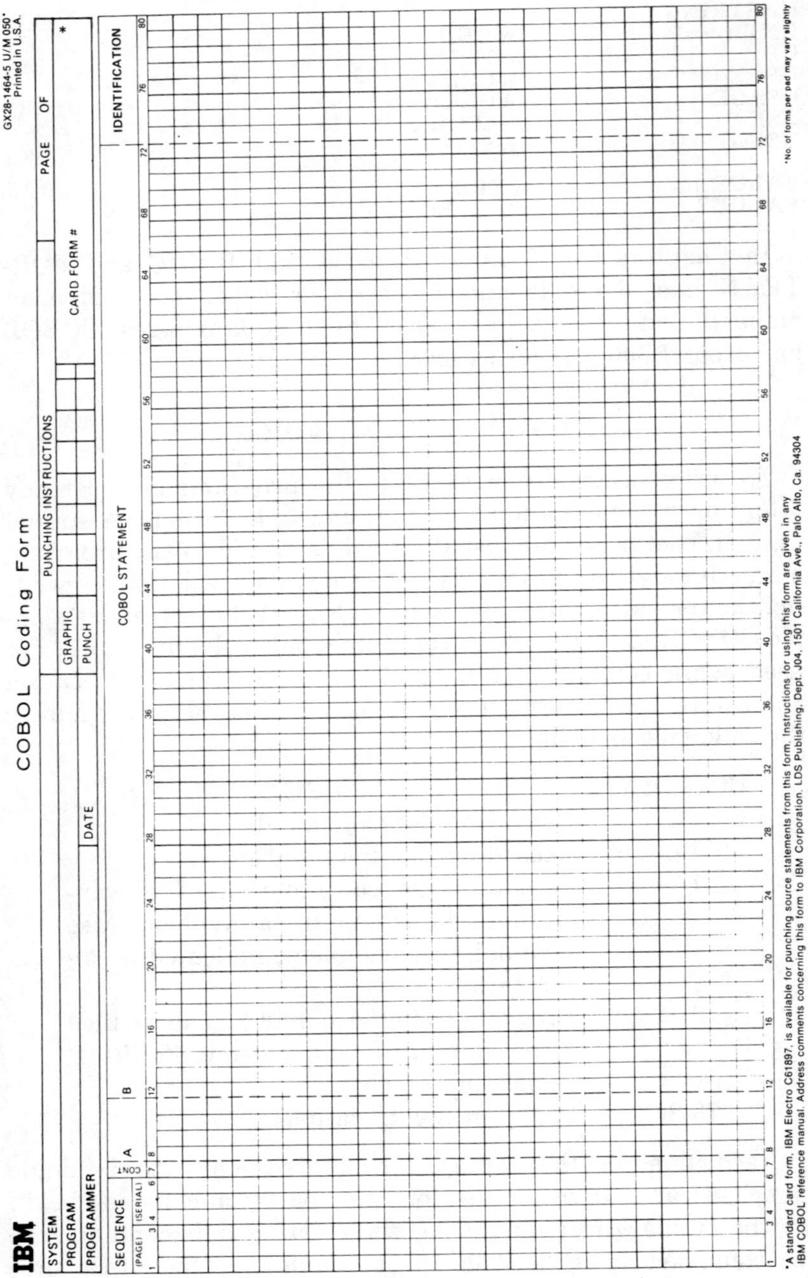
IBM

COBOL Coding Form

GX28-1464-5 U/M 050*
Printed in U.S.A.

SYSTEM		PUNCHING INSTRUCTIONS			PAGE OF
PROGRAM		GRAPHIC			CARD FORM # *
PROGRAMMER	DATE	PUNCH			

SEQUENCE (PAGE) (SERIAL)	CONT.	A	B	COBOL STATEMENT	IDENTIFICATION
1 3 4 6	7	8	12 16 20 24 28 32 36 40 44 48 52 56 60 64 68	72	76 80

*A standard card form, IBM Electro C61897, is available for punching source statements from this form. Instructions for using this form are given in any IBM COBOL reference manual. Address comments concerning this form to IBM Corporation, LDS Publishing, Dept. J04, 1501 California Ave., Palo Alto, Ca. 94304

*No. of forms per pad may vary slightly

Fig. 11-2. A COBOL coding form.

STRUCTURE OF A COBOL PROGRAM

A COBOL program consists of four parts, called divisions:

1. The IDENTIFICATION DIVISION is used to attach a unique identification such as program name, program number, program version, programmer's name, installation, etc., to the program.
2. The ENVIRONMENT DIVISION is used to specify the computer on which the program is to be compiled and executed.
3. The DATA DIVISION is used to define the characteristics and format of data to be processed.
4. The PROCEDURE DIVISION is used to describe the internal processing that is to be performed. All input/output operations, computational operations, logical decisions, and data movement instructions must be defined in this section.

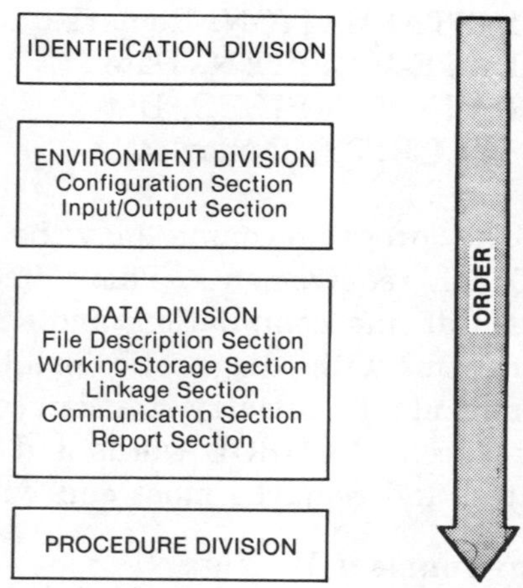

Fig. 11-3. Major divisions of a COBOL program.

All four divisions must be present in the order specified in Fig. 11-3. In summary, the four divisions of a COBOL program provide identification, a description of the equipment being used, a description of the data being processed, and a set of procedures specifying how the data are to be processed. A more detailed description of each division follows.

Identification Division

The IDENTIFICATION DIVISION identifies a program and the outputs from a compilation. It is the shortest of the major COBOL divisions. It allows the programmer to assign the program a name and to supply other information serving to identify the program, such as the author, the date the program was written, the date the program was compiled, and such other information as desired under the paragraphs in the general format. This division is similar to the COMMENT statement in FORTRAN and the REM statement in BASIC.

The following format shows the structure of the IDENTIFICATION DIVISION. It consists of six paragraphs, of which only the first is required; the others are all optional, but must appear in the following order:

```
IDENTIFICATION DIVISION.
PROGRAM-ID. Name.
AUTHOR. Name.
INSTALLATION. Remarks.
DATE-WRITTEN. Date.
DATE-COMPILED. Date.
SECURITY. Remarks.
```

The program name may be any word meeting regular COBOL requirements. This name is associated with the program during compilation, and serves to identify the compiled program with diagnostic printouts and computer-oriented comments. Each entry starts in column 8 (A margin) and both the specified COBOL words and programmer-supplied names, dates, and remarks must end with a period.

Environment Division

The ENVIRONMENT DIVISION specifies a standard method of expressing those aspects of a data-processing problem that depend on the physical characteristics of a specific computer. This division allows specification of the configuration of the compiling computer and the computer on which the program is to be executed. In addition, information relating to input/output control, special hardware characteristics, and control techniques can be specified.

The ENVIRONMENT DIVISION is divided into two sections: the CONFIGURATION SECTION, and the INPUT/OUTPUT SECTION. The CONFIGURATION SECTION specifies the computer that is used to compile the source program and to execute the machine-language program. This section is divided into three paragraphs: the SOURCE-COMPUTER paragraph, which describes the computer configuration on which the source program is compiled; the OBJECT-COMPUTER paragraph, which describes the computer configuration that will be used to execute the program; and the SPECIAL-NAMES paragraph, which relates the implementor-names used by the compiler to the mnemonic-names used in the source program. The following is the general structure of the CONFIGURATION SECTION. All paragraphs except SPECIAL-NAMES are always required.

```
ENVIRONMENT DIVISION
CONFIGURATION SECTION.
SOURCE COMPUTER. Computer name.
OBJECT COMPUTER. Computer name.
SPECIAL-NAMES
   Compiler name IS mnemonic name.
```

Having identified the configuration, the programmer must then define input/output techniques and associated files with external media. This is accomplished by the INPUT/OUTPUT SECTION, which is divided into two paragraphs: the FILE-CONTROL paragraph, which names and associates the files with external media; and the I/O-CONTROL paragraph, which defines special control techniques to be used in the object program. The general structure of this section is as follows:

```
INPUT/OUTPUT SECTION.
FILE-CONTROL.
   SELECT file-name ASSIGN TO hardware-name.
I/O-CONTROL.
   APPLY input/output techniques ON file-name.
```

Data Division

The DATA DIVISION describes the data that the object program is to accept as input, to manipulate, to create, or to

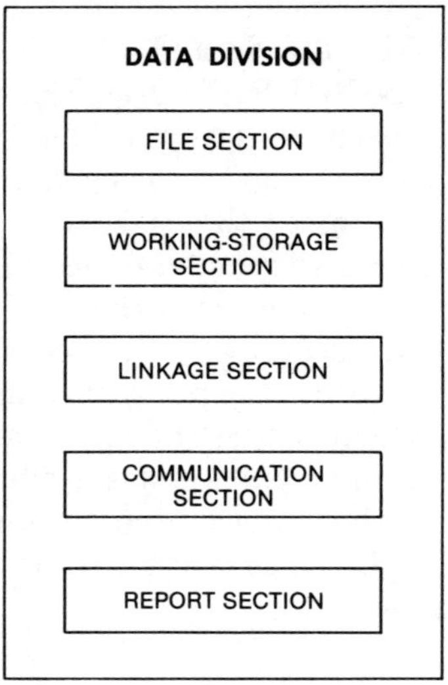

Fig. 11-4. Structure of the DATA DIVISION.

produce as output. This division is usually much longer than the IDENTIFICATION or ENVIRONMENT DIVISIONS and is subdivided into five sections: FILE SECTION, WORKING-STORAGE SECTION, LINKAGE SECTION, COMMUNICATION SECTION, and REPORT SECTION. See Fig. 11-4 for an illustration of the structure of the DATA DIVISION.

The FILE SECTION defines the contents of data files stored on an external medium. Each file is defined by a file description followed by a record description or a series of record descriptions. Perhaps at this point we should define the terms *file* and *record*. A file is a collection of related information about some subject that is directed toward some purpose. Two types of files are usually needed to maintain most recorded business information: *master files* and *transaction files*. A master file is a permanent recording that shows the status of any segment of information. With manual bookkeeping, a ledger book is an example of a master file and may include inventory, payroll earnings, and accounts receivable. Transaction files are made up of daily or periodic transactions that are assembled, then recorded into the permanent file of master records. Transaction files may be made up of invoices of sales to customers, or records of goods received for inventory, etc. A file consists of a collection of records providing information about a group

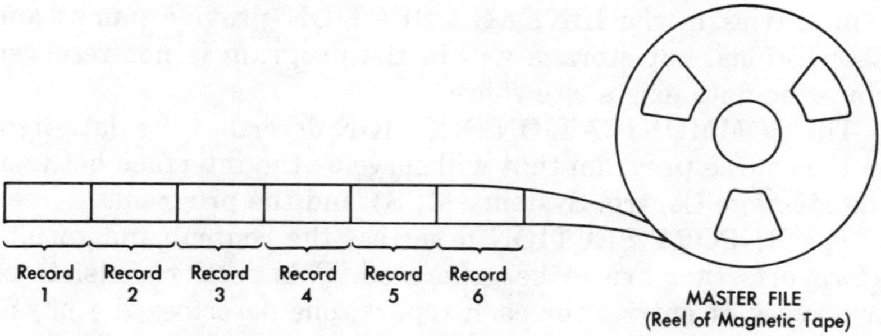

Fig. 11-5. A master file showing the breakdown into many records.

of stock items, related accounts, etc. A file, then, is composed of a collection of many records. This point is illustrated in Fig. 11-5.

Because a variety of files may be used by a program, each with a different format, the programmer must describe each of these files to the computer using the following format:

```
FD file name . . .
01 record name . . .
    02 description of record item . . .
```

The FD stands for file description.

The WORKING-STORAGE SECTION describes records and noncontiguous data items which are not part of external files but are developed and processed internally. The skeleton format for this section is as follows:

```
WORKING-STORAGE SECTION.
77 field name.
      .
      .
      .
01 record name.
      .
      .
      .
```

The LINKAGE SECTION describes data passed from one program to another. This section is identified by, and must begin with, the section header LINKAGE SECTION and a period, followed by noncontiguous data item description entries, and then by record description entries. Record description entries in the LINKAGE SECTION provide names and descriptions, but storage within the program is not reserved since the data exists elsewhere.

The COMMUNICATION SECTION describes the data item in the source program that will serve as the interface between the Message Control System (MCS) and the program.

The REPORT SECTION describes the content and format of reports that are to be generated. This section consists of two types of entries for each report; one describes the physical aspects of the report format, the other type describes conceptual characteristics of the items which make up the report and their relation to the report format.

Considerable care must be taken in developing the DATA DIVISION of a program. It provides a standard technique to describe files and data within files; however, careful planning of file structure and precision in the item descriptions is still required of the programmer.

Procedure Division

The last part of a COBOL program is the PROCEDURE DIVISION, where step-by-step instructions for computer operation are written in meaningful English with verbs denoting actions, sentences describing procedures, and conditional statements specifying alternate paths of action.

The principal subdivision of the PROCEDURE DIVISION is the *paragraph*. This is a program segment of at least one sentence, introduced by a name, called a paragraph or *procedure* name. *Sentences* exist within paragraphs. A sentence consists of one or more *statements,* which are syntactically valid combinations of words and symbols beginning with a COBOL verb; e.g., ADD, COMPUTE, or SEARCH.

The following five arithmetic operators may be used in developing COBOL statements:

Arithmetic Operator	*Meaning*
+	Addition
–	Subtraction
*	Multiplication
/	Division
**	Exponentiation

Parentheses may be used to specify the order in which elements are to be evaluated. Expressions within parentheses are evaluated first, and, within a nest of parentheses, evaluation proceeds from the least inclusive set to the most inclusive set.

STATEMENTS

Following are brief descriptions of several COBOL statements:

ACCEPT

This statement causes data to be read from an appropriate peripheral device.

ADD

This statement causes two or more numeric operands to be summed and the result to be stored.

ALTER

This statement modifies a predetermined sequence of operations.

CALL

This statement causes control to be transferred from one object program to another, within the run unit.

CANCEL

This statement releases the memory areas occupied by the referred-to program.

CLOSE

This statement terminates the processing of input and output files with optional rewind and/or lock where applicable.

COMPUTE

This statement assigns to one or more data items the value of an arithmetic expression.

COPY

This statement incorporates text into a COBOL source program.

DELETE

This statement logically removes a record from a mass storage file.

DISPLAY

This statement causes data to be written on an appropriate peripheral device.

DIVIDE

This statement divides one numeric data item into others and sets the values of data items equal to the results.

ENTER

This statement provides a means of allowing the use of more than one language in the same program.

EXIT

This statement provides a common end point for a series of procedures.

EXIT PROGRAM

This statement marks the logical end of a called program.

GENERATE

This statement directs the Report Writer Control System (RWCS) to produce a report in accordance with the report description that was specified in the REPORT SECTION of the DATA DIVISION.

GO TO

This statement causes program control to be transferred from one part of the PROCEDURE DIVISION to another.

IF

This statement causes a condition to be evaluated. The subsequent action of the object program depends on whether the value of the condition is true or false.

INITIATE

This statement causes the RWCS to begin the processing of a report.

INSPECT

This statement provides the ability to tally, replace, or tally and replace occurrences of single characters, or groups of characters, in a data item.

MERGE

This statement combines two or more identically sequenced files on a set of specified keys, and during the process makes records available, in merge order, to an output procedure or file.

MOVE

This statement transfers data, in accordance with the rules of editing, to one or more data areas.

MULTIPLY

This statement causes numeric data items to be multiplied and sets the values of data items equal to the results.

OPEN

This statement initiates the processing of both input and output files. It performs checking and/or writing of labels and other input/output operations.

PERFORM

This statement is used to depart from the normal sequence of execution in order to execute one or more procedures, either a specified number of times or until a specified condition is satisfied, and to return control to the normal sequence.

READ

For sequential access, this statement makes available the next logical record from a file. For random access, the READ statement makes available a specified record from a mass storage file.

RELEASE

This statement transfers records to the initial phase of a SORT operation.

RETURN

This statement obtains either sorted records from the final phase of a SORT operation, or merged records during a MERGE operation.

REWRITE

This statement logically replaces a record existing in a mass storage file.

SEARCH

This statement is used to search a table for a table element that satisfies the specified condition, and to adjust the associated index-name to indicate that table element.

SET

This statement establishes reference points for table-handling operations by setting index-names associated with table elements.

SORT

This statement creates a sort file by executing input procedures or by transferring records from another file, sorts the records in the sort file on a set of specified keys, and in the final phase of the sort operation, makes available each record from the sort file, in sorted order, to some output procedures or to an output file.

START

This statement provides a basis for logical positioning within a relative or indexed file, for subsequent sequential retrieval of records.

STOP

This statement halts the object program either permanently or temporarily.

STRING

This statement provides juxtaposition of the partial or complete contents of two or more data items into a single data item.

SUBTRACT

This statement is used to subtract one, or the sum of two or more, numeric data items from one or more items, and set the values of one or more items equal to the results.

SUPPRESS

This statement causes the RWCS to inhibit the presentation of a report group.

TERMINATE

This statement terminates the processing of a report.

UNSTRING

This statement causes contiguous data in a sending field to be separated and placed into multiple receiving fields.

USE

This statement specifies procedures for input/output error handling that are, in addition to the standard procedures, provided by the input/output control system. It is also used to specify PROCEDURE DIVISION statements that are executed just before a report group named in the REPORT SECTION of the DATA DIVISION is produced.

WRITE

This statement releases a logical record for an output or input/output file. It can also be used for vertical positioning of a printer mechanism.

A SAMPLE PROGRAM

Before we examine a sample COBOL program, let us examine the skeleton format of a complete program shown in Fig. 11-6. This format illustrates the four divisions of a COBOL program and the relative order that each division appears in the program. All four divisions must be present in the program in the indicated order.

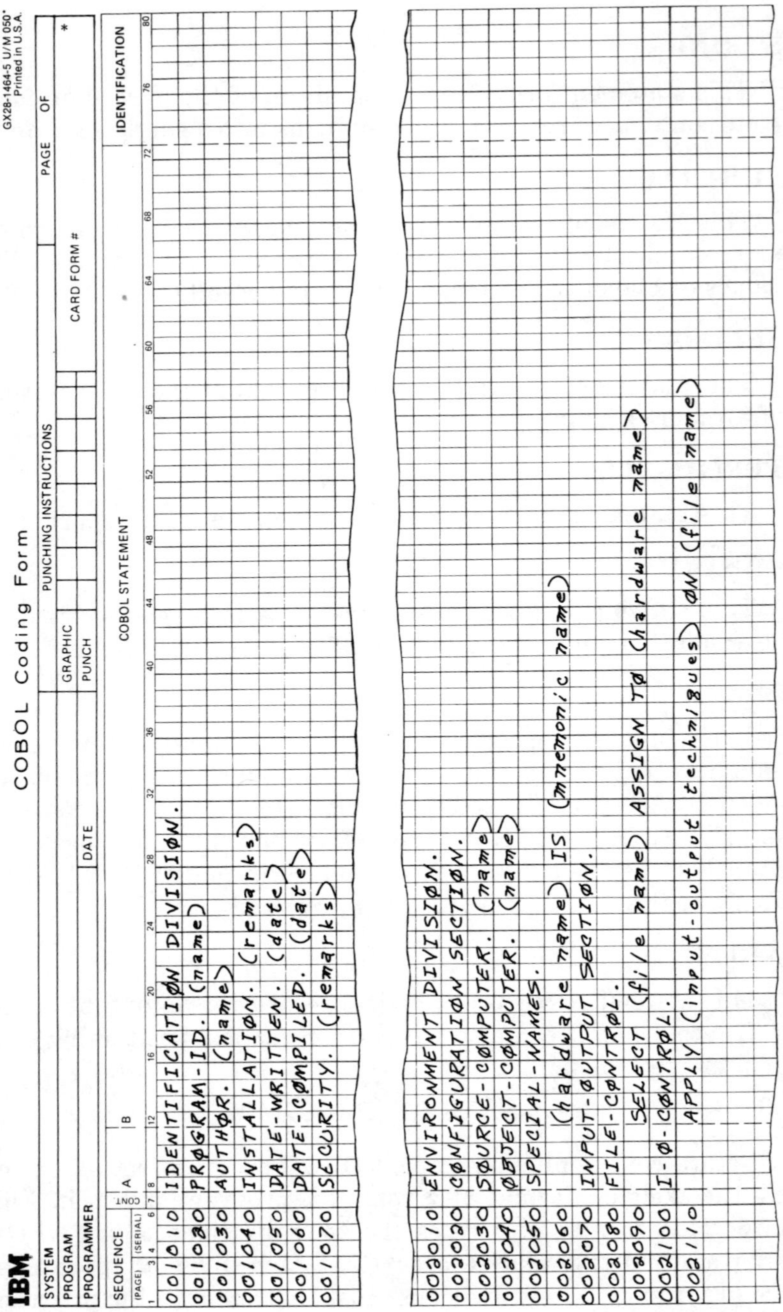

IBM

COBOL Coding Form

GX28-1464-5 U/M 050*
Printed in U.S.A.

SYSTEM | PROGRAM | PROGRAMMER | DATE | PUNCHING INSTRUCTIONS | GRAPHIC | PUNCH | CARD FORM # | PAGE OF | *

SEQUENCE (PAGE) (SERIAL) | CONT | A | B | COBOL STATEMENT | IDENTIFICATION

```
001010 IDENTIFICATIØN DIVISIØN.
001020 PRØGRAM-ID. (name)
001030 AUTHØR. (name)
001040 INSTALLATIØN. (remarks)
001050 DATE-WRITTEN. (date)
001060 DATE-CØMPILED. (date)
001070 SECURITY. (remarks)

002010 ENVIRONMENT DIVISIØN.
002020 CØNFIGURATIØN SECTIØN.
002030 SØURCE-CØMPUTER. (name)
002040 ØBJECT-CØMPUTER. (name)
002050 SPECIAL-NAMES.
002060     (hardware name) IS (mnemonic name)
002070 INPUT-ØUTPUT SECTIØN.
002080 FILE-CØNTRØL.
002090     SELECT (file name) ASSIGN TØ (hardware name)
002100 I-Ø-CØNTRØL.
002110     APPLY (input-output techniques) ØN (file name)
```

Fig. 11-6. Skeleton format of a

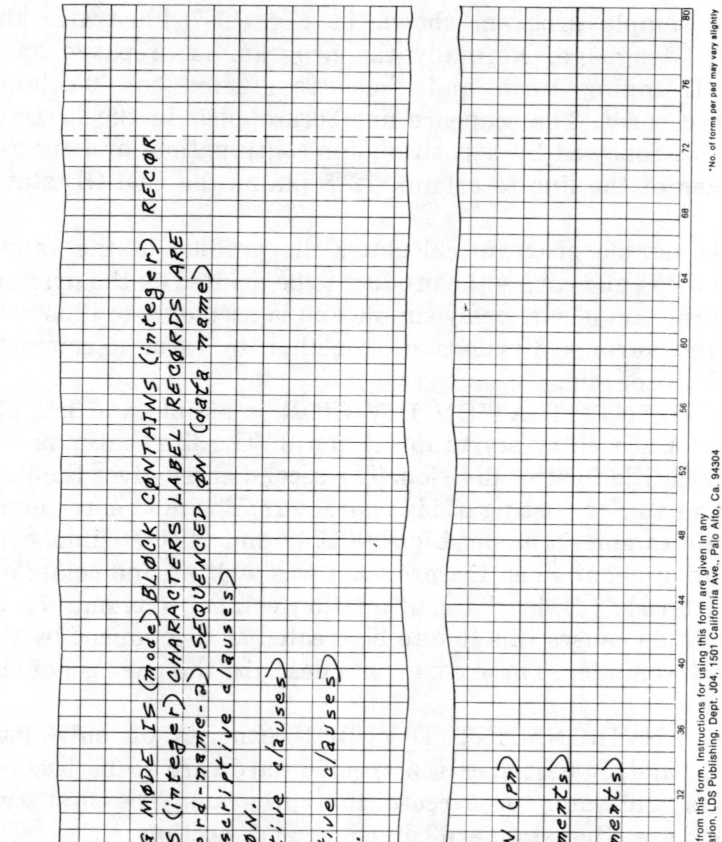

source program written in COBOL.

The sample program shown in Fig. 11-7 illustrates the COBOL language. Normally the program is prepared on a COBOL coding form and then transferred to 80-column punched cards. The sequence numbers appear in the first six columns, followed by a position for continuation, and the remainder of the line to column 72 contains the COBOL statement.

This sample program calculates the product of the values 643 and 761 and causes the product to be printed on the printer. This program is extremely simple and is used only to illustrate how the various divisions go together to form a complete COBOL program.

The IDENTIFICATION DIVISION is simple and has six entries. Each entry starts in column 8. The first entry is the standard title for this division. The second entry gives the program a name consisting of six characters. The next entry gives the programmer's name. Lines 001040 and 001050 supply information about when the program was written and compiled. The asterisk (*) in the continuation column (column 7) at line 001060 causes this line to be treated as a comment by the COBOL compiler. These comments describe the purpose of the program.

The ENVIRONMENT DIVISION consists of only four entries, and, it describes the specific hardware to be used to compile and later to execute this program. The first two entries are the standard division and section titles. The SOURCE-COMPUTER paragraph starts at line 001100, and, it indicates that the source computer is an IBM System/370. The OBJECT-COMPUTER paragraph specifies on line 001110 that an IBM System/370 computer is also to be used to execute the program.

The DATA DIVISION consists of five paragraphs starting on line 001120 with the standard title for this division. In this division we have identified names for the values used in the program. The first name is NUMBER-ONE and has been assigned the value of 643. The second name is NUMBER-TWO and has been given the value of 761. In this division, we also reserved an area in which to store the product. This area is given the name TOTAL and is a large enough storage area to contain any six-digit number. The names defined in the DATA DIVISION will be used in the following division.

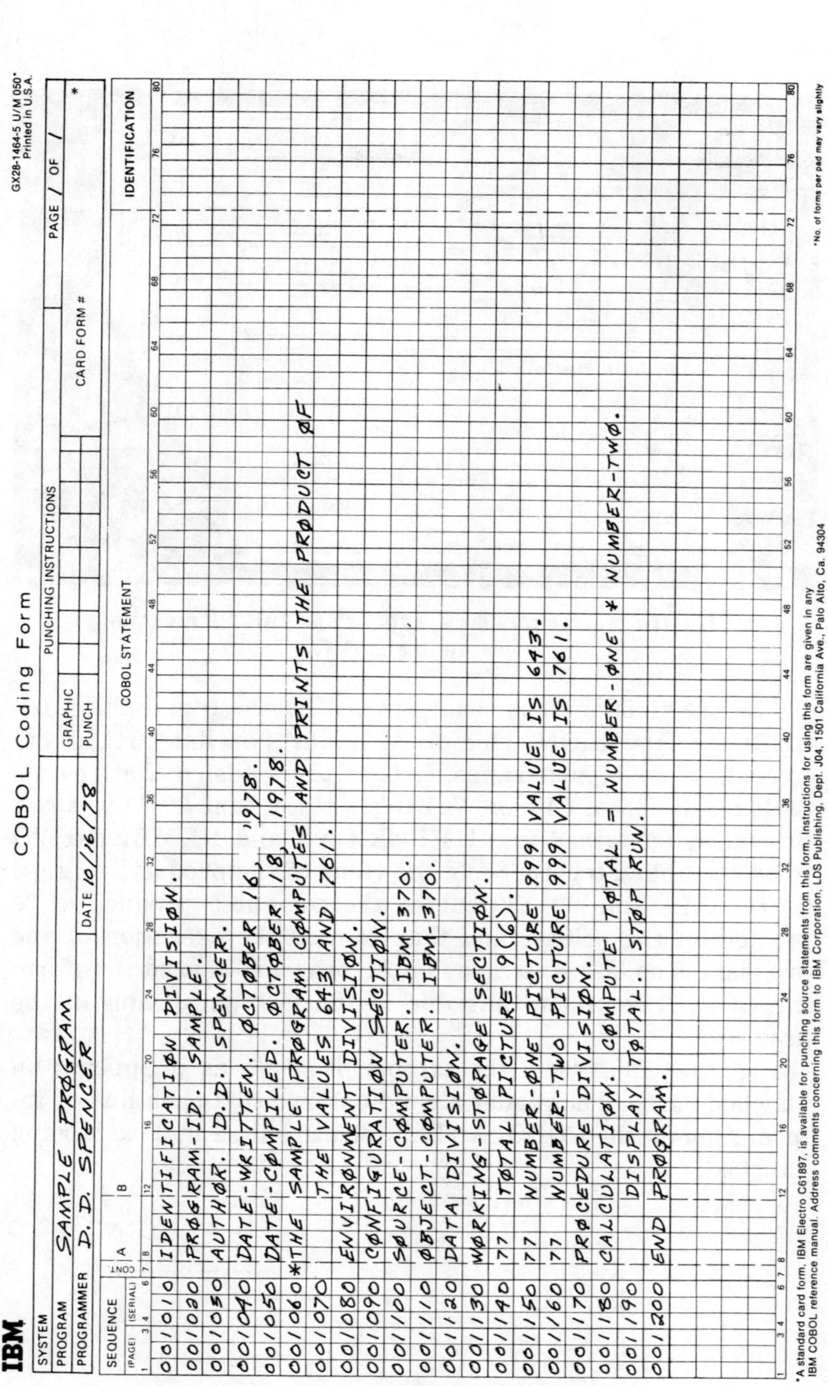

IBM — COBOL Coding Form — GX28-1464-5 U/M 050* Printed in U.S.A.

SYSTEM — PUNCHING INSTRUCTIONS — PAGE 1 OF 1

PROGRAM: SAMPLE PRØGRAM — GRAPHIC — PUNCH — CARD FORM #

PROGRAMMER: D. D. SPENCER — DATE 10/16/78

SEQUENCE (PAGE) (SERIAL) — CONT. — A — B — COBOL STATEMENT — IDENTIFICATION

```
001010 IDENTIFICATIØN DIVISIØN.
001020 PRØGRAM-ID. SAMPLE.
001030 AUTHØR. D.D. SPENCER.
001040 DATE-WRITTEN. ØCTØBER 16, 1978.
001050 DATE-CØMPILED. ØCTØBER 18, 1978.
001060*THE SAMPLE PRØGRAM CØMPUTES AND PRINTS THE PRØDUCT ØF
001070     THE VALUES 643 AND 761.
001080 ENVIRØNMENT DIVISIØN.
001090 CØNFIGURATIØN SECTIØN.
001100 SØURCE-CØMPUTER. IBM-370.
001110 ØBJECT-CØMPUTER. IBM-370.
001120 DATA DIVISIØN.
001130 WØRKING-STØRAGE SECTIØN.
001140 77  TØTAL PICTURE 9(6).
001150 77  NUMBER-ØNE PICTURE 999 VALUE IS 643.
001160 77  NUMBER-TWØ PICTURE 999 VALUE IS 761.
001170 PRØCEDURE DIVISIØN.
001180 CALCULATIØN. CØMPUTE TØTAL = NUMBER-ØNE * NUMBER-TWØ.
001190     DISPLAY TØTAL. STØP RUN.
001200 END PRØGRAM.
```

*A standard card form, IBM Electro C61897, is available for punching source statements from this form. Instructions for using this form are given in any IBM COBOL reference manual. Address comments concerning this form to IBM Corporation, LDS Publishing, Dept. J04, 1501 California Ave., Palo Alto, Ca. 94304

*No. of forms per pad may vary slightly

Fig. 11-7. A sample COBOL program.

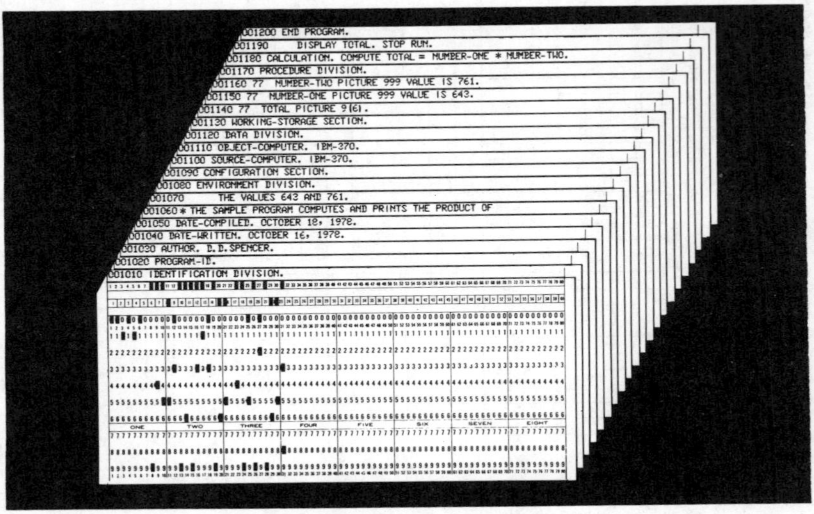

Fig. 11-8. Source card deck of the sample COBOL program shown in Fig. 11-7.

The last division in our sample COBOL program is the PROCEDURE DIVISION. This division starts on line 001170 and consists of four paragraphs. It is in this division that the actual calculation of 643 and 761 takes place. Line 001180 causes the values contained in NUMBER-ONE and NUMBER-TWO to be multiplied together and the value of the product assigned to TOTAL. Line 001190 causes the computed product to be printed on the printer and then to stop the execution of the program. The last statement in the program is used to inform the COBOL compiler that this is the last paragraph in the program.

Fig. 11-8 illustrates the sample program as it appears on punched cards. The reader should observe that each line of information on the COBOL coding form resulted in a card being punched.

Chapter 12

Computer Concepts

Courtesy Sperry Univac, a Division of Sperry Rand Corp.

The majority of present computer applications fall into the category of *information systems.* In these applications (Table 12-1 lists a few of them), the computer is used as a massive filing system. The files are updated and analyzed by the computer, information is retrieved rapidly, and individual documents or reports are prepared automatically from information in the files. Since the 1950s, computers have been the central controlling element of such systems. Today, computers handle information processing in a variety of different ways: by allowing time sharing between several users, by providing data processing in real-time, etc. A few methods for processing information will be discussed in this chapter.

"ALL I WANTED YOU TO DO WAS TELL ME WHICH PROGRAMMING LANGUAGE TO USE!!!"

TIME SHARING

Time sharing is the simultaneous shared use of a computer system by independent users. A time-sharing computer system enables several users to share space in the computer memory and to share computation time. Among the many advantages offered by this type of system are:

1. Users can prepare their own programs in an easy-to-learn conversational language. This eliminates having the problem solved by a professional programmer.
2. Since time-sharing users receive their answers immediately, there is no time delay as found in batch-processing systems. What is the time delay in an average batch-processing computer system? First, users must define their problems and provide data to a programmer who, after a short period of time, produces a computer program. The program is written (or coded) in a programming language for the specific computer being used. The program is then punched on either cards or paper tape and sent to the computer center for processing. After a few hours, the program will be run on the computer. If the program is incorrect (it almost always is on the first attempt), the programmer must debug the program and correct the problem. After several days, the program will be working properly and the problem answers will be satisfactory.

Table 12-1. Information Systems Applications

Credit Card Processing	Newspaper Printing
Record Keeping	Menu Planning
Book Publishing	Law Data Bank
Movie Production	Stock Market Analysis
School Administration	Test Grading
Production Control	Report Preparation
Scheduling	Market Research
Accounting	Election Returns
Inventory Control	Income Tax Returns
Reservation Control	Language Translation
Sales Analysis	Hospital Administration
Billing & Invoicing	Economic Analysis
Actuarial Research	Census Data Analysis
Library Search & Retrieval	Medical Data Bank
Personnel Files	Patent Search

3. Time sharing places a powerful computer at the hands of many users who would not normally be able to afford the use of a computer system.
4. The manufacturers and suppliers of time-sharing systems often furnish many "application" programs for use by the user.

The time-sharing concept is based on the principle that there is enough capacity in a computer system for multiple users, provided that each user console is active only a small fraction of the time. The components of a time-sharing system are the operating system (time-sharing executive, language compilers, application programs, etc.), hardware (computer, data communications equipment, auxiliary storage, etc.), and remote-user terminals (teletypewriters, typewriters, crt display devices, etc.). It is the responsibility of the operating system to determine what each user is attempting to do and to schedule all communications between the computer system and the user. In a simple system, the user programs are stored in an auxiliary storage and transferred in and out of the computer main memory as needed. The operating system would determine what programs needed swapping and when this swapping must occur.

Users of a time-sharing system have the illusion that each is the only one using the system. This illusion is false, however, as each user has the use of the computer for only a specified amount of time. The computer picks up orders from one user, works on this problem for a short period of time such as $\frac{1}{20}$ of a second, and stores the partial answer. The computer then moves to the next user, receives the orders, works on the second problem for $\frac{1}{20}$ of a second, and moves to the third user, etc. When a specific user's problem is completed, the results are transmitted to the user's console. The computer accomplishes the orders of several users so fast that they all receive the impression the system is working for them full time.

In a typical time-sharing system, the users communicate with the computer by means of remote consoles. The computer may only be a few yards from the console or it may be several thousand miles away. Communications between these remote consoles and the computer system is via the normal telephone service. A remote unit such as a teletypewriter is connected with the computer by using a dataphone set which may be leased from the local telephone company. The dataphone is a modulator-demodulator unit used for converting the keyboard signals of the teletypewriter into two-level tones for transmission over the voice-grade telephones lines. As a demodulator, it converts the received signals to activate the print mechanism of the teletypewriter.

Courtesy Scientific Data Systems, Inc.

Fig. 12-1. Two engineering designers work with a time-sharing computer system to solve a complex problem. The computer is located several miles from the Teletype terminal they are using.

Fig. 12-1 shows two engineering designers using a Model 33 Teletype terminal which is connected to a time-sharing computer system. This Teletype terminal is a typical remote unit and can print information at a rate of 10 characters per second (100 words per minute). A user can use this unit to prepare programs, check out programs, or run previously written programs.

The time-sharing computer uses the same basic equipment as a computer used for batch processing. However, not all machines suitable for batch-processing work are for use in time-sharing systems. This may be because certain hardware features are not available or that time-sharing software is not available.

Hardware items that are peculiar to time-sharing computer systems are data communications control units (for gathering and routing all input/output communications between the computer and remote units), memory protection features, remote terminal units, and large auxiliary storage units. In addition, the computer equipment must be reliable. When equipment failure occurs in a normal batch-processing computer system, only a few users voice their complaints. In a time-sharing system it is possible to expect complaints from several hundred irate users whenever the time-sharing system is not functioning properly.

A typical time-sharing hardware system is diagrammed in Fig. 12-2. This system contains the equipment normally found in a computer system (central processing unit, auxiliary storage devices, and input/output equipment) plus the data communications equipment and remote terminal units. The data communications equipment performs similar to a telephone exchange in routing incoming calls to the computer and outgoing information to the correct remote unit.

The largest present users of time-sharing systems are universities, large industrial companies, small engineering companies, small research firms, and small businesses.

To engineers, students, businessmen, or any other user, the time-sharing system is just a useful tool. It allows them to solve their problems more rapidly. The users want to simply use an application program that has been written by someone else or they want to write programs easily. With a language such as BASIC, the user communicates with the computer in a conversational mode. In this mode, the user communicates or con-

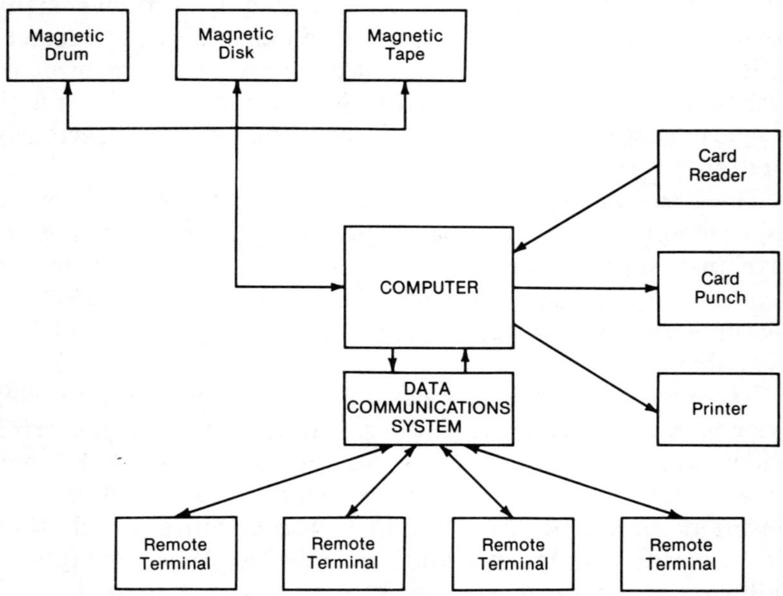

Fig. 12-2. Hardware configuration of a typical time-sharing system.

verses directly with the computer in terms of requests and acknowledgment dialogues. The user can prepare a program, one instruction at a time or several at a time, and can change any instruction in the computer at any time.

In the field of education, time sharing makes computers available to many students. This allow students to become familiar with the use of a computer and to use this capability in the solution of problems in their prime area of interest. As the use of computers in industry, government, and business increases, the need for training becomes more acute. Time sharing is certainly not limited to university students only, as students in secondary and elementary schools are easily able to learn how to use these systems.

The use of time-sharing systems varies with the manufacturer; however, they all follow a similar pattern. First, the user dials the computer by using either a telephone mounted on the teletypewriter or a telephone connected to a dataphone set. This call goes through the normal telephone exchange network and establishes contact with the computer system. When contact is made, the user will be asked for identification and to select the programming system to be used. If a program that is already written and stored in the time-sharing system library is to be used, the user simply requests to execute the program. If, however, a new program is being prepared, the user will type the program in some conversational programming language and, when complete, inform the computer that the program is to be executed. The computer will then run the program and transmit the program results to the remote unit. The user also has the option of storing this newly created program in the system library for use on some future occasion.

BATCH PROCESSING

Batch processing is a method of processing data in which transactions are accumulated for a predetermined period of time and prepared for input to the computer for processing as a single unit. Input is collected in batches and sorted in the same sequence as it is to be processed. For example, all memos of transactions (invoices, sales slips, etc.) are collected. The batch of memos is then sorted numerically or alphabetically for posting to accounts. The indicated time period may be any length—an hour, a day, a week, or a month. In batch processing, however, there is often some delay between the occurrence of original events and the eventual processing of the transactions. This type of processing is contrasted with real-time processing in which transactions are dealt with as they arise and are automatically applied to files held in a direct-access storage device.

Batch processing has several important advantages. It makes mechanization of processing operations more feasible by assuring that a large number of items will be processed at one time. Preparation time for processing data is reduced since a few large processing runs are made instead of numerous smaller processing runs.

MULTIPROCESSING

A *multiprocessing* computer system is one that contains two or more interconnected central processing units, each with its own arithmetic and logic units, and each capable of independent operation (see Fig. 12-3A).

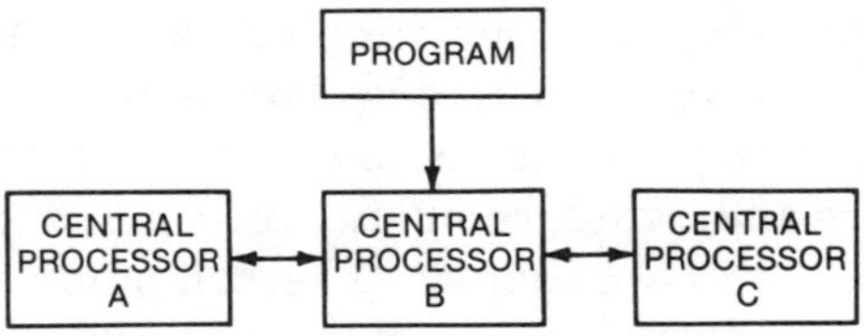

(*A*) *Multiprocessing.*

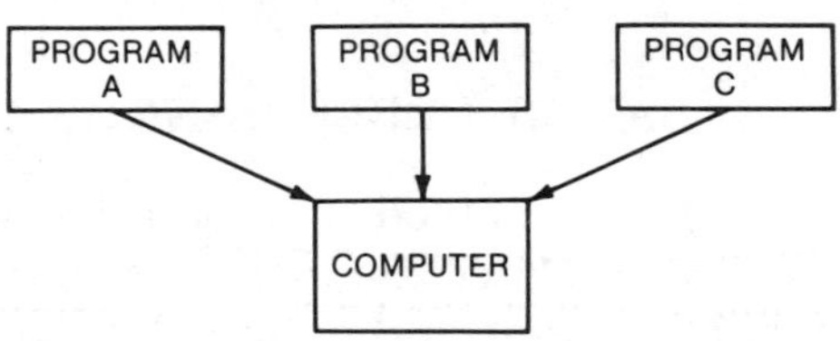

(*B*) *Multiprogramming.*

Fig. 12-3. Comparison of multiprocessing and multiprogramming configurations.

A computer system operating in a multiprocessing configuration must be able to interpret and execute its own programmed instructions. In addition, facilities must be available to transfer data from one CPU to another, to transfer data and instructions to and from internal storage, and to transfer data and instructions to and from a common auxiliary storage device.

The requirements for multiprocessing in terms of both equipment and programs are extensive. One of the first multiprocessors consisted of ten small computers, each capable of performing input, output, and processing, while connected to a main central processing unit. The main CPU included many multiply, add, shift, and test units which could operate at the same time to improve processing speed.

Multiprocessing offers data-processing capabilities that are not available when only one central processing unit is used. With a multiprocessing system, many complex operations can be performed at the same time.

MULTIPROGRAMMING

There is an extreme difference in the speeds at which a computer is able to perform calculations and the speeds at which even the fastest input/output devices can operate. In the time taken to print one line on a line printer working at 1200 lines per minute, a computer could perform 10,000 additions. *Multiprogramming* is a technique developed to relieve this imbalance and to further increase the utilization of the computer.

Multiprogramming is the concurrent execution of two or more programs simultaneously residing in the internal storage unit of a computer (see Fig. 12-3B). The basic principle of multiprogramming is that the programs in internal storage share the available time of the central processing unit and the input/output units. Each program is written as a completely independent program. While input/output operations of one program are being handled, the CPU is essentially idle and can handle some non-input/output processing of another program at the same time. For example, a program to read data from punched cards and transcribe it to magnetic tape will only require the use of the computer for a small fraction of the program running time. The remainder of the time represents input/output transfer time during which other programs can use the central processing unit.

Benefits to be gained from multiprogramming include the elimination of *off-line* equipment normally used to transcribe data onto a faster medium for input. While this activity is proceeding, using limited numbers of input/output devices and little processing time, other more productive programs can use the remaining input/output devices and central processing unit time.

REAL-TIME PROCESSING

Real-time is a term used to describe a system that controls an ongoing process and delivers its outputs not later than the time when these are needed for effective control. An example of a real-time system is an airline reservations system, in which each reservation must be processed by the system immediately after it is made so that a complete, up-to-date picture of available seating is maintained by the computer at all times, With a real-time airline reservations system, a customer can request space for a specific date between cities. A reservations agent then inserts a flight card in the computer, querying it on seat availability. Instantaneously, the computer searches for the appropriate flight record and transmits the latest availability information back to the agent. This information is then displayed for the agent on a crt viewing screen. When a seat is sold, the agent presses a button and the computer center then updates the seat inventory for that flight. Fig. 12-4 illustrates the computer-controlled terminals used by an airline reservations system.

A real-time system network is also being used in the railroad industry where, in a matter of seconds, recording of and access to freight car location and movement information can be accomplished. The system enables a railroad to supply shippers with freight car location, as well as approximate time of freight car arrival within seconds after an inquiry is received. The system also makes it possible to eliminate many handwritten daily reports that have been a burden on operating personnel since the inception of railroads.

Many department stores, insurance companies, and banks use real-time systems. Banks and other financial establishments use these systems to send transactions from branches to a central computer installation. Real-time terminals are being used on bank counters to check customers' balances and sometimes to produce statements or to process the customer transactions on-line.

Courtesy American Airlines

Fig. 12-4. Remote crt terminals at an airline reservations center.

Real-time data-processing equipment also controls dissemination of the New York Stock Exchange trading data, runs stock tickers, and even "speaks" to member subscribers over the Exchange's telephone quotation service. Trading information, which was previously transmitted by pneumatic tubes and voice, is now sped to a computer center in the Exchange via direct electronic signals from *data readers* on the trading floor. The system prints sales on exchange tickers across the United States in as little time as a half-second after a special reporting card is "read" on the floor.

Common elements of all these applications of real-time systems include a file to store information, a computer to process it, and communications lines and terminals to provide access to or for someone remotely located.

The impetus for acquiring a real-time operation is the need for immediate information. With a real-time system, information managers have the capability of making human judgments based on the most recent data.

Real-time systems normally require the use of data communications equipment to feed data into the system from remote terminals, direct-access storage devices to store incoming data in large volumes, and computers capable of executing the programs needed to validate data and control the input data at the same time as this data is being used for the particular application.

Real-time systems have definite advantages over more conventional methods of processing data. These systems provide immediate interaction between human and machine or between machine and machine (computer to computer, terminal to computer, etc.).

OPERATING SYSTEMS

When computers were first developed, they were usually put to work solving jobs that had previously required a great deal of routine human activity. For example, basic accounting, record keeping, and problem solving were a few of these early applications. By and large, the automatic processing of such jobs proved the speed, economy, and reliability of electronic data processing.

A few years later, computer users began to use computers for applications that went far beyond the mere mechanization of manual operations. Process control systems, medical diagnosis systems, management information systems, computer-assisted instruction (CAI) systems, and storage and retrieval systems are a few recent examples.

Today, as a result of this rapid progress, most data-processing installations are facing an increase in the number of conventional applications as well as an increase in the scope and complexity of new system applications. To cope with these problems, a data-processing system must efficiently apply all of its resources—hardware, information, and human. These resources represent a considerable investment and must be used efficiently. Hardware and information resources must be readily available, so that the CPU can be kept busy processing data. Human resources must be relieved of tasks that the computing system can perform.

An *operating system* is an organized collection of programs and data that are specifically designed to manage the resources of a computer system and to facilitate the creation of computer programs and control their execution in that system. The primary purpose of operating systems is to reduce the cost of running problems (production programs) by increasing the use of the various computer system components and by avoiding lost time. Through the use of operating systems, the computer user delegates part of the burden of improved information processing efficiency to the computer itself.

For an operating system to achieve the high efficiencies of which present information processing systems are capable, it should be able to handle the following functions:

- Scheduling and performing input/output and related functions for programs.
- Interpreting human operator commands and/or control cards which describe to it the work to be done.
- Handling requests for all allocation of system resources.
- Controlling the stacking of jobs for continuous processing.
- Allocating space for external storage devices.
- Governing the operation of compilers, assemblers, and other manufacturer-provided software.
- Readying programs for execution.
- Monitoring the execution of processing programs.
- Protecting the various programs from one another.
- Providing a variety of user services.

Operating systems range in complexity from simple systems, which manage only simple functions, to very complex ones. In general, the more sophisticated the computer system, the more complex is the operating system required to manage its use. The philosophy underlying the operating system is that the computer should perform those operator tasks that it can do faster and more accurately, and that the computer should be kept operating as continuously and as effectively as possible.

A small-scale computer system may have a very minimal operating system which deals primarily with input/output activities. Minicomputers and microcomputers may not have operating systems, since they may be dedicated to particular tasks. In most medium- and large-scale systems, however, the operating system controls the total computer environment.

Perhaps the most complex operating system in existence is that used in the IBM System/370 computer. Operating System/370 (OS/370) is designed to be used with the largest and most powerful configurations of IBM System/370 computers. The OS/370 spans a range from the medium-scale computers using sequential scheduling up to the very largest computers operating with multiprogramming.

One of the major features of an operating system is that the computer operator can stack the jobs for continuous processing (batch processing), which, of course, greatly reduces the setup time between jobs. The system will then take advantage of all the facilities offered in the system by calling special programs, routines, and data as needed. The operator uses a *job-control language* to give instructions to the computer. The job-control language statements permit the computer operator to communicate wishes to the computer in a language that both parties can understand. The user may, for instance, use job-control language to request that a PL/1 program be compiled or that a program that has been stored in the auxiliary memory of the computer be executed. No matter what the request is, the operating system software processes job-control language statements. After checking the job-control statements to be sure that valid requests have been made, the operating system software locates, in auxiliary storage, needed programs and brings (loads) them into the internal memory of the computer.

Other operating system software is responsible for initiating input/output operations, checking and creating file labels, processing interrupt signals, responding to end-of-file conditions, error recovery, printing control messages for the computer operating, and a variety of other tasks.

The utility system component of an operating system assists the computer user by performing library maintenance, diagnostics, sorting and merging, and job reporting. Library maintenance routines consist of software that can add, delete, or copy programs into or from the various program libraries located in auxiliary storage. Diagnostic software provides the computer user with error messages when conditions exist that make it difficult or impossible for the computer to continue processing a job.

The sort and merge programs are designed to reorder data files. Job-reporting software records information that will be used to evaluate the efficiency with which the computer system is run and to bill computer users. This software stores the name of every program run on the computer, when the program was run and how much time it took, and the name of the person or department responsible for having the program run.

The operating system functions mentioned in this section are merely an indication of the type of programs that are included in operating systems. Additional operating system software is required for computer systems that support such features as time sharing, multiprogramming, virtual memory, or remote processing. In all cases, operating system software exists to provide the computer user with a workable system.

STRUCTURED PROGRAMMING

Structured programming is concerned with improving the programming process through better organization of programs and better programming notation to facilitate correct and clear descriptions of data and control structures.

Improved programming languages and organized programming techniques should help one produce programs that are (1) more understandable and therefore more easily modified and documented, (2) more economical to run because good organization and notation makes it easier for a compiler to "understand" the logic of the program, and (3) more correct and therefore more easily debugged.

The physical structure of a well-organized program corresponds to the sequence of steps in the algorithm being implemented. At a lower level, all parts of the implementation of one idea are grouped in a structure that clearly indicates how the various parts are selected and sequenced, and the relation of this idea to neighboring ideas.

The program should be expressed in the most natural and appropriate representation. The program should not contain a GOTO statement when a better representation is available. A program designer should, however, use a GOTO statement when the alternates are worse. Whenever a GOTO statement is used in a program, it should be accompanied by enough comments to make its purpose perfectly clear.

Some program designers limit their conception of structured programs to programs with structured control, and ignore the equally important factor of structured data. When the data has to be manipulated to fit the available data structure representations, the program becomes less readable. The program designer should inform the reader and the computer how to represent his data structure representations into computer representations, and then go about using his representations in his program.

A good language for structured programming has a carefully thought out assortment of control structures and data-structure definition facilities. If a language provides one kind of iterative control statement for counter-controlled loops, and others for loops controlled by a decision value of an expression, then the former should be used when the loop is expected to terminate as a result of the counter reaching its terminal value. The others should be used when some other condition is expected to terminate the loop. This makes it easier for a reader to distinguish between the "nature" of the control being exercised by the loop.

When a line of code is a continuation of a previous line or a subsidiary idea, it should be indented from the left margin established by the principal statement. When an indented code might be so complex or long as to obscure the principal level of control, then one should consider making this code into a procedure. A good "rule of thumb" is to try to get each principal idea to fit on a single page.

Structured programming is often associated with "top-down programming." Although this technique is a useful tool for explaining a program and illustrates how much nicer it is to explain a structured program than a haphazardly written one, it is unlikely that the art of programming can be restricted to the use of a single technique.

Chapter 13

Systems Design

Courtesy Data General Corp.

A *systems study* is the investigation made in a business to determine and develop needed informational improvements in specified areas. In some cases, the needed improvements will involve using a computer to achieve objectives. There are at least three reasons for making a systems study. First, substantial investment may be involved in using a computer, and a proper study reduces the risk of loss. Second, many of the common pitfalls associated with inadequate planning may be avoided. Finally, the study may point the way to substantial benefits.

In this chapter, we will examine an approach for a business to follow in conducting a system study.

SYSTEMS ANALYSIS AND DESIGN

Systems analysis and design is the evaluation and creation of computer-based information systems. Its relationship with computer programming is shown in Fig. 13-1. The process begins with the *recognition* of a *problem* or an opportunity (step 1). The problem may be specific, such as payroll for 120 employees, or the general idea that control could be enhanced by a more effective computer-based information system. In either case, the next step is *systems analysis* (step 2), which is to learn enough about the present system to design a better one. This step involves collecting, organizing, and evaluating facts about a system and the environment in which it operates. The systems analysis step is intended to evaluate the necessity and the economic and technological feasibility of a solution to the problem. The written report produced in the systems analysis step is the *feasibility study.*

The third step is *systems design.* Once it is determined that the project is feasible, a general outline of the proposed solution (feasibility study) is used to produce a detailed design. This detailed design is literally the specifications that are supplied to programming (step 5).

The fourth step is *equipment selection and acquisition.* The object of this step is to select and acquire the computer system that will do the job effectively at the lowest possible cost. This step is accomplished by converting the feasibility study to a nonhardware-oriented specification. To obtain the lowest price, computer vendors are invited to submit bids based on the speci-

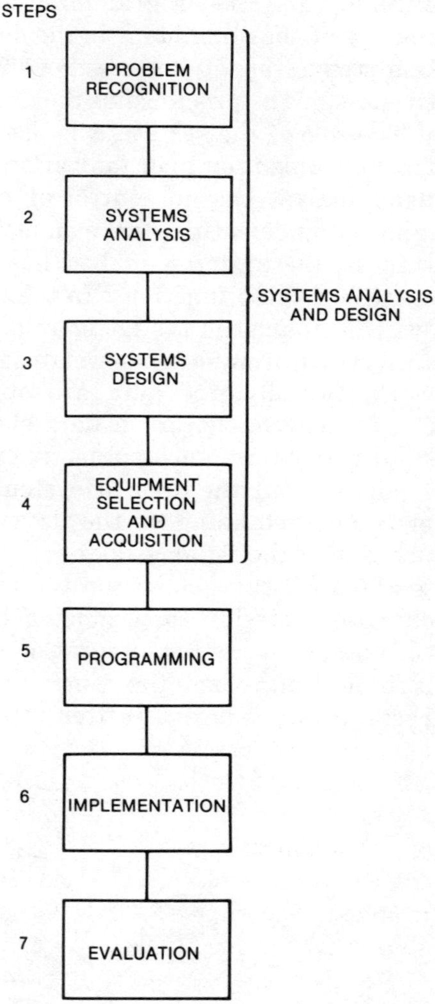

Fig. 13-1. Steps in the process of developing a computer-based system.

fications. The user evaluates the bids and selects the vendor from which to buy or lease the equipment.

The first four steps—problem recognition, systems analysis, systems design, and equipment selection and acquisition—constitute systems analysis and design. The remaining three steps are *programming*, *implementation*, and *evaluation*. The objectives of the programming and implementation steps (steps 5 and 6) are to write, test, and check out (debug) the programs for the new system. More personnel resources are expended for the programming and implementing steps than for any of the other steps in the development cycle. The evaluation step (step 7) involves reviewing and checking the effectiveness of the process and the finished product.

The role of the *systems analyst* in the last three steps varies from organization to organization. In some businesses, the systems analyst has no control or authority over the programming, implementing, or evaluating. However, in other instances, the systems analyst has total responsibility for and control of these functions. In this chapter, we will consider the systems analyst in the latter role.

Systems analysts accumulate a great deal of data as they work. Initially, the data are objective and appear as grid charts, flowcharts, or on data sheets. However, systems analysts also obtain much subjective information. They draw conclusions about the present system. First, they acquire a complete understanding of the data flow of the system. Second, they know the actions taken by each work center in the system. Third, they know the total activity of the system from data organization to product delivery. Fourth, they identify the possible areas for integration of functional areas. This step is important when the work progresses to systems design. Fifth, they produce a written report—the feasibility study.

" SORRY, OUR PRESIDENT IS OUT OF TOWN, OUR FIRST VICE-PRESIDENT IS OUT SICK, AND OUR SECOND VICE-PRESIDENT IS A COMPUTER. "

FEASIBILITY STUDY

The *feasibility study* analyzes the practicality and economics of installing a new system in one or more application areas within an organization. It is a familiar technique used for years by systems personnel. Its name describes its function—a study to determine the feasibility of a request for a change from one method to another in accomplishing certain processing functions. The request normally involves a major system change. Performing a study has the effect of averting certain problems because:

1. It forces the requestor to examine in detail the system under consideration and to reduce the proposal to writing.
2. It induces a broader look at the system under study. Many related functions must be examined, such as data conversion and input, audit and control, and the interrelationship with other departments and system functions.
3. It includes the participation and contribution of members of the user department. To often, the request for a new system technique comes from a source outside of the department most directly affected.
4. It prohibits a one-sided proposition from being adopted. Public acknowledgment that a study is in progress alerts other interested parties and gives them a chance to participate.
5. It enables the study to be reviewed in terms of other studies being performed and allows corporate management to properly forecast potential future expenditures.

A feasibility study should be as factual as possible and all-inclusive in examining the many factors that affect system selection. The study results in a document of a few pages, or a substantial report of many pages, depending on the magnitude of the system investigated. The study should outline the scope of the system, the objectives that such implementation hopes to accomplish, and the desired results as far as its contribution to overall corporate processing is concerned. In addition, it should be a vehicle to obtain approval from the user department manager and any other responsible individuals. Included with the goals must be an estimate of systems personnel-hours required, a general assignment of personnel, and a plan for integration of this request with other current and future projects.

Frequently, the study can deteriorate into a one-sided attempt to place an application on the computer, so it is important to outline both advantages. Such seemingly incidental factors as user training, user-department documentation, program maintenance, and forms design and cost should be included. The finished study should allow management to make an unbiased decision.

As the systems analyst or the systems team approaches a feasibility study, there are four basic solutions to the request for a computer system implementation:

1. *Develop a computer system as a solution*—In these days of microcomputers, minicomputers, large disk-storage units, virtual storage, multiprogramming, time sharing, and improved programming techniques, a computer may be the most obvious (although not necessarily the best) solution. Generally, the request for a system is proposed on the assumption that a computer system would be designed and implemented.
2. *Develop a manual system as a solution*—If a new system must be designed, then it is often less expensive and simpler to develop a manual system and operate it at least until it is error free. In addition, performing the job manually allows the user to develop a better understanding of what the system entails. Historical information can be accumulated, and the initial data base can be developed under the manual system. Later, automation of the system as experience and volume grow may offer the most efficient solution. Systems people should not be blinded by the computer. Sometimes, modifications to a manual system can accomplish corporate purposes.
3. *Develop an integrated manual and computer system as a solution*—With any computer system, there is some manual effort in its initial processes, but it may be determined that other intermediate steps or validation techniques could be performed more economically.

   Occasionally, when computerizing a system, one small part may require an inordinate amount of time for programming and testing, or it may require a large amount of hardware resources. To do this manually would be the best solution.

4. *Do not change the current method*—Frequently, a manual system or a manual/computer system cannot be improved enough to justify the expense involved in the change. Do not change something for the sake of change. It is important that the information processing manager select or recommend the method that is most beneficial to the company, whether it be computer, manual, or a combination. This selection cannot be done by viewing only cost savings as the determiner, but by evaluating all factors.

User-department participation in feasibility studies is important to success. This participation not only provides a better and more comprehensive study and system but also makes the user department feel that the system is its own.

Participation should be by a designated individual or individuals to provide continuity. On major projects it is important, if not imperative, that a member of the user department be assigned to work full time on the study. This lets the user staff member identify with the system from the beginning, understand why certain things are done or are not done, and have a say about how and what should be done. It also dispels any feelings among user-department personnel that a system is being imposed upon them. In addition, the participation promotes cooperation during the design, training, conversion, and implementation phases of the project.

A system must be designed for the user, not for the convenience of the computer. The best computer system can fail without user-department cooperation.

Several important steps need to be taken before actually starting a feasibility study. First, the systems analyst together with the requestor and appropriate systems and user-department personnel should:

1. Define, review, and confirm the study scope, objectives, and desired results in a preliminary form that includes the purpose, extent, and limitation of the study. This phase should point out the possible effects of the proposed system on other systems, sections, and departments. It may also result in dropping the project or significantly widening its scope.

2. Develop a preliminary study approach, timetable, and personnel requirements. This step will document a proposed study approach and estimate the following requirements of the study: total personnel-months, total elapsed time, number of systems personnel, number of user-department personnel, and number of other personnel.
3. Review the previous steps with management. The scope, objectives, desired results, study approach, timetable, and estimated personnel requirements should be reviewed with the user department head and head of the systems department. The objective of this review is to obtain approval for making the study, the scope and desired results of the study, and commitment of personnel and projected start date.

"WHAT MAKES YOU THINK I'M LYING ABOUT THE CAPABILITIES OF OUR COMPUTER SYSTEM?"

When time and personnel requirements are significant, a cost estimate for the feasibility study may be required. In many companies, for any significant project, it is necessary to obtain high-management approval and an assignment of project priority from the total company view.

All full-time team members of a feasibility study should be selected and be given any necessary education or orientation. It is helpful to give nonsystems team members a course in information processing systems or at least a short course covering flowcharts, vocabulary, and methods of documentation. It is also a good idea to have a member of the user department spend some time outlining the department work that the study will affect.

Once the team has been formed, the study plan can be reviewed, modified if necessary, and made formal. From this an outline of the various steps to be followed can be produced, including the company areas and/or departments to be contacted and external visits or contacts to be made to avoid duplication of work already done.

A timetable should be set up. It will either reinforce the original estimates or allow them to be modified prior to the actual start of the study.

One of the most important steps to include in the outline and timetable is periodic review and reporting. This should not be just a frequency, it should be specific dates and times; for instance, the first and third Monday of each month at 10:00 a.m. in the conference room. A set time will ensure that meetings occur, whereas a vague "once a month" may never come. Without reporting and review by the whole team and the respective section or department heads, a study may go off on an unwanted tangent or the timetable may become so warped that it cannot be fulfilled.

After establishing goals and objectives, the feasibility study team begins to collect information about the current system and its environment. All information gathered, including minutes of meetings, should be documented, categorized, indexed, and copied so that each member of the team has a complete set. Included in this documentation should be any suggestions or comments on the design of the system that have been made during the fact-finding phase. In most cases, some of the information will need expansion. This additional information should be documented and indexed, and, if appropriate, cross-keyed to previous documentation. As in all systems work, "documentation" is the byword.

Using the facts and documentation developed in earlier steps and any additional information needed, begin to develop possible solutions. Identify the areas of difficulty and examine their implications. This step helps determine the requirements of the system. A good system does not have to be automatic from beginning to end. Manual intervention may easily overcome some of the problem areas at certain points.

Develop as many alternative solutions and approaches as possible. Weed out those that are obviously unworkable. Then evaluate the remaining solutions from the standpoint of technical, economic, administrative, and implementation feasibility. Be sure to project the volumes for the current system and for the proposed systems three to five years in advance. A system that is marginal now may be a real money-saver at the increased volumes. In addition, it may show the total inability of the current system to cope with future volumes. After this preliminary evalution, select the preferred solutions for further evaluation. For the chosen solutions, you must next design approaches to the overall design, a systems-approach programming implementation, and evaluation.

First, develop the personnel requirement for analysts, programmers, training and followup, and user-department personnel. Second, using the estimated personnel requirement, develop a detailed schedule for the completion of the system. Actually, both the first and second points are handled together, as one depends on the other. Do not forget vacations and allowances for sick time, meetings, and any other factor that may require time of the project personnel. If omitted, these items can quickly wreck the best schedule.

Develop an economic evaluation. Develop all costs for the system, both recurring and nonrecurring. Costs deriving from the implementation of the system include:

- Cost of the computer hardware system.
- Cost of the software system.
- Additions to the programming and systems staff.
- Site preparation.
- Staff training.
- Systems analysis and design.
- Software development and checkout.
- User training.
- Security.
- Physical facilities (floor space, lighting, heating, and air conditioning).
- Conversion.
- Printed forms.

The final report on the feasibility of a system should be produced professionally. A hastily typed, slapped-together document with sloppy handwritten material makes poor backup and starts readers off with a negative attitude. A good feasibility report contains at least the following:

1. A *summary* that states the recommended solution to the request or problem. This summary should be the first page of the report.
2. A list of any *new equipment* necessary, with details of why the particular equipment was chosen.
3. An estimated *cost* of the system, including a future projection of the costs and savings for the next three to five years.
4. A list of *intangible benefits.*
5. If new jobs have been created, then new *job descriptions* should be written. Identify old jobs that are no longer necessary.
6. A recommended *schedule* for design, programming, system checkout, training, conversion, implementation, and documentation.
7. An estimate of the *useful life* of the system.
8. Indicate the future growth pattern and the *ease of system expansion.*
9. A list of the *advantages* and *disadvantages* of the system.
10. A *conclusion* which provides some detail.
11. An *index* if the report is large enough to warrant it.

During the preparation phases of a system feasibility study, the systems analyst's greatest assets are an *open mind* and a *willingness to be convinced.* One should avoid tunnel vision by looking at all solutions.

Chapter 14

The Computer Center

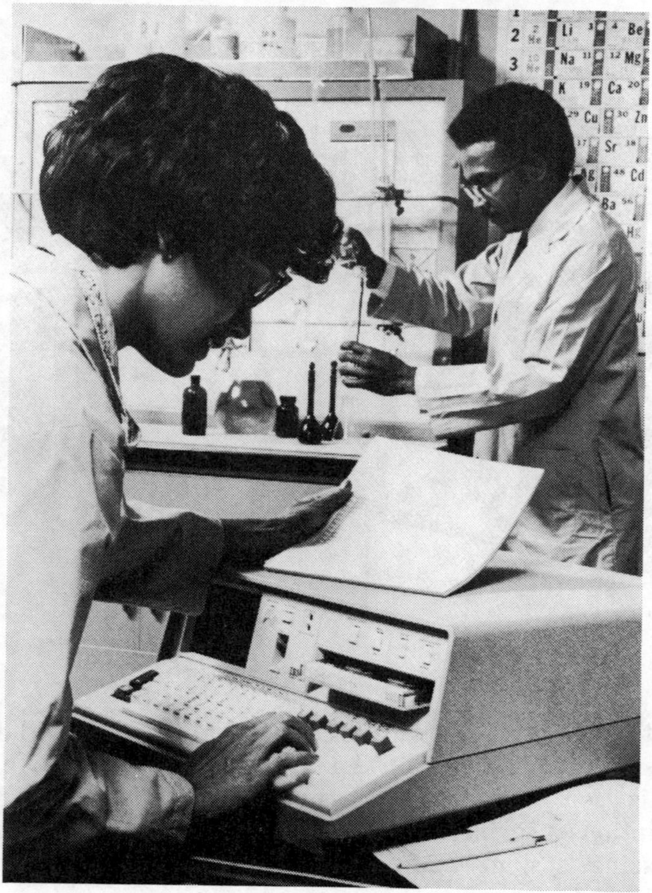

Courtesy IBM Corp.

A data-processing center is significant in the overall organization of a company not only because of the expense of the equipment, software, and personnel but also because of its role as a service department which accepts input data, performs processing and storage, and provides information (see Fig. 14-1). If the function is not well managed, it can seriously impair the activities of the entire organization.

All of the principles of good organization and management that apply to any business or organization apply to the management of data-processing facilities. While data processing may be unique in the type of service that it renders and possibly in its location in the overall organizational structure, it is nevertheless composed of people, machines, responsibilities, and production deadlines.

Courtesy IBM Corp.

Fig. 14-1. A data-processing center.

In this chapter, we will discuss the placement of the data-processing function within the structure of a company and the organization of a data-processing center. The following job descriptions are included in this chapter: manager of data processing, systems analyst, programmer, computer operator, and clerical jobs.

ORGANIZATIONAL CONCEPTS

There is no universal or standard pattern for the location of the data-processing center within the organizational structure of a company. Individual company differences influence the nature and location of the data-processing function.

Traditionally, the data-processing functions were placed under the financial managers, primarily because most of the original information processing applications were related to accounting functions (e.g., payroll, accounts receivable, and general accounting). It was, therefore, somewhat natural that financial managers (usually the controller) should play a large role in the administration of data-processing activities.

Today, there is a trend in the more advanced data-processing functions to have a vice-president devote full time to the responsibility (see Fig. 14-2). The designation of a vice-president of data processing can have a positive effect because it reflects a progressive attitude toward data-processing activities. It recognizes the need to be flexible and to cope with changes, new technologies, and the state of the economy. The emergence and importance of data-processing activities in many organizations warrants suitable organizational status for these functions.

A major requirement is to develop data-processing awareness in all managers and in the rank and file, so that they can appreciate the role of the computer. The managers of a company should be able to identify and articulate problems with the systems analysts and programmers.

Unless data processing has top management backing, the organization will be ineffective in its total systems and management information efforts and in its capability to cope with newer technologies. A lesser reporting relationship will not

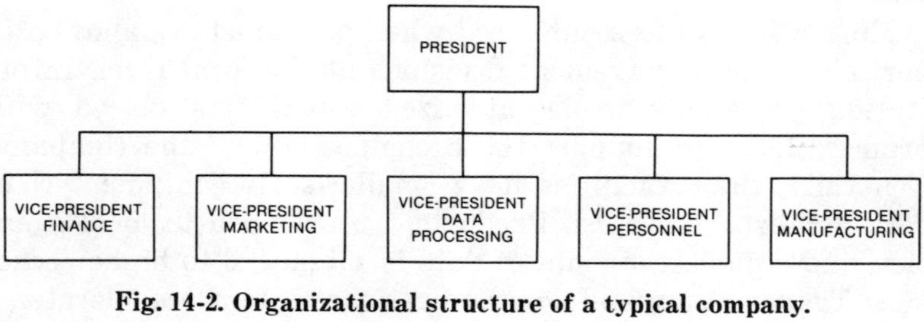

Fig. 14-2. Organizational structure of a typical company.

have the authority, influence, and knowledge of management's requirements to attain full benefit from the new technology and to get the support of the departments of the company affected by proposed changes. In many small businesses, the function of the vice-president of information may be combined with one or more additional responsibilities (e.g., vice-president of marketing, personnel, and information).

A company or organization may either centralize or decentralize management and staff activities. When centralized, management is concentrated at one location to obtain the benefits of greater specialization and ease of coordination, communication, and top-level decision making. Generally, if management is centralized, information processing is also centralized so that it can support the staff. In fully centralized computer operations, all data to be processed are submitted or transmitted to one central location—the principal offices of the company. Information is provided to the staff agencies at the central location, and certain reports may be forwarded to field locations. Communications and data transmission costs are usually high. Centralized computer facilities ordinarily have larger-scale computer systems than do comparable decentralized locations. Specialized applications dealing with simulation, modeling, operations research, or other management science techniques may be in use.

On the other hand, in a decentralized operation, the authority and responsibility for results may be as far down the line as efficient management permits. Decentralization may imply that the size and volume of the organization's data-processing needs are too unwieldly to control from a central point. It may take too long to send facts up the line and wait for the decision to come back down. The basic concept of decentralization is that facts are gathered and decisions are made on the scene of action.

Motivation is often enhanced when personnel are allowed to participate in management decisions at the local level. Information processing is decentralized when it is placed with branch offices to support those components of the company. Generally, these facilities have smaller-scale equipment than do centralized facilities. Products are provided to local agencies, and a modest amount of data is submitted to higher echelons. Transmission and communications costs are moderate.

Some people have envisioned the role of the computer as encouraging a swing to the centralized concept because unlimited amounts of data are readily available at the home office. The lower cost and higher processing output of newer computers (especially minicomputers and microcomputers), however, encourage the decentralized concept. Communications costs are

"THAT'S RIGHT, MR. DAVIS... ACCORDING TO OUR COMPUTER, YOU ARE NONEXISTENT."

beginning to approach hardware costs for highly centralized operations. Data transmission costs are lower when decentralized units support widely separated branches or divisions.

DATA-PROCESSING ORGANIZATION

The internal organization of the data-processing function may vary, depending on the size and nature of the business it services. Since these and other factors may influence the exact organizational structure of the data-processing function, only a general type of organization is shown (see Fig. 14-3).

COMPUTER-CENTER PERSONNEL

Most companies and organizations have job descriptions which identify job titles and clearly describe all job functions required of an employee. Although titles vary between com-

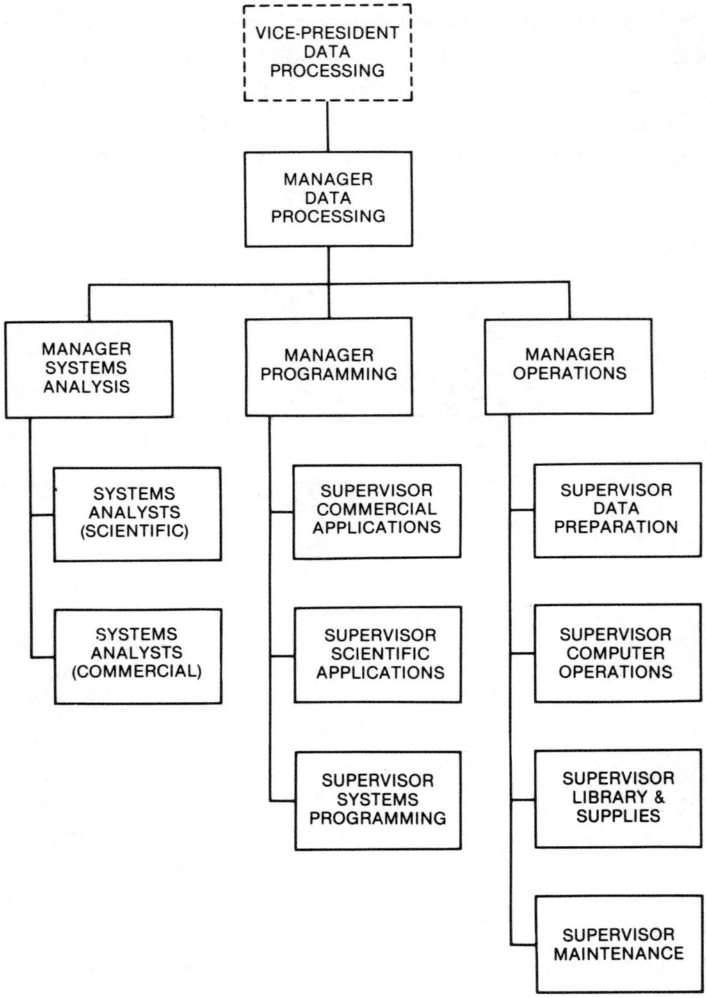

Fig. 14-3. Organizational structure of a typical data-processing function.

puter installations, the following general job descriptions cover the most common data-processing positions.

Manager of Data Processing

At the head of most computer installations or departments is someone who coordinates and directs the overall efforts of systems analysts, programmers, computer operators, and others involved with the use of the computer. Such department heads may have titles like *manager of data processing, manager of computer services,* etc. They generally report to a top executive of the organization.

Management of data processing requires considerable experience, good management skills, and, in most companies, a college degree. Salaries vary widely depending on the size of the staff and the organizational level within the company.

Systems Analyst

The work of the *systems analyst* involves both the collection of facts regarding the information requirements of the computer user and the analysis of those facts. Systems analysts formulate efficient patterns of information flow from its sources to the computer, define the computer process necessary to turn the raw data into useful information, and plan the distribution and use of the resulting information.

In smaller computer installations, the functions of systems analysis and programming are frequently combined; while in the larger installations, they are usually separate. No matter what the title, persons performing the analysis have to understand the problem and interpret it correctly, and, at the same time, know how to use the computer effectively. They must bring to every problem a deep insight that will enable them to reduce it to its fundamental information-flow terms.

An engineering-scientific analyst may work on such problems as tracking a satellite or controlling a nuclear process. The analyst must consult with and understand top-level scientists and mathematicians and develop mathematical equations that describe the problem and its solution. Such an analyst, of course, must have at least one degree in mathematics, physics, or an appropriate engineering science.

On the other hand, while a formal educational background in business administration is helpful for systems analysts who specialize in business data processing, it is not always required. Business experience and the ability to reason logically are important, however. Typical of the projects that a business systems analyst may work on are the development of an integrated production, inventory control, and cost analysis system.

An area of increasing importance, as businesses grow bigger and more diversified, is operations research. This field is an especially challenging specialty, involving the analyst in the highest echelons of decision making in any business or organization. The analyst must formulate a mathematical model of a management problem and use it to provide a quantitative basis for making decisions. Many organizations require that systems analysts have two or more years of programming experience in addition to a college degree.

"THIS ABOVE ALL, MY SON: STOCK UP ON SPARE PARTS FOR YOUR MINICOMPUTER!"

Programmer

After the analysts have laid out the solution for a problem or the design of an information processing system, it goes to a *programmer*. It is the programmer's job to devise a detailed plan for solving the problem on the computer. This plan is called the *program,* and in final form it consists of a series of coded, step-by-step instructions that make the computer perform the desired operations. In most instances, the analysts or the programmer will have prepared a flowchart which graphically illustrates the flow of data through the system and what actions are to be taken when a given condition is met or not met. The programmer generally employs one of several com-

Courtesy IBM Corp.

Fig. 14-4. A programmer "debugging" (finding and correcting errors) in a computer program.

puter languages to communicate with the machine. The programmer checks the program by preparing sample data and testing it on the computer. The programmer also "debugs" the program by making several trial runs with actual data from the project (see Fig. 14-4). To complete the entire programming process for a large project may take several months or longer, and the program may take up several volumes of flowcharts and listings of program steps.

Programmers often work as part of a team, with different levels of responsibility (see Fig. 14-5). Depending on the size

Courtesy IBM Corp.

Fig. 14-5. Programmers often work as part of a team.

of the project, there may be a programming manager or a senior programmer leading the team, with a staff of programmers, junior programmers, coders, and trainees. The term *coder* is sometimes used instead of junior programmer. The name derives from the fact that machine instructions are often called machine *codes*. A coder takes detailed flowcharts and produces coded instructions.

In some organizations, coders and programmer trainees translate the programmers' instructions into the codes understood by the particular computer being used. The junior programmers write instructions from the detailed flowcharts developed by the programmers and sometimes receive the opportunity to write specific parts of a broad program. In this way, they develop the skills and experience needed to develop programs on their own. Those who take a full range of computer courses leading to a computer science degree at a college or university can generally skip the initial training-level positions in their first job and go right into full-fledged programming assignments.

The varieties of problems programmers deal with, the different computers they may work with, and the various information processing languages they must know demand a high degree of ingenuity, experience, imagination, and, above all, the ability to think logically. Well-trained and experienced programmers can write programs for many different types of problems.

Computer Operator

Look into any busy data-processing center, and you will see several men and women pushing buttons, changing magnetic tapes, flicking through punched cards, and in other ways supervising the operations of the computer (see Fig. 14-6). Computer operators, those who push the buttons and watch the lights, actually do much more than that. They review computer programs and instruction sheets to determine the necessary equipment setup for the job. When the control panel lights indicate that the machine has stopped for some reason, the console operator must investigate and correct the stoppage, or call in a maintenance engineer if the cause is equipment malfunc-

Courtesy NCR Corp.

Fig. 14-6. Computer operators using the equipment in a computer center.

tion. The console operator keeps a log of the work done by the computer and writes reports on its use. In large installations, the console operator is assisted by tape librarians and handlers and the operators of peripheral equipment (sorters, collators, high-speed printers, tape-drive units, etc.).

Courtesy Department of Health, Education, and Welfare

Fig. 14-7. Tape librarians maintaining magnetic-tape files.

Computer operators usually serve an apprenticeship, during which their main duties are inserting punched cards in card readers and punches, inserting forms in printers, mounting reels of magnetic tape on tape drives, and generally readying peripheral devices for operation. More-experienced operators are usually responsible for actually manipulating the controls that actuate the computer system. The console operator holds a position of much responsibility since mistakes can be time-consuming and costly. Employers require a high-school education, and many of them prefer some college. A college degree is very helpful for those who aspire to progress into programming or systems analysis. Many computer operators have successfully advanced to positions as supervisors of operations, programmers, and managers of data-processing centers.

Clerical

Clerical jobs vary, but usually include manual coding of data, verification of totals used for accounting controls, maintaining libraries of magnetic-tape files (see Fig. 14-7), and maintaining operating schedules and logs of operation. These tasks provide good on-the-job training for high-school graduates who wish to learn something about computing. These tasks are sometimes "apprenticeship" jobs for computer operators.

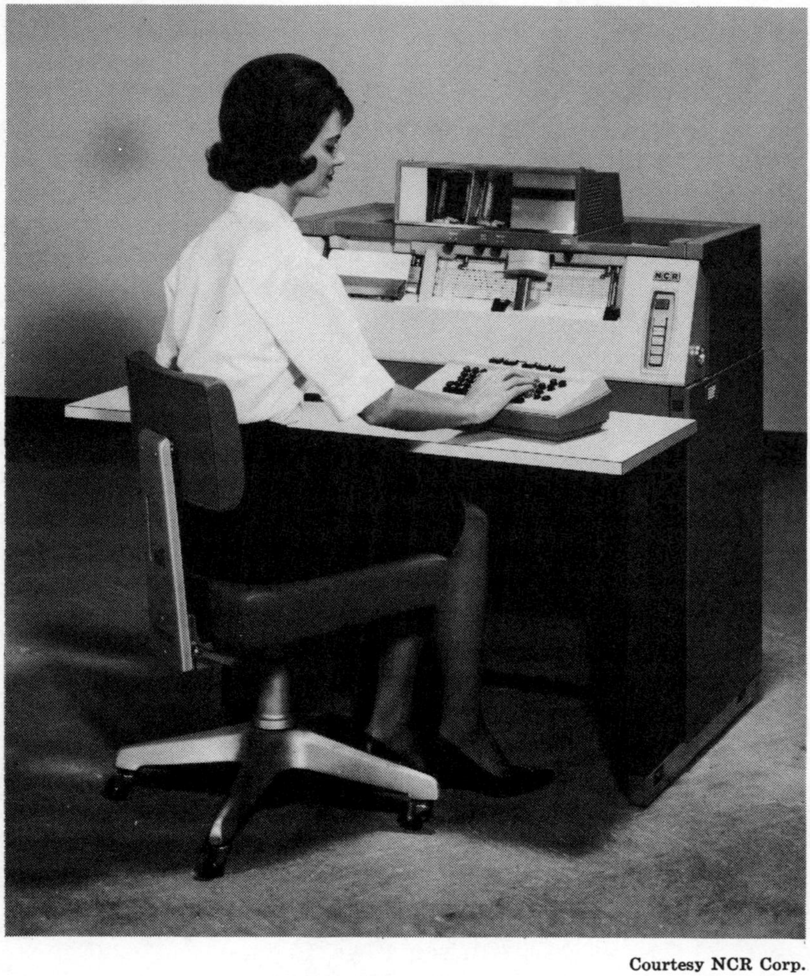

Courtesy NCR Corp.

Fig. 14-8. Keypunch operator.

Keypunching

Keypunching of data into punched cards or paper tape and operating other key-driven, data-recording devices require an ability to type reasonably well (30 to 40 words per minute) and an ability to work in a fairly noisy environment. After two or three weeks of intensive training, a high-school graduate may start as a keypunch operator (see Fig. 14-8).

Chapter 15

The Future

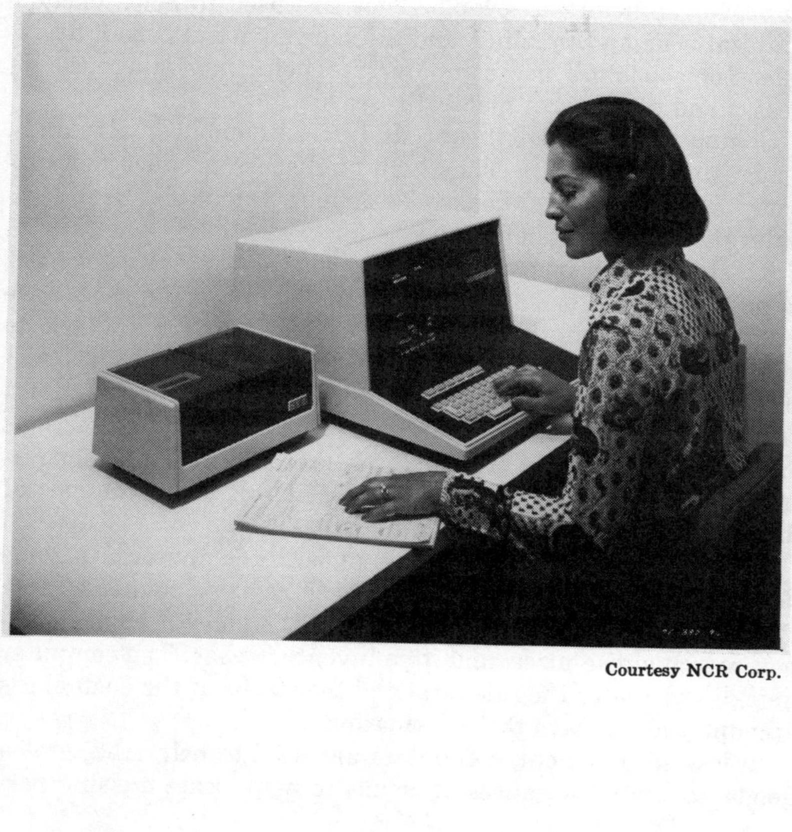

Courtesy NCR Corp.

Computers have been used to process data since only the late 1940s. In about thirty years they have become a major factor in our economy. They influence our lives in the fields of science, business, education, medicine, industry, and many other fields. Computers are used by corporations, schools, small businesses, governmental agencies, hospitals, and thousands of other establishments.

In the field of education, computers enable students and teachers to perform more effectively. With their assistance, persons may delve more deeply into areas that were once thought too time-consuming for hand-calculation methods. Imaginative new devices and techniques have been developed to help students learn. As an example, students may sit at a typewriter-like device (called a terminal) and communicate directly with a computer.

In the field of medicine, computers are being used to help improve the health of people. They are used to help schedule hospital beds and to admit and discharge patients from hospitals. Some doctors use computers to help them diagnose illnesses and to perform medical research.

Computers help engineers design automobiles, airplanes, bridges, and buildings. They help publishers produce newspapers, magazines, and books. Telephone companies use computers to route telephone calls.

The business world affects us all, whether or not we wish it to do so, and the business world functions with the assistance of computer systems. Business concerns use computers to maintain records, pay employees, keep track of inventory, control manufacturing, and perform hundreds of other functions.

A bank may record hundreds of thousands of transactions daily. Computers have become essential to the continued operation of banks. Rapid, accurate processing of large volumes of data is necessary in the banking business.

Retail businesses find increasing use for computers. In some department stores, a clerk using a cash register connected to a computer keys in a type-of-sale code, customer account number, merchandise price, and item inventory code. The computer quickly calculates the sale total and the status of the customer's account and displays the information.

In law enforcement, computers are used to help trace stolen goods, to study the causes of crime, to help locate missing per-

"IT'S A DISPOSABLE COMPUTER... YOU SOLVE ONE PROBLEM AND THROW IT AWAY!"

sons and wanted fugitives, and to research methods of preventing crime.

Computers are used to reserve seats on airplanes, to help keep track of passenger baggage, and to help pilots safely fly airplanes. A computer aboard the giant Boeing 747 jetliner has been programmed to actually "fly" the airplane.

In the area of entertainment and novelty, computers have been programmed to play chess, compose original music, write poetry, and draw pictures.

But what about the future? If computers have made such a large impact on our present daily lives, what can we expect from them next? Let us consider the trends in computer hardware and software, and then look at some possible future uses of computers.

COMPUTER HARDWARE TRENDS

Computer technology throughout the world has improved at an unbelievably fast pace during the past two decades. In the 1960s, computers were used in ways not even envisioned in the 1950s. In the next two decades, one can expect the computer to be used in many applications not envisioned today. Every few years a rapid change in computer hardware and technology occurs, thus making older systems obsolete. In this way, the computer industry is quite similar to the automobile industry, which replaces its older models each year.

The ENIAC (*E*lectronic *N*umerical *I*ntegrator *A*nd *C*alculator) contained 19,000 vacuum tubes, weighed about 30 tons, and filled an area of over 139.35 m^2 (1500 square feet; the size of an average three-bedroom home). This enormous device, developed in 1946, could perform 5000 additions per second. Today, computers are much smaller, much lighter, and can perform as many as 100,000,000 additions per second. The new machines are more reliable than the old, require less power to operate, and produce considerably less heat. All the early computers had to be placed in air-conditioned rooms. Today, computers can be placed anywhere—in an office, in one's home, in an airplane, on a ship, in a missile or spacecraft, in a bank, or in a hospital.

The IBM System/360 Model 195 is an example of a large computer. This machine can process instructions at a rate of one every 54 billionths of a second. In that time, light, traveling at a rate of 344,991 km (186,281 miles) per second, can move only 16.15 m (53 feet). The Model 195 can solve 15 problems simultaneously. Its capacity would allow the literary content of a library with more than 3,000,000 books to be stored, and it would be able to locate and read any one of these books in less than one second. This multimillion-dollar computer can be used in a variety of applications—airline reservations, weather predictions, space exploration, etc.

In contrast with the large computers are *minicomputers* and *microcomputers*. Minicomputers cost only a few thousand dollars, are about the size of a small suitcase, and can perform operations similar to the large computers at rates approximating as many as 600,000 additions per second. What is the future of minicomputers and microcomputers?

The minicomputer is currently very widely used in industry, process control, and education. Continued expansion is expected in its use in industrial plants, hospitals, laboratories, secondary and elementary schools, colleges, manufacturing plants, government, military, and other areas. In business, the minicomputer will be used to a much greater extent than it is now. The small businessman will be more tempted to develop his own computer center with a minicomputer now that computer manufacturers are beginning to offer software and systems support for these machines.

Since the cost of the minicomputer, when contrasted to a larger computer, is extremely low, minicomputers will be available for use by personnel other than professional programmers. Because these machines are relatively inexpensive, management will not be concerned with idle CPU time. In elementary and secondary schools and colleges, the minicomputer will be used in many new and different ways.

Many larger businesses and governmental agencies will use a network of minicomputers, located throughout the country or world. The trend will be toward decentralization of the data-processing function. Many businesses have found that a network of minicomputers can often do the job more economically than one large computer system. In a network, if one minicomputer becomes "ill," a substitute is readily available. Due to the economy of the minicomputer, management would not be overly concerned if one was used as a "spare." When not needed in the network, the minicomputer could be assigned other tasks.

Since microcomputers are much smaller and cheaper than minicomputers, entirely new application areas are developing for their use. Although microcomputers are often slower than minicomputers, they are lower in cost, more flexible, and require less design time. We can expect to see several billion of these machines in use at the turn of the century. Some of the future uses of microcomputers will be to control intelligent terminals, building-security systems, automobile electrical systems, medical equipment, retail cash registers, fire and burglary alarm systems, and the "home computer system."

Future computers will probably make extensive use of *firmware;* that is, special programs (called *microprograms*) within the hardware that will be able to simulate many types of ma-

chines. When this revolution occurs, it will make programming a computer and conversion from one computer to another much easier. Users will simply utilize a basic language instruction that will be interpreted through hardware (using a firmware concept) to emulate other machines.

It seems reasonable to predict that future computers will be faster, more reliable, cheaper, and easier to use. In order to simplify them, one can expect computer manufacturers to develop new human/machine interface devices.

Credit-card readers, keyboard numbering devices, and small display terminals will undoubtedly be widely employed in future computers. A simple miniterminal consists of a display used in conjunction with a touch-tone telephone. This display might be limited to displaying 20 to 100 characters, or even just ten- or twelve-digit numbers. Simple terminals like these could be used in low-cost computer communications systems, the type that might be found in homes in the 1980s.

Cathode-ray-tube and television displays will be much more common in future computer applications, and the cost of these devices should decrease considerably. The *plasma panel,* another type of display device, can be expected to be used as a low-cost terminal for computer systems during the late 1970s and 1980s.

Semiconductor memories are available on many computers today. It is believed that this type of memory will find widespread use in future computer memory systems. The primary characteristic of tomorrow's computers will thus be much the same as today's—an improved price/performance ratio.

When Christopher Columbus set foot in the New World in 1492, he did not know where he was or how he got there. It took the world years to learn of his courageous journey. When Neil Armstrong stepped on the surface of the moon in 1969, he knew exactly where he was, having followed a precisely preplanned route, and the entire world was watching him. In less than 500 years, people's ability to communicate has advanced from its most primitive forms to an astounding level of sophistication.

Computer centers are now being connected to one another via communications facilities. An airline reservations office in London, England, can communicate with a computer center in New York via satellite. Large companies can link facilities on opposite sides of the Pacific Ocean.

This developing relationship between computer and telecommunications technology is one of the most important events of our times. The two technologies complement each other; in combination, their power is multiplicative, not additive. Computers will one day control immense communications switching centers, and these in turn will make available the power of computers to millions of users in remote locations. The present trend toward large-scale, time-shared computers and the development of advanced, so-called "intelligent" terminals seem to indicate that within the next decade a large portion of the computers used will be communications-oriented.

The major computer problems of the future will be carryovers from the present. First, there is the people problem: the need to teach students the use of computer processing techniques and to train vast numbers of people to become productive members of the computer industry. Then, there are the social implications of private and governmental data banks, vast nationwide information networks and the threats they pose, if any, to the privacy of individuals. And with data traffic exceeding voice traffic in the 1970s, data communications faces the problem of overloaded and unreliable transmission lines, which could seriously hamper the growth of computer processing.

In summary, there will be dramatic progress in every important area of hardware for computers. Furthermore, the cost of any particular computation or operation will decrease steadily and significantly for the next several decades. The most will be decreased at least by a factor of 100 and probably by a factor of 1000. A smaller decrease will occur in the cost of terminals, perhaps by only a factor of 10 or 20. Even so, this means that the cost of a very powerful computer system will be well within the price range of a small business or of an average family.

COMPUTER SOFTWARE TRENDS

It is doubtful if many major software functions will be developed in the next few years. Complex operating systems for machines such as the IBM System/370 have been designed to meet user needs for some time to come. In other words, the software designers have adequately specified all the major functions needed for applications foreseeable in the immediate future.

Programming languages are the primary means by which a person communicates with a computer. The use of current programming languages is not likely to change drastically for a number of years. In 1980, users will probably still be using FORTRAN, COBOL, BASIC, PL/1, RPG, and APL. Two of the newer programming languages, PASCAL and LOGO, will probably be used more widely in educational institutions.

As computers become more common in schools, homes, and businesses, one can expect more people to learn computer languages. Within the next decade, BASIC will very likely have widespread use in secondary and elementary schools. For the distant future, we should expect to see the development and use of natural languages (for example, English) as well as languages designed for specific application areas (for example, languages for solving medical problems, educational problems, engineering problems, etc.).

Recently, a number of researchers have designed and implemented "two-dimensional" programming languages (picture- and symbol-oriented) as opposed to the previously mentioned "one-dimensional" languages (text- and character-oriented). These may become increasingly important in human/machine communications.

In future computers, one can also expect that many functions now performed by software will be implemented by *microprograms* in a read-only computer memory (firmware). Today, several of the microcomputers (Commodore PET, Radio Shack TRS-80, etc.) have BASIC language interpreters in ROM (*R*ead-*O*nly *M*emory).

In the future, computer manufacturers will supply more application-oriented software with their machines. Let us look at how computers might be used in the future home, the future hospital, the future bank, etc.

FUTURE APPLICATIONS

Home

The future home might be similar to that of Mr. and Ms. Winslow. This home contains three bedrooms, a family room, a kitchen, two bathrooms, and a large play room. Located in the kitchen is a family control center, the heart of which is a computer. There is a keyboard input device, a voice recognition/response device, and a storage device. Ms. Winslow (or Mr. Winslow, if he's the family cook) uses the center to conjure up nutritionally balanced, tasty, eye-pleasing meal plans. She simply supplies the computer with an appropriate code for any of several major food categories. The computer then causes a printout with a full dinner menu planned around entrees such as ham, beef, chicken, trout, lobster, veal, lamb, pork, game, eggs, and cheese. For finicky or allergy-prone diners, substitutions can be obtained by entering additional costs. Ms. Winslow is always free to place new menus in the computer memory.

Ms. Winslow also uses the center for typing her shopping lists, writing letters, monitoring appliances, calculating requirements for drapery material, obtaining suggestions for re-

arranging room furniture, keeping track of the household budget, ordering grocery and clothing items from the computerized store, and as a ready address and telephone file.

Mr. Winslow uses the computer to keep track of his investments, to prepare tax reports, to take a course in business law, to take care of his checkbook accounting, and to solve problems related to his work. For example, he can use the computer to prepare budgets and manpower forecasts for his different business projects. He, like the rest of the family, may also use the computer in his spare time to learn a foreign language; e.g., Spanish. The computer retrieves from its memory a teaching program for Spanish, remembering where the student left off at the end of the last lesson. The Spanish lessons are programmed to proceed at just the pace that matches a student's learning rate.

The computer center can drive clocks throughout the house, control the air-conditioning and heating system, change television channels at predetermined times, control the stereo music center, open and close doors and windows, perform family medical diagnoses, monitor the home burglar alarm, monitor phone calls, and store family medical records.

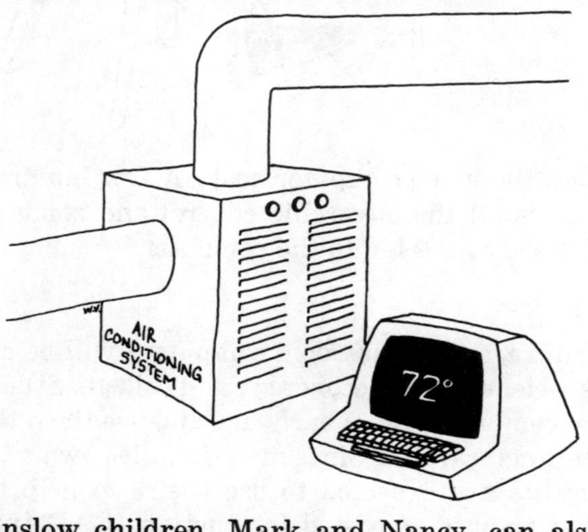

The Winslow children, Mark and Nancy, can also use the computer center. Mark is in elementary school and checks all his arithmetic and language problems by computer. He also uses the computer to give him drill in arithmetic problems and new mathematical concepts such as fractions and square roots.

Nancy, who is in college, can use the computer as a homework aid in practically all her courses. When their lessons are done, the children can play a game of tic-tac-toe, blackjack, backgammon, Ping-Pong, chess, or Space War with the computer.

What does the home computer cost? A few hundred dollars, which includes all the electronic control and communications devices that are connected to the computer.

Education

In the future, small classroom computers will be common in all schools—elementary, secondary, and college. Students learn to program computers at an early age and use them throughout their educational careers. Since most families own a home computer, students are expected to use theirs to help them with homework. *C*omputer-*A*ssisted *I*nstruction (CAI) in which the computer presents tutorial and drill practice information to the student, is a feature of all schools. For example, you may engage in the following conversation with a computer. The underlined remarks are yours:

HELLO
HI
HOW ARE YOU THIS MORNING?
FINE. HOW ARE YOU?
OK. ARE YOU BUSY TODAY?
FAIRLY BUSY. I AM COMMUNICATING WITH 1263 USERS
RIGHT NOW.
WILL YOU HELP ME WITH A PROBLEM?
OF COURSE. TELL ME THE PROBLEM.
I HAVE AN ITEM IN MY STORE THAT COSTS $18. TELL ME
THE SELLING PRICE I SHOULD CHARGE SO I WILL HAVE A PROFIT
OF 12% OF THE SELLING PRICE.
$20.45. DO YOU WANT TO KNOW HOW I COMPUTED THIS ANSWER?
NO THANKS. YOU TOLD ME WHAT I WANT TO KNOW.
DO YOU HAVE ANOTHER PROBLEM?
YES. WHAT SHOULD I BUY MY MOTHER-IN-LAW FOR
HER BIRTHDAY?
SORRY. I DO NOT GET INVOVED WITH IN-LAW PROBLEMS.
DO YOU HAVE ANOTHER PROBLEM?
NO. GOODBYE FOR NOW.
SO LONG.

The computer almost seems literally to understand what you want. It does not, really, because the computer has been pro-

grammed to give the proper responses. Nevertheless, you are now able to have realistic conversations with the computer.

Entertainment

In the future, you will have a wide choice over what you hear or watch on your home entertainment center. You can watch the news, a sporting event, a musical play, a travelog, an educational program, a soap opera, or a movie. You can dial programs you have missed or those you would like to see again. You can even select the commercials that you want to watch. You can also just listen to a good musical program. The cost is by the program, and the computer, of course, automatically deducts the proper cost from your bank checking account.

Small computers and tv receivers can also be connected together. An entire week of favorite television programs can be programmed and the computer assigned to do one of several ingenious things: signal an alarm prior to air time, turn on the set, or control the videotape recorder.

Entertainment parks, such as Disney World in Orlando, Florida, will use computers to control rides (like Space Mountain) and to move the arms, legs, ears, and eyes of all their animated characters (see Fig. 15-1).

Fig. 15-1. Future animated characters will either be controlled by computers, or will use movement instructions produced by computers.

Transportation

In the future, computers will be used to control the operations of ships. It will be technically feasible to have unmanned ships sailing from San Francisco to Kobe, Japan.

Computers will handle most of the operating details of jetliners, allowing the captain of the ship to keep watch only for unusual occurrences. Computers switch equipment on and off, control aircraft centers of gravity, communicate with other airplane computers enroute, determine the proper speed and altitude of the plane, run through preflight checklists, and perform automatic takeoffs and landings. The onboard computer takes account of winds, storms, temperature, and other aircraft. When landing, the computer automatically adjusts the speed and angle of descent of the plane so that a perfect landing can be made without any action on the pilot's part. Maintenance computers give advance notice of needed repairs or replacement of aircraft components, and have practically eliminated flight delays or cancellation of flights because of mechanical problems.

Future surface transportation systems will be available that permit speeds of 250 mph through densely populated cities. Computers will be used to design, test, and run these systems. Their bullet-shaped vehicles produce almost no pollutant byproducts and are relatively vibration-free.

Medicine

Future hospitals will use centralized computer systems to perform a large amount of patient care. A patient entering the hospital will be admitted, diagnosed, and monitored by the computer. Electroencephalogram (brain-wave recording) analysis will be performed by computer. Electrocardiograms (heart waveforms) will be read and interpreted accurately by computer. Phonocardiograms (heart sounds and murmurs) will be processed and analyzed by computer. The timing and relative amplitudes of heart sounds are displayed on a crt device along with the onset, duration, relative amplitudes, and relative frequency information of any systolic or diastolic murmurs that have been detected.

In the future, doctors will have display terminals connected to medical information banks for consultation purposes. You

will be able to "dial the doctor" and be connected to a medical computer system which can make a first-level medical diagnosis. This system asks questions, prescribes medication, and gives instructions on whether to go to the hospital emergency room immediately or to your family doctor or clinic tomorrow. Some medical systems will even have access to your own medical history. Computers will help stamp out all forms of diseases so that people can enjoy healthier, more satisfying lives.

Robots

In the future, robots will be walking, making decisions, and thinking, as it were, for themselves. Their minds are composed of programmed computers. They use television-like cameras for eyes to send inputs to the computer. For example, if a robot on an exploration trip bumps into an obstacle which it has not previously sensed, the television camera and cat-whisker antennas (wire sensors) send data to the computer that in effect ask, "What do I do now?" The computer then switches to an "I'll-walk-around-it" or a "Let-me-take-a-look" program.

Domestic robots will be available to perform a variety of routine household chores. These chores include preparing some meals, mowing the lawn, cleaning up after meals, babysitting, washing clothes, watering plants, or even fixing the toaster. Robots will be used to perform tasks that are boring, dangerous, or that have to be performed in hostile environments, such as the floor of the ocean. When NASA sends a space vehicle to Mars, robots may be the first to explore this dangerous terrain. The temperature of the surface of Venus is about 900°F;

Jupiter has a poisonous atmosphere and crushing gravity; pressures on the bottom of the ocean can crush vessels with steel hulls several inches thick. People are unable to explore these areas, but robots impervious to heat, poisons, and pressure are able to.

Mobile robots will be used in industry to perform operations in various manufacturing processes.

Business

In the future, computers linked to common information banks will be common in law and medicine as well as in education institutions. Criminal justice information systems will allow all allied organizations to share information, expand local data files, and analyze interdependent problems, such as personnel utilization and court docketing. Medical information systems will provide doctors and hospitals with a central source of up-to-date data concerning all known diseases and medical procedures. School terminals connected to a central educational system will allow access to vast amounts of general information.

You will be able to "dial the encyclopedia" and obtain rapid access to a body of factual information at least as large as a good current encyclopedia. The requests can be spoken, and the response is either spoken or displayed on a visual device.

You will be able to "dial the store" and obtain delivery on thousands of items from peanut butter to sirloin steak to sandpaper to furniture. Thus, you will be able to shop by catalog and obtain the bulk of your needs without leaving your home.

Hotels will use computerized systems to keep track of room reservations, hotel personnel, disposable items, food and beverage items, and to compute customer bills upon checkout.

Information banks will be available that contain detailed information on available positions and persons seeking employment. These systems cover jobs at all levels and will be a major method of the government in the analysis and control of the economy.

Law-enforcement agencies will use computer systems to identify criminals (by fingerprints, voiceprints, pictures, and handwriting) as well as to obtain instantaneous information on stolen items, traffic violations, etc.

Miscellaneous Uses

Future cities will be designed with the aid of computers. Mathematical models of atmospheric pollution patterns will be used to predict where heavy industry and new population centers should be located to minimize environmental damage and optimize healthful living conditions. Small computers, about the size of a watch, will become available to everyone. These computers will cost only about $50 (at the current value of the dollar).

Computers will be able to analyze a person's voice, handwriting, fingerprints, and photograph and make a positive identification.

Computers will be used to combine voice analysis and language translation into a translator device for conversations in two different natural languages. These translation devices will be used primarily by tourists, businessmen, and scientists.

In the future, the cause-and-effect relations of weather will be better understood, and computers will be used to accurately analyze and predict the weather as well as explore ways to modify weather patterns.

Supermarkets will use computer systems to keep track of inventory and to speed up the food checkout process.

APPENDIXES

Appendix A

Number Systems

Most modern computers use the binary digit as a basic unit of information. The reason for this is that the two digits of the binary number system are easier to represent and use electronically than are the ten Arabic numerals of the decimal system. However, since people normally use the decimal number system, it is necessary to provide a method for the computer user to communicate with the computer. This usually results in the computer using an internal code of binary notation, whereas input and output information to the computer is handled in either decimal, octal, or hexadecimal notation. Of course, this involves a translation of the input and output information.

In most cases, it will be sufficient for one to think and use decimal values. In some cases, however, such as shifting, scaling numbers, logical operations, reading memory dumps, console debugging, etc., a knowledge of binary, octal, and hexadecimal representation is necessary.

BINARY NUMBER SYSTEM

In the binary number system, the base (radix) is 2 and digits can have one of two values: 0 or 1. Binary numbers are the common internal system for digital computation due to the relative simplicity of recording, storing, and recognizing variables of only two values. The value of a binary number is computed by multiplying the value of each digit by the corresponding power of 2 and summing all of the products. The positional weights of a binary number (powers of 2) can be represented as shown in Fig. A-1.

It can be seen from Fig. A-1 that the powers of 2 are of ascending order to the left of the binary point, and of descending order to the right of the binary point. The positive and negative powers of 2 and their decimal equivalents are shown in Table A-1.

The presence of a 1 in a digit position of a binary number indicates that the corresponding power of 2 is used in determining the value of the binary number. A 0 in a digit position indicates that the corresponding power of 2 is absent from the binary number.

As an example, the binary number, 101100, can be expressed as follows:

$$\begin{aligned}101100 &= 1\times 2^5 + 0\times 2^4 + 1\times 2^3 + 1\times 2^2 + 0\times 2^1 + 0\times 2^0\\ &= 1\times 32 + 0\times 16 + 1\times 8 + 1\times 4 + 0\times 2 + 0\times 1\\ &= 32 + 0 + 8 + 4 + 0 + 0\\ &= 44\end{aligned}$$

The binary number 101100 is equivalent to the decimal number 44.

A binary fractional number can be represented using negative powers of 2 for the corresponding 1s in the binary number. For example, the binary fractional number, .1010, has the

Table A-1. The Powers of 2 and Their Decimal Equivalents

Positive Power of 2	Decimal Equivalent	Negative Power of 2	Decimal Equivalent
2^9	512	2^{-1}	1/2
2^8	256	2^{-2}	1/4
2^7	128	2^{-3}	1/8
2^6	64	2^{-4}	1/16
2^5	32	2^{-5}	1/32
2^4	16	2^{-6}	1/64
2^3	8	2^{-7}	1/128
2^2	4	2^{-8}	1/256
2^1	2	2^{-9}	1/512
2^0	1		

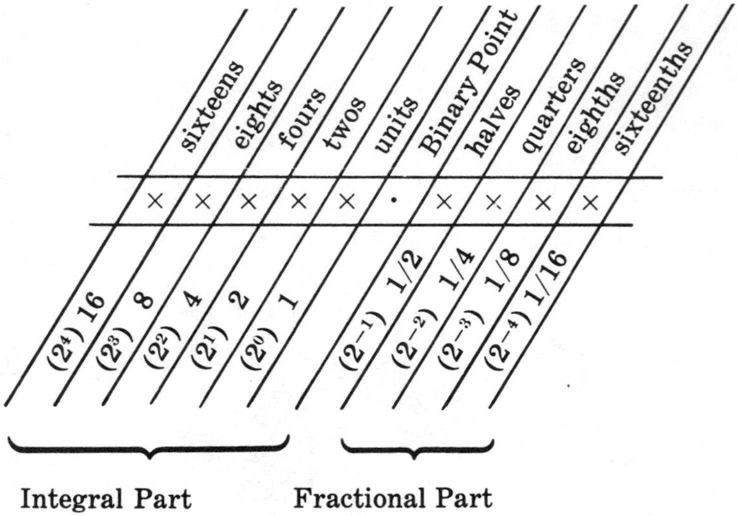

Fig. A-1. The positional weights of a binary number (powers of 2).

equivalent value, .625, and is determined in the following manner:

$$\begin{aligned} .1010 &= 1 \times 2^{-1} + 0 \times 2^{-2} + 1 \times 2^{-3} + 0 \times 2^{-4} \\ &= 1 \times 1/2 + 0 \times 1/4 + 1 \times 1/8 + 0 \times 1/16 \\ &= \quad 1/2 + \quad 0 + \quad 1/8 + \quad 0 \\ &= \quad 4/8 + \quad 1/8 \\ &= 5/8 \\ &= .625 \end{aligned}$$

A mixed binary number is composed of a binary integral value and a binary fractional value separated by a binary point. It is not necessary, but perhaps more convenient in the case of a mixed number, to consider the integral part separate from the fractional part and then combine the two parts to form a mixed number. The mixed binary number 101101.101, which has an integral part of 101101 and a fractional part of .101, can be expressed as:

$$\begin{aligned} &101101.101 = \\ &101101 \quad = 1\times2^5 + 0\times2^4 + 1\times2^3 + 1\times2^2 + 0\times2^1 + 1\times2^0 \\ &\qquad\qquad = 1\times32 + 0\times16 + 1\times8 + 1\times4 + 0\times2 + 1\times1 \\ &\qquad\qquad = \quad 32 + \quad 0 + \quad 8 + \quad 4 + \quad 0 + \quad 1 \\ &\qquad\qquad = \quad 45 \end{aligned}$$

The integral part of the mixed number 101101.101 is 45.

$$\begin{aligned} .101 &= 1 \times 2^{-1} + 0 \times 2^{-2} + 1 \times 2^{-3} \\ &= 1 \times 1/2 + 0 \times 1/4 + 1 \times 1/8 \\ &= \quad 1/2 + \quad 0 + \quad 1/8 \\ &= 5/8 \\ &= .625 \end{aligned}$$

The fractional part of the mixed number 101101.101 is .625. When these results are combined, the decimal equivalent of the binary number is obtained:

$$101101.101_2 = 45.625_{10}$$

DECIMAL NUMBER SYSTEM

The familiar decimal number system is based on a radix of 10 and is composed of the digits 0, 1, 2, 3, 4, 5, 6, 7, 8, and 9. Each position of a decimal number has a weight of some power of 10. For example, the decimal number 8136 is described as follows:

8 1 3 6

$$\begin{aligned} 6 \times 10^0 &= 6 \times 1 = 6 \\ 3 \times 10^1 &= 3 \times 10 = 30 \\ 1 \times 10^2 &= 1 \times 100 = 100 \\ 8 \times 10^3 &= 8 \times 1000 = 8000 \\ & \overline{\quad 8136} \end{aligned}$$

It can readily be seen in the foregoing example that each digit position has a value equal to the product of the digit appearing in the position and a corresponding power of 10. The powers of 10 are of ascending order to the left of the decimal point, and are of descending order to the right of the decimal point. The positional weights of a decimal number (powers of 10) can be represented as shown in Fig. A-2.

Any decimal number can be considered as the sum of the products obtained by multiplying the digits by the corresponding powers of the base. As an illustration of positional notation of a decimal number, consider the following decimal values:

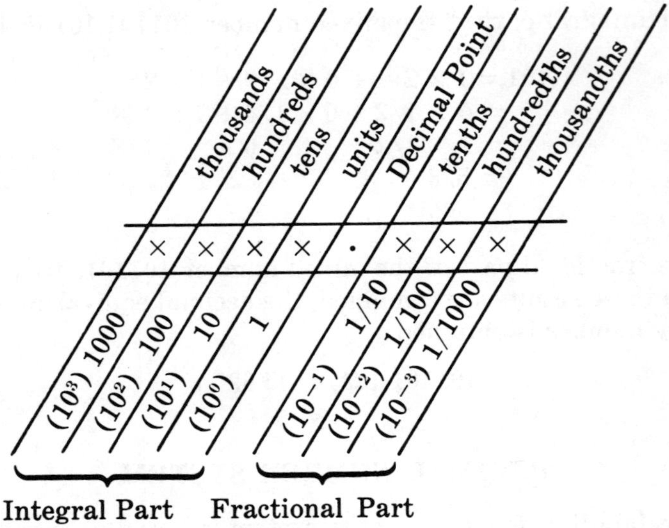

Fig. A-2. The positional weights of a decimal number (powers of 10).

$$\begin{aligned} 6321 &= 6 \times 10^3 + 3 \times 10^2 + 2 \times 10^1 + 1 \times 10^0 \\ &= 6 \times 1000 + 3 \times 100 + 2 \times 10 + 1 \times 1 \\ &= 6000 + 300 + 20 + 1 \end{aligned}$$

Thus far, only decimal integers have been considered. Numbers of this type have an assumed decimal point to the right of the least significant digit. A decimal fraction has each digit position to the right of the decimal point. Each digit position of a fractional number has a negative power of 10 assigned to it. For example, the fractional number 0.4327 can be broken down as follows:

$$\begin{aligned} 0.4327 &= 4 \times 10^{-1} + 3 \times 10^{-2} + 2 \times 10^{-3} + 7 \times 10^{-4} \\ &= 4 \times 1/10 + 3 \times 1/100 + 2 \times 1/1000 + 7 \times 1/10{,}000 \\ &= 4/10 + 3/100 + 2/1000 + 7/10{,}000 \\ &= \frac{(4000 + 300 + 20 + 7)}{10{,}000} \\ &= \frac{4327}{10{,}000} \\ &= 0.4327 \end{aligned}$$

The decimal point of a mixed number (integral part plus fractional part) is used merely as a reference to show where the positive powers of 10 end and the negative powers of 10 begin.

The mixed number 437.618 really means:

$$4\times10^2 + 3\times10^1 + 7\times10^0 + 6\times10^{-1} + 1\times10^{-2} + 8\times10^{-3}$$
$$4\times100 + 3\times10 + 7\times1 + 6\times1/10 + 1\times1/100 + 8\times1/1000$$
$$400 + 30 + 7 + 6/10 + 1/100 + 8/1000$$

HEXADECIMAL NUMBER SYSTEM

The hexadecimal number system is based on a radix of 16 and uses 16 digits. The digits 0 through 9 are used in the usual sense and the other six digits are represented by the symbols A, B, C, D, E, and F.

The positional weights of a hexadecimal number (powers of 16) can be represented as shown in Fig. A-3.

The decimal value of a hexadecimal number is determined by multiplying the value of each digit by the corresponding power of 16 and summing all the products. For example, the

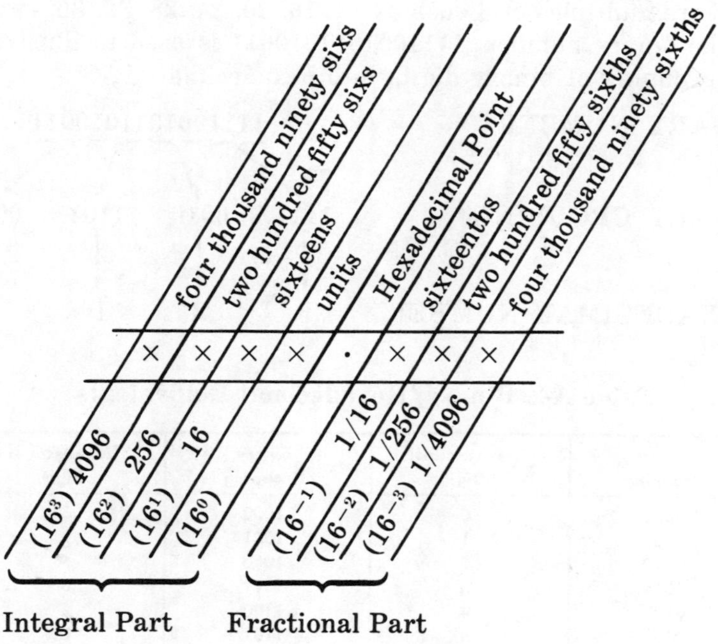

Fig. A-3. The positional weights of a hexadecimal number (powers of 16).

equivalent decimal value of the hexadecimal number 95.4 can be determined in the following manner:

9 5 . 4

$$4 \times 16^{-1} = 4 \times \frac{1}{16} = \frac{4}{16} = .25$$

$$5 \times 16^{0} = 5 \times 1 = 5 = 5.$$

$$9 \times 16^{1} = 9 \times 16 = 144 = 144.$$

$$149.25$$

If a binary number is divided into groups of four bits, proceeding in either direction from the binary point, each group can be replaced directly by its hexadecimal equivalent. These groupings are shown in Table A-2.

This form of grouping is extremely useful when used to represent values of an 8-bit byte of information. This unit of information is the basic unit of many modern computers. It is also very useful in representing words of binary computers that are multiples of 4 such as 12, 16, 20, 24, 28, 32, 36, etc.

The binary number, 1111001011010011 is used to illustrate the grouping of binary digits into hexadecimal digits:

BINARY NUMBER	1111001011010011			
BINARY GROUPING	1111	0010	1101	0011
HEXADECIMAL NUMBER	F	2	D	3

Table A-2. Binary/Hexadecimal Equivalents

Binary Grouping	Hexadecimal Digit	Binary Grouping	Hexadecimal Digit
0000	0	1000	8
0001	1	1001	9
0010	2	1010	A
0011	3	1011	B
0100	4	1100	C
0101	5	1101	D
0110	6	1110	E
0111	7	1111	F

Thus, the hexadecimal number F2D3 is the equivalent of the binary number 1111001011010011.

OCTAL NUMBER SYSTEM

The octal number system is based on a radix of 8 and uses the digits 0, 1, 2, 3, 4, 5, 6, and 7. The positional weights of an octal number (powers of 8) can be represented as shown in Fig. A-4.

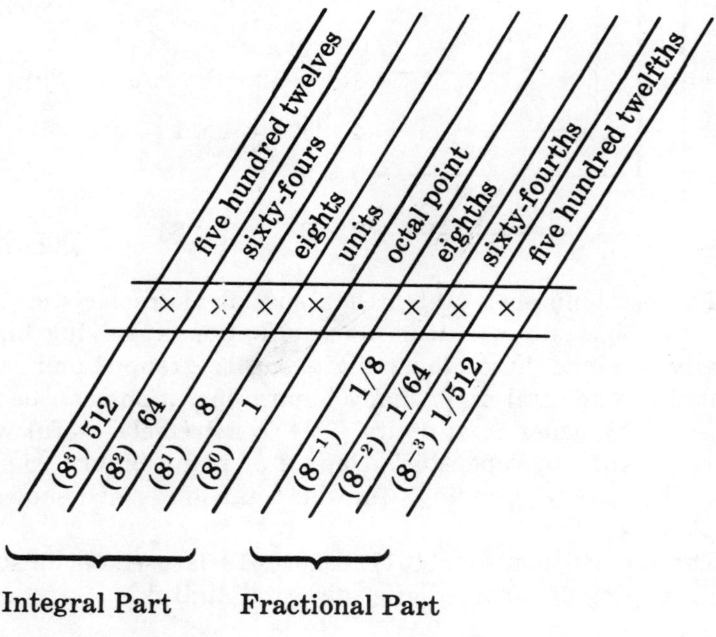

Fig. A-4. The positional weights of an octal number (powers of 8).

Table A-3. Binary/Octal Equivalents

Binary Grouping	Octal Digit
000	0
001	1
010	2
011	3
100	4
101	5
110	6
111	7

The octal number, 204.763, can be converted into its decimal equivalent by the following method:

2 0 4 · 7 6 3

$$3 \times 8^{-3} = 3 \times \frac{1}{8^3} = .006$$
$$6 \times 8^{-2} = 6 \times \frac{1}{8^2} = .094$$
$$7 \times 8^{-1} = 7 \times \frac{1}{8} = .875$$
$$4 \times 8^{0} = 4 \times 1 = 4.$$
$$0 \times 8^{1} = 0 \times 8 = 0.$$
$$2 \times 8^{2} = 2 \times 64 = 128.$$
$$\overline{132.975}$$

The octal number system has special characteristics that make it especially useful in many situations involving binary numbers. Since three binary digits can be grouped and represented as one octal digit, many binary operations can be represented by using octal digits. This is extremely useful when working with the operator's console of many binary computers. The binary groupings for the octal digits are shown in Table A-3.

The binary number, 110111101011010 is used to illustrate the grouping of binary digits into octal digits:

BINARY NUMBER	110111101011010				
BINARY GROUPING	110	111	101	011	010
OCTAL NUMBER	6	7	5	3	2

Thus, the octal number 67532 is the equivalent of the binary number 110111101011010. It should be obvious that the writing and reading of binary numbers can be simplified by using octal notation.

Appendix B

Glossary

Accumulator—A register in which the result of an arithmetic or logic operation is formed.

Acronym—A word formed from the first letter or letters of the words describing some item; e.g., FORTRAN from *FORmula TRAN*slation.

Address—A name, label, or number that identifies a location in storage.

Analysis—The investigation of a problem by some consistent, systematic procedure.

Analyst—A person skilled in the definition and development of techniques for the solving of a problem, especially those techniques for solutions on a computer.

ANSI—*A*merican *N*ational *S*tandards *I*nstitute. An organization that acts as a national clearinghouse and coordinator for voluntary standards in the United States.

APL—*A P*rogramming *L*anguage. A higher-level, terminal-oriented programming language.

Application—The system or problem to which a computer is applied.

Arithmetic Unit—The portion of the central processing unit where arithmetic and logical operations are performed.

ASCII Code—*A*merican *S*tandard *C*ode for *I*nformation *I*nterchange. A seven-bit code used on many present-day computers.

Assembler—A computer program used to translate a program written in a symbolic programming language into a machine-language program.

Assembly Language—A programming language which allows a computer user to write a program using mnemonics instead of numeric instructions. It is a low-level, symbolic programming language which closely resembles machine-code language.

Auxiliary Storage—A storage that supplements the internal storage of the central processing unit. Also called *secondary storage.*

Background Processing—Processing of a low-priority program that takes place only when no higher-priority or real-time processing function is present.

Base—The radix of a number system. See *Radix.*

BASIC—*B*eginners *A*ll-purpose *S*ymbolic *I*nstruction *C*ode. An easy-to-learn and easy-to-use programming language developed at Dartmouth College. BASIC can be used to solve business problems as well as scientific applications.

Batch Processing—A technique by which items to be processed must be coded and collected into groups prior to processing.

Binary—(1) A condition or situation having only two possibilities. (2) A number representation system with a radix of 2.

Binary Digit—In binary notation, either of the digits, 0 or 1.

Bit—An abbreviation of "*bi*nary digi*t*."

Bit Rate—The rate at which binary digits, or pulse representations, appear on communications lines or channels.

Block—A set of things, such as digits, characters, or words, handled as a unit.

Branch—A technique used to transfer control from one sequence of a program to another.

Buffer—A storage device used to compensate for a difference in the rate or sequence of data flow when transmitting data from one device to another.

Bug—A term used to denote a mistake in a computer program or a malfunction in a computer hardware component.

Bus—A channel or path for transferring data and electrical signals.

Byte—A grouping of adjacent binary digits operated on as a unit by the computer. The most common size of byte contains eight binary digits.

Card—A storage medium in which data is represented by means of holes punched in vertical columns in a paper card.

Card Punch—An output device used to punch cards.

Card Reader—An input device used to transmit punched-card data to the central processing unit of a computer.

Carriage—A control mechanism for a typewriter or printer that automatically feeds, skips, spaces, or ejects paper forms.

Central Processing Unit—That portion of the hardware of a computing system containing the control unit, arithmetic unit, and internal storage unit. Abbreviated CPU.

Character—A symbol, mark, or event which a data-processing machine can read, write, or store. It is used to represent data to a machine.

Circuit—A system of conductors and related electrical elements through which electrical currents flow.

Closed Shop—The operation of a computer facility where actual program running service is the responsibility of a group of specialists, thereby effectively separating the phase of task formulation from that of computer implementation. The programmers are not allowed in the computer room to run or oversee the running of their programs. Contrasted with *open shop.*

COBOL—*CO*mmon *B*usiness-*O*riented *L*anguage. A higher-level programming language developed for programming business problems.

Coder—A person who prepares instruction sequences from detailed flowcharts and other algorithmic procedures prepared by others, as contrasted with a programmer who prepares the procedures and flowcharts.

Coding—The process of translating problem logic represented by a flowchart into computer instructions and data.

Coding Form—A form on which the instructions for programming a computer are written. Also called a *coding sheet.*

COM—*C*omputer *O*utput *M*icrofilm. Refers to a method of converting computer output to microfilm form.

Compatible—A term applied to a computer system which implies that it is capable of handling both data and programs devised for some other type of computer system.

Compiler—A computer program used to translate high-level, source-language programs into machine-language programs suitable for execution on a particular computing system.

Compiler Language—See *Higher-Level Language.*

Computer—A calculating device which processes data represented by a combination of discrete data (in digital computers) or continuous data (in analog computers).

Computer Operator—A person who manipulates the controls of a computer and performs all operational functions that are required in the computing system, such as loading a tape transport, placing cards in the input hopper, removing printouts from the printer rack, etc.

Computer Program—See *Program.*

Computer Programmer—A person who designs, writes, debugs, and documents computer programs.

Computer Science—The field of knowledge that involves the design and use of computer equipment, including software development.

Computer System—A central processing unit together with one or more peripheral devices.

Console—That part of a computer used for communications between the computer operator or maintenance engineer and the computer.

Control Unit—The portion of the central processing unit that directs the step-by-step operation of the entire computing system.

Conversational Mode—A mode of operation where a user is in direct contact with a computer, and interaction is possible between human and machine without the user being conscious of any language or communications barrier.

Counter—A device such as a storage location or a register used to represent the number of occurrences of an event.

CPU—*C*entral *P*rocessing *U*nit.

CRT—*C*athode *R*ay *T*ube. An electronic vacuum tube with a screen for visual display of output information in graphical or alphanumeric form. Display is produced by means of proportionally deflected electron beams.

Cycle—An interval of time in which an operation or set of events is completed.

Data—A representation of facts or concepts in a formalized manner suitable for communication, interpretation, or processing by people or by automatic means.

Data Base—A comprehensive data file containing information in a format applicable to a user's needs and available when needed.

Data Processing—A term used in reference to operations performed by data-processing equipment.

Data-Processing Center—An installation of computer equipment which provides computing services for users.

Debug—To detect, locate, and remove all mistakes in a computer program and any malfunctions in the computing system hardware itself.

Diagnostics—Statements printed by an assembler or compiler indicating mistakes detected in a source program.

Digit—One of the symbols of a number system used to designate a quantity.

Digital—Pertaining to the utilization of discrete integral numbers in a given base to represent all the quantities that occur in a problem or a calculation.

Digital Computer—A computer that operates on discrete data by performing arithmetic and logic processes on the data.

Digital Plotter—An output unit which graphs data by an automatically controlled pen. Data is normally plotted as a series of incremental steps.

Direct-Access Storage—Pertaining to the process of obtaining data from or placing data into storage where the time required for such access is independent of the location of the data most recently obtained or placed in storage. Also called *random-access storage.*

Disc—Another spelling of disk.

Disk—See *Magnetic disk.*

Diskette—See *Floppy Disk.*

Disk Pack—The vertical stacking of a series of magnetic disks in a removable self-contained unit.

Display Unit—A device that provides a visual representation of data. See *CRT*.

Dump—Printing all or part of the contents of a storage device.

EBCDIC—*E*xtended *B*inary *C*oded *D*ecimal *I*nterchange *C*ode. An eight-bit code used for data representation in several computers including the IBM System/360 and System/370.

Emulate—To imitate one system with another, such that the imitating system accepts the same data, executes the same programs, and achieves the same results as the imitated system.

Execute—To perform the operations specified by computer instructions (programs).

File—An organized collection of related data. For example, the entire set of inventory master data records makes up the inentory master file.

Fixed-Word Length—The condition in which a machine word always contains a fixed number of bits, characters, bytes, or digits.

Floppy Disk—A flexible disk (diskette) of oxide-coated mylar that is stored in paper or plastic envelopes. The entire envelope is inserted in the disk unit. Floppy disks are low-cost storage units that are widely used with microcomputers and minicomputers.

Flowchart—A graphical representation for the solution of a problem. It is used primarily to help in the development of a computer program by illustrating how a computer program logic is laid out, and to provide documentation for the program.

Foreground Processing—The automatic execution of the computer programs that have been designed to preempt the use of the computing facilities.

FORTRAN—*FOR*mula *TRAN*slation. A higher-level programming language designed for programming scientific-type problems.

Hard-Copy—A printed copy of computer output; e.g., printed reports, listings, or documents.

Hardware—The physical equipment in a computer system; e.g., mechanical, electrical, or magnetic devices. Contrasted with *software.*

Higher-Level Language—A computer programming language that is intended to be independent of a particular computer. See *Procedure-Oriented Language.*

Hollerith Code—A punched card based on a code developed by Dr. Herman Hollerith for tabulating census data for the U.S. Census Bureau.

Information—Data that have been organized into a meaningful sequence.

Information Retrieval—A technique of classifying and indexing useful data in mass storage devices, in a format amenable to interaction with the user(s).

Input—The introduction of data from an external source into the internal storage unit of a computer.

Input/Output—A general term for the peripheral devices used to communicate with a digital computer, and the data involved in the communication.

Input Unit—A device used to transmit data into a central processing unit; e.g., a card reader, a teletypewriter, a paper-tape reader, an MICR reader, or an optical scanning reader.

Instruction—A set of characters used to define a basic operation and to tell the computer where to find the data needed to carry out the operation.

Integer—A whole number which may be positive, negative, or zero. It does not have a fractional part. Examples of integers are 26, −417, and 0.

Integrated Circuit—A microminiature electronic circuit produced on a single chip of silicon.

Intelligent Terminal—An input/output device in which a number of computer processing characteristics are physically built into, or attached to, the terminal unit.

Interface—A common boundary between two pieces of hardware or between two systems.

Internal Storage—Addressable storage directly controlled by the central processing unit of a digital computer. It is an integral part of the central processing unit. The CPU uses interval storage to store programs while they are being executed. Also called *primary storage, immediate-access storage,* and *main storage.*

Interpreter—(1) A machine that is used to sense information recorded in a punched card and print the information on the face of the card. (2) A computer program that translates and executes each source-language expression before translating and executing the next one.

Interrupt—To temporarily disrupt the normal execution of a program by a special signal from the computer.

K—When referring to storage capacity, 2^{10}; in decimal notation, 1024.

Keypunch—A keyboard-operated device that is used to punch holes in punched cards to represent data.

Light Pen—A stylus used with crt display devices to add, modify, and delete information on the face of the crt screen.

Line Printer—An output unit used to record computer output in the form of printed characters.

Loop—A sequence of program instructions which are repeated until a predetermined terminal condition is achieved.

LSI—*L*arge-*S*cale *I*ntegration. Logic used in microprocessors, microcomputers, and other computers.

Machine Address—An address that is permanently assigned by the machine designer to a storage location. Also called *absolute address.*

Machine Independent—A term used to indicate that a program is developed in terms of the problem rather than in terms of the characteristics of the computer system.

Machine Language—Basic language of a computer. Programs written in machine language require no further interpretation by a computer.

Macroinstruction—An instruction, in a source language, that is equivalent to a specified sequence of machine-language instructions.

Magnetic Core—A tiny doughnut-shaped piece of magnetizable material capable of storing one binary digit.

Magnetic-Disk Unit—A device used to read and write data on thin magnetic disks, the surfaces of which have been coated with a magnetizable material.

Magnetic-Drum Unit—A device used to read and write data on a cylinder, the surface of which is covered with a magnetizable material.

Magnetic Ink—An ink that can be magnetized. It is used for printing magnetic characters on forms such as checks, utility bills, invoices, etc. These magnetic characters are subsequently read by magnetic-ink character-reading equipment.

Magnetic-Tape Unit—A device used to read and write data in the form of magnetic spots on reels of tape coated with a magnetizable material.

Main Frame—The part of the computer that contains the arithmetic unit, internal storage unit, and control functions. See *Central Processing Unit.*

Main Storage—See *Internal Storage.*

Mark-Sense Card—A card designed to permit data to be entered on it with an electrographic pencil.

Memory—A term often used to refer to the storage facility of a computer. See *Storage.*

MICR—*M*agnetic *I*nk *C*haracter *R*ecognition. A system of coding in which numeric and special characters are printed with magnetizable ink.

Microcomputer—A computer consisting of a central processing unit, storage, and input/output circuitry. A microcomputer contains at least one microprocessor. It functions much the same way as a minicomputer.

Microelectronics—The field that deals with techniques for producing miniature circuits; e.g., integrated circuits, thin-film techniques, and solid-logic modules.

Microprocessor—The control and processing portion of a minicomputer or microcomputer, which is usually built with LSI circuitry on one chip. An example is the 8080 chip manufactured by Intel Corp.

Microsecond—One millionth of a second. Abbreviated *μs.*

Millisecond—One thousandth of a second. Abbreviated *ms.*

Minicomputer—A small and relatively inexpensive digital computer.

Mistake—A human failing; e.g., faulty arithmetic, incorrect keypunching, incorrect formula, or incorrect computer instructions.

Modem—A contraction of *MO*dulator/*DEM*odulator. Its function is to interface with data-processing devices and convert data to a form compatible for sending and receiving on transmission facilities.

Monolithic Integrated Circuit—A class of integrated circuits wherein the substrate is an active material such as the semiconductor, silicon.

Multiprocessing—Independent and simultaneous processing accomplished by a computer configuration consisting of more than one arithmetic and logic unit, each being capable of accessing a common memory.

Multiprogramming—Pertaining to the concurrent execution of two or more programs by a computer. The programs operate in an interleaved manner within one computer system.

Nanosecond—One billionth of a second. Abbreviated *ns*.

Network—The interconnection of a number of points by data communications facilities.

Nonvolatile Storage—A storage medium that retains its data in the absence of power.

Number Base—See *Radix*.

Octal—A numbering system based on a radix of 8.

Off-Line—Peripheral units which operate independently of the central processing unit. Devices not under the control of the central processing unit.

On-Line—Peripheral devices operating under the direct control of the central processing unit.

Open Shop—A computer installation at which computer operation can be performed by a qualified person. Contrasted with *closed shop*.

Operand—A unit of data that is to be operated upon.

Operating System—Software that controls the execution of computer programs and which may provide scheduling, input/output control, compilation, data management, debugging, storage assignment, accounting, and other similar functions.

Operation Code—The portion of an instruction which designates the operation to be performed by a computer; e.g., add, subtract, or move. Also called a *command*.

Optical Scanning—The translation of printed or handwritten characters into machine language.

Output Unit—A device capable of recording data coming from the internal storage unit of a computer; e.g., card punch, line printer, crt display, magnetic disk, or teletypewriter.

Paper Tape—A continuous strip of paper into which data is recorded as a series of holes along its length. Data is read by a paper-tape reader sensing the pattern of holes, which repsent coded data.

Paper-Tape Punch—An output unit used to encode data in paper tape.

Paper-Tape Reader—An input unit used to sense information coded in paper tape.

PL/1—*P*rogramming *L*anguage/*1*. A general-purpose programming language initially specified for the IBM System/360 computer; however, it is now available on several machines.

Point-of-Sale (POS) Terminal—An intelligent input/output device that is used to capture data in retail stores; i.e., supermarkets or department stores. POS is a term used to indicate that data regarding a sale is entered directly into the computerized system without having to be converted to another form first.

Printer—See *Line Printer.*

Procedure—A precise step-by-step method for effecting a solution to a problem.

Procedure-Oriented Language—A programming language designed for the convenient expression of procedures used in the solution of a wide class of problems; e.g., FORTRAN, COBOL, APL, and PL/1.

Program—All of the instructions required to solve a specific problem on a computer.

Programming—The process of translating a problem from its physical environment to a language that a computer can understand and obey. The process of planning the procedure for solving a problem. This may involve, among other things, an analysis of the problem, preparation of a flowchart, coding of the problem, establishing input/output formats, establishing testing and checkout procedures, allocation of storage, preparation of documentation, and supervision of the running of the program on a computer.

Programming Analyst—See *Analyst.*

Programming Language—A language used to prepare computer programs.

Radix—The quantity of characters or digit symbols required by a number system. Same as *base.*

Random-Access Storage—See *Direct-Access Storage.*

Raw Data—Data that has not been processed.

Read—To sense data from an input medium such as punched cards, magnetic tape, punched paper tape, or MICR form.

Reader—Any device capable of transcribing data from an input medium.

Real-Time System—A system where transactions are processed as they occur.

Record—A group of related items of data treated as a unit; e.g., the inventory master record. A complete set of such records forms a file.

Register—A temporary storage device used by the computer to store a specified amount of data, such as one word.

RPG—*R*eport *P*rogram *G*enerator. A language designed with built-in logic to produce report-writing programs given input and output descriptions.

Run—A single, continuous performance of a computer program.

Secondary Storage—Devices that are used to store large quantities of data and programs. To be processed, these data and programs must first be loaded into primary storage. Also called *auxiliary storage.*

Semiconductor Memory—A computer memory that uses silicon integrated-circuit chips.

Simulate—To represent the functioning of one system by another; i.e., to represent a physical system by the execution of a computer program, or to represent a biological system by a mathematical model.

Software—The computer programs, procedures, and documentation concerned with the operation of a computer system; e.g., assemblers, compilers, operating systems, diagnostic routines, program loaders, manuals, library routines, and circuit diagrams. Software is the name given to the programs that cause a computer to carry out particular operations. Contrasted with *hardware.*

Solid State—The electronic components that convey or control electrons within solid materials; e.g., transistors germanium diodes, and integrated circuits.

Storage—The retention of data so that the data can be obtained at a later time.

Storage Capacity—The number of items of data that a storage device is capable of containing. Frequently defined in terms of computer words, or by a specific number of bytes or characters.

Storage Device—A device used for storing data within a computer system; e.g., core storage, magnetic-disk unit, magnetic-tape unit, magnetic-drum unit, etc.

Storage Location—A position in storage where a character, byte, or word may be stored.

Storage Unit—The portion of the central processing unit that is used to store instructions and data.

Structured Programming—Techniques concerned with improving the programming process through better organization of programs and better programming notation to facilitate correct and clear description of data and control structures.

Subroutine—A set of instructions that directs the computer to carry out a well-defined mathematical, logical, or special operation. It may be used over and over in the same program and in different programs.

System—An organized collection of machines, methods, and personnel required to accomplish a specific objective.

Systems Analysis—The examination of an activity, procedure, method, technique, or a business to determine what must be accomplished and how the necessary operations may best be accomplished by using electronic data-processing equipment.

Systems Analyst—A person skilled in solving problems with a digital computer. He/she analyses and develops information systems.

Systems Programs—Computer programs provided by a computer manufacturer. Examples are operating systems, assemblers, compilers, debugging aids, input/output programs, etc.

Tape—A strip of material, which may be punched or coated with a magnetically sensitive substance, and which is used for data input, storage, or output. The data are usually stored serially in several channels across the tape transversely to the reading or writing motion.

Telecommunications—Pertaining to the transmission of data over long distances through telephone and telegraph facilities.

Teletypewriter—A keyboard printing unit that is often used to enter information into a computer and to accept output from a computer. The widest usage of the teletypewriter is as an input/output device in minicomputer systems, a remote terminal in a time-sharing system, and an operator console for computer systems.

Terminal—A point in a system or communications network at which data can either enter or leave.

Thin Film—A high-speed storage device consisting of a molecular deposit of materials on a substrate.

Time Sharing—A method of operation whereby a computer system automatically distributes processing time among many users simultaneously.

Track—The path along which data is recorded, as in magnetic disks and magnetic drums.

Transistor—A solid-state electronic device developed at Bell Telephone Laboratories in 1948.

Typewriter—An input/output device that is capable of being connected to a digital computer and used for communications purposes.

Variable—A quantity that can assume any of a given set of values.

Verifier—A machine that is used to check the correctness of manually recorded data.

Virtual Memory—A technique for managing a limited amount of high-speed memory and a (generally) much larger amount of lower-speed memory in such a way that the distinction is largely transparent to a computer user. The technique entails some means of swapping segments of program and data from the lower-speed memory (which would commonly be a drum or disk) into the high-speed memory, where it would be interpreted as instructions or operated upon as data. The unit of program or data swapped back and forth is called a *page*. The high-speed memory from which instructions are executed is *real* memory, while the lower-speed memory (drums or disks) is called *virtual* memory.

Volatile Storage—A storage medium in which data cannot be retained without continuous power dissipation.

Word—An ordered set of characters which occupies one storage location and is treated by the computer circuits as a unit. Ordinarily, a word is treated by the control unit as a quantity. Word lengths may be fixed or variable depending on the particular computer.

Word Length—The number of bits, bytes, or characters in a word.

Write—To transfer information, usually from internal storage to an output device.

Index